THE PENGUIN FREUD LIBRARY

General Editors:
Angela Richards (1973–82)
Albert Dickson (1982–)

VOLUME 7

ON SEXUALITY

THREE ESSAYS ON THE THEORY OF SEXUALITY
AND OTHER WORKS

Sigmund Freud

Sigmund Freud was born in 1856 in Moravia. Between the ages of four and eighty-two his home was in Vienna: in 1938 Hitler's invasion of Austria forced him to seek asylum in London, where he died in the following year. His career began with several years of brilliant work on the anatomy and physiology of the nervous system. He was almost thirty when, after a period of study under Charcot in Paris, his interests first turned to psychology, and another ten years of clinical work in Vienna (at first in collaboration with Breuer, an older colleague) saw the birth of his creation, psychoanalysis. This began simply as a method of treating neurotic patients by investigating their minds, but it quickly grew into an accumulation of knowledge about the workings of the mind in general, whether sick or healthy. Freud was thus able to demonstrate the normal development of the sexual instinct in childhood and, largely on the basis of an examination of dreams, arrived at his fundamental discovery of the unconscious forces that influence our everyday thoughts and actions. Freud's life was uneventful, but his ideas have shaped not only many specialist disciplines, but the whole in   e of the last half-century.

THE PENGUIN FREUD LIBRARY
VOLUME 7

•

ON SEXUALITY

THREE ESSAYS ON THE THEORY OF SEXUALITY

AND OTHER WORKS

Sigmund Freud

•

Translated from the German
under the general editorship of James Strachey

The present volume
compiled and edited by Angela Richards

PENGUIN BOOKS

PENGUIN BOOKS

Published by the Penguin Group
Penguin Books Ltd, 27 Wrights Lane, London W8 5TZ, England
Penguin Books USA Inc., 375 Hudson Street, New York, New York 10014, USA
Penguin Books Australia Ltd, Ringwood, Victoria, Australia
Penguin Books Canada Ltd, 10 Alcorn Avenue, Toronto, Ontario, Canada M4V 3B2
Penguin Books (NZ) Ltd, 182–190 Wairau Road, Auckland 10, New Zealand

Penguin Books Ltd, Registered Offices: Harmondsworth, Middlesex, England

Three Essays on the Theory of Sexuality and other works
Present English translations first published in *The Standard Edition of the Complete
Psychological Works of Sigmund Freud* by the Hogarth Press and the Institute of
Psycho-Analysis, London, as follows:
Three Essays on the Theory of Sexuality, Volume VII (1953); 'The Sexual
Enlightenment of Children', 'On the Sexual Theories of Children'; 'Character and
Anal Erotism', 'Family Romances', Volume IX (1959); 'Contributions to the
Psychology of Love, I, II, and III', Volume XI (1957); 'Two Lies Told by Children',
Volume XII (1958); 'On Transformations of Instinct as Exemplified in Anal Erotism',
Volume XVII (1955); 'The Infantile Genital Organization', 'The Dissolution of the
Oedipus Complex', 'Some Psychical Consequences of the Anatomical Distinction
Between the Sexes', Volume XIX (1961); 'Fetishism', 'Libidinal Types', 'Female
Sexuality', Volume XXI (1961).
'Sigmund Freud: A Sketch of his Life and Ideas' first published in *Two Short
Accounts of Psycho-Analysis* in Pelican Books 1962
This collection, *On Sexuality*, first published in Pelican Books 1977
Reprinted in Penguin Books 1991
5 7 9 10 8 6

Printed in England by Clays Ltd, St Ives plc
Set in Monotype Bembo

CONTENTS

VOLUME 7
ON SEXUALITY

THREE ESSAYS ON THE
THEORY OF SEXUALITY
(1905)

CONTENTS

INTRODUCTION TO
THE PENGUIN FREUD LIBRARY

The Penguin Freud Library (formerly *The Pelican Freud Library*) is intended to meet the needs of the general reader by providing all Freud's major writings in translation together with an appropriate linking commentary. It is the first time that such an edition has been produced in paperback in the English language. It does not supplant *The Standard Edition of the Complete Psychological Works of Sigmund Freud*, translated from the German under the general editorship of James Strachey, in collaboration with Anna Freud, assisted by Alix Strachey and Alan Tyson, editorial assistant Angela Richards (Hogarth Press, twenty-four volumes, 1953–74). The *Standard Edition* remains the fullest and most authoritative collection published in any language. The present edition does, however, provide a large enough selection to meet the requirements of all but the most specialist reader – in particular it aims to cater for students of sociology, anthropology, criminology, medicine, aesthetics and education, all of them fields in which Freud's ideas have established their relevance.

The texts are reprinted unabridged, with corrections, from the *Standard Edition*. The editorial commentary – introductions, footnotes, internal cross-references, bibliographies and indexes – is also based upon the *Standard Edition*, but it has been abridged and where necessary adapted to suit the less specialized scope and purposes of the *Penguin Freud Library*. Some corrections have been made and some new material added.

Selection of Material

This is not a complete edition of Freud's psychological works – still less of his works as a whole, which included important contributions to neurology and neuropathology dating from the early part of his professional life. Of the psychological writings, virtually all the major works have been included. The arrangement is by subject-matter, so that the main contributions to any particular theme will be found in one volume. Within each volume the works are, for the main part, in chronological sequence. The aim has been to cover the whole field of Freud's observations and his theory of psychoanalysis: that is to say, in the first place, the structure and dynamics of human mental activity; secondly, psychopathology and the mechanism of mental disorder; and thirdly, the application of psychoanalytic theory to wider spheres than the disorders of individuals which Freud originally, and indeed for the greater part of his life, investigated – to the psychology of groups, to social institutions and to religion, art and literature.

In his 'Sigmund Freud: A Sketch of his Life and Ideas' (p. 13ff. below), James Strachey includes an account of Freud's discoveries well as defining his principal theories and tracing their development.

Writings excluded from the Edition

The works that have been excluded are, (1) The neurological writings and most of those very early works from the period before the idea of psychoanalysis has taken form. (2) Writings on the actual technique of treatment. These were written specifically for practitioners of psychoanalysis and for analysts in training and their interest is correspondingly specialized. Freud never in fact produced a complete text on psychoanalytic treatment and the papers on technique only deal with selected points of difficulty or theoretical interest. (3) Writings which cover the same ground as other major works which have been included; for example, since the *Library* includes the *Introductory Lectures on Psychoanalysis* and the *New Lectures*, it was decided to leave out several of the shorter expository works in which Freud surveys the whole subject. Similarly, because *The Interpretation of Dreams* is included, the shorter writings on this topic have been omitted. (4) Freud's private correspondence, much of which has now been published in translation.[1] This is not to imply that such letters are without interest or importance though they have not yet received full critical treatment. (5) The numerous short writings such as reviews of books, prefaces to other authors' works, obituary notices and little *pièces d'occasion* – all of which lose interest to a large extent when separated from the books or occasions to which they refer and which would often demand long editorial explanations to make them comprehensible.

All of these excluded writings (with the exception of the works on neurology and the private letters) can be found in the *Standard Edition*.

Editorial Commentary

The bibliographical information, included at the beginning of the Editor's Note or Introduction to each work, gives the title of the German (or other) original, the date and place of its first publication and the position, where applicable, of the work in Freud's *Gesammelte Werke*, the most complete edition at present available of the works in German (published by S. Fischer Verlag, Frankfurt am Main). Details of the first translation of each work into English are also included, together with the *Standard Edition* reference. Other editions are listed only if they contain significant changes. (Full details of all German editions published in Freud's lifetime and of all English editions prior to the *Standard Edition* are included in the *Standard Edition*.)

The date of original publication of each work has been added to the half-title page, with the date of composition included in square brackets wherever it is different from the former date.

Further background information is given in introductory

1. [See the list, p. 26 *n*. below, and the details in the Bibliography, p. 393 ff.]

notes and in footnotes to the text. Apart from dealing with the time and circumstances of composition, these notes aim to make it possible to follow the inception and development of important psychoanalytic concepts by means of systematic cross-references. Most of these references are to other works included in the *Penguin Freud Library*. A secondary purpose is to date additions and alterations made by Freud in successive revisions of the text and in certain cases to provide the earlier versions. No attempt has been made to do this as comprehensively as in the *Standard Edition*, but variants are given whenever they indicate a definite change of view. Square brackets are used throughout to distinguish editorial additions from Freud's text and his own footnotes.

It will be clear from this account that I owe an overwhelming debt to the late James Strachey, the general editor and chief translator of the *Standard Edition*. He indeed was mainly responsible for the idea of a *Pelican Freud Library*, and for the original plan of contents. I have also had the advantage of discussions with Miss Anna Freud and the late Mrs Alix Strachey, both of whom gave advice of the greatest value. I am grateful to the late Mr Ernst Freud for his support and to the Publications Committee of the Institute of Psycho-Analysis for help in furthering preparations for this edition.

ANGELA RICHARDS, 1977

SIGMUND FREUD

A SKETCH OF HIS LIFE AND IDEAS

SIGMUND FREUD was born on 6 May 1856 in Freiberg, a small town in Moravia, which was at that time a part of Austria–Hungary. In an external sense the eighty-three years of his life were on the whole uneventful and call for no lengthy history.

He came of a middle-class Jewish family and was the eldest child of his father's second wife. His position in the family was a little unusual, for there were already two grown-up sons by his father's first wife. These were more than twenty years older than he was and one of them was already married, with a little boy; so that Freud was in fact born an uncle. This nephew played at least as important a part in his very earliest years as his own younger brothers and sisters, of whom seven were born after him.

His father was a wool-merchant and soon after Freud's birth found himself in increasing commercial difficulties. He therefore decided, when Freud was just three years old, to leave Freiberg, and a year later the whole family settled in Vienna, with the exception of the two elder half-brothers and their children, who established themselves instead in Manchester. At more than one stage in his life Freud played with the idea of joining them in England, but nothing was to come of this for nearly eighty years.

In Vienna during the whole of Freud's childhood the family lived in the most straitened conditions; but it is much to his father's credit that he gave invariable priority to the charge of Freud's education, for the boy was obviously intelligent and was a hard worker as well. The result was that he won a place in the 'Gymnasium' at the early age of nine, and for the last six of the eight years he spent at the school he was regularly top of his class. When at the age of seventeen he passed out of school his career was still undecided; his education so far had been of the most general kind, and, though he seemed in any case destined for the University, several faculties lay open to him.

Freud insisted more than once that at no time in his life did he feel 'any particular predilection for the career of a doctor. I was moved, rather,' he says, 'by a sort of curiosity, which was, however, directed more towards human concerns than towards natural objects.'[1] Elsewhere he writes: 'I have no knowledge of having had any craving in my early childhood to help suffering humanity . . . In my youth I felt an overpowering need to understand something of the riddles of the world in which we live and perhaps even to contribute something to their solution.'[2] And in yet another passage in which he was discussing the sociological studies of his last years: 'My interest, after making a lifelong *détour* through the natural sciences, medicine, and psychotherapy, returned to the cultural problems which had fascinated me long before, when I was a youth scarcely old enough for thinking.'[3]

What immediately determined Freud's choice of a scientific career was, so he tells us, being present just when he was leaving school at a public reading of an extremely flowery essay on 'Nature', attributed (wrongly, it seems) to Goethe. But if it was to be science, practical considerations narrowed the choice to medicine. And it was as a medical student that Freud enrolled himself at the University in the autumn of 1873 at the age of seventeen. Even so, however, he was in no hurry to obtain a medical degree. For his first year or two he attended lectures on a variety of subjects, but gradually concentrated first on biology and then on physiology. His very first piece of research was in his third year at the University, when he was deputed by the Professor of Comparative Anatomy to

1. [*An Autobiographical Study* (1925*d*), near the opening of the work.]
2. ['Postscript to *The Question of Lay Analysis*' (1927*a*).]
3. ['Postscript (1935) to *An Autobiographical Study*' (1935*a*).]

investigate a detail in the anatomy of the eel, which involved the dissection of some four hundred specimens. Soon afterwards he entered the Physiological Laboratory under Brücke, and worked there happily for six years. It was no doubt from him that he acquired the main outlines of his attitude to physical science in general. During these years Freud worked chiefly on the anatomy of the central nervous system and was already beginning to produce publications. But it was becoming obvious that no livelihood which would be sufficient to meet the needs of the large family at home was to be picked up from these laboratory studies. So at last, in 1881, he decided to take his medical degree, and a year later, most unwillingly, gave up his position under Brücke and began work in the Vienna General Hospital.

What finally determined this change in his life was something more urgent than family considerations: in June 1882 he became engaged to be married, and thenceforward all his efforts were directed towards making marriage possible. His fiancée, Martha Bernays, came of a well-known Jewish family in Hamburg, and though for the moment she was living in Vienna she was very soon obliged to return to her remote North-German home. During the four years that followed, it was only for brief visits that he could have glimpses of her, and the two lovers had to content themselves with an almost daily interchange of letters. Freud now set himself to establishing a position and a reputation in the medical world. He worked in various departments of the hospital, but soon came to concentrate on neuroanatomy and neuropathology. During this period, too, he published the first inquiry into the possible medical uses of cocaine; and it was this that suggested to Koller the drug's employment as a local anaesthetic. He soon formed two immediate plans: one of these was to obtain an appointment as *Privatdozent*, a post not unlike that of a university lecturer in England, the other was to gain a travelling bursary which would enable him to spend some time in Paris where the reigning figure was the great Charcot. Both of these aims, if they were realized, would, he felt, bring him real advantages, and in 1885, after a hard struggle, he achieved them both.

The months which Freud spent under Charcot at the Salpêtrière (the famous Paris hospital for nervous diseases) brought another change in the course of his life and this time a revolutionary one. So far his work had been concerned entirely with physical science and he was still carrying out histological studies on the brain while he was in Paris. Charcot's interests were at that period concentrated mainly on hysteria and hypnotism. In the world from which Freud came these subjects were regarded as barely respectable, but he became absorbed in them, and, though Charcot himself looked at them purely as branches of neuropathology, for Freud they meant the first beginnings of the investigation of the mind.

On his return to Vienna in the spring of 1886 Freud set up in private practice as a consultant in nervous diseases, and his long-delayed marriage followed soon afterwards. He did not, however, at once abandon all his neuropathological work: for several more years he studied in particular the cerebral palsies of children, on which he became a leading authority. At this period, too, he produced an important monograph on aphasia. But he was becoming more and more engaged in the treatment of the neuroses. After experimenting in vain with electrotherapy, he turned to hypnotic suggestion, and in 1888 visited Nancy to learn the technique used with such apparent success there by Liébeault and Bernheim. This still proved unsatisfactory and he was driven to yet another line of approach. He knew that a friend of his, Dr Josef Breuer, a Vienna consultant considerably his senior, had some ten years earlier cured a girl suffering from hysteria by a quite new procedure. He now persuaded Breuer to take up the method once more, and he himself applied it to several fresh cases with promising results. The method was based on the assumption that hysteria was the product of a psychical trauma which had been forgotten by the patient; and the treatment consisted in inducing her in a hypnotic state to recall the forgotten trauma to the accompaniment of appropriate emotions. Before very long Freud began to make changes both in the procedure and in the underlying theory; this led eventually to a breach with Breuer, and to the ultimate development by Freud of the whole system of ideas to which he soon gave the name of psychoanalysis.

From this moment onwards – from 1895, perhaps – to the very end of his life, the whole of Freud's intellectual existence revolved around this development, its far-reaching implications, and its theoretical and practical repercussions. It would, of course, be impossible to give in a few sentences any consecutive account of Freud's discoveries and ideas, but an attempt will be made presently to indicate in a disconnected fashion some of the main changes he has brought about in our habits of thought. Meanwhile we may continue to follow the course of his external life.

His domestic existence in Vienna was essentially devoid of episode: his home and his consulting rooms were in the same house from 1891 till his departure for London forty-seven years later. His happy marriage and his growing family – three sons and three daughters – provided a solid counterweight to the difficulties which, to begin with at least, surrounded his professional career. It was not only the nature of his discoveries that created prejudice against him in medical circles; just as great, perhaps, was the effect of the intense anti-semitic feeling which dominated the official world of Vienna: his appointment to a university professorship was constantly held back by political influence.

One particular feature of these early years calls for mention on account of its consequences. This was Freud's friendship with Wilhelm Fliess, a brilliant but unbalanced Berlin physician, who specialized in the ear and throat, but whose wider interests extended over human biology and the effects of periodic phenomena in vital processes. For fifteen years, from

1887 to 1902, Freud corresponded with him regularly, reported the development of his ideas, forwarded him long drafts outlining his future writings, and, most important of all, sent him an essay of some forty thousand words which has been given the name of a 'Project for a Scientific Psychology'. This essay was composed in 1895, at what might be described as the watershed of Freud's career, when he was reluctantly moving from physiology to psychology; it is an attempt to state the facts of psychology in purely neurological terms. This paper and all the rest of Freud's communications to Fliess have, by a lucky chance, survived: they throw a fascinating light on the development of Freud's ideas and show how much of the later findings of psychoanalysis were already present in his mind at this early stage.

Apart from his relations with Fliess, Freud had little outside support to begin with. He gradually gathered a few pupils round him in Vienna, but it was only after some ten years, in about 1906, that a change was inaugurated by the adhesion of a number of Swiss psychiatrists to his views. Chief among these were Bleuler, the head of the Zurich mental hospital, and his assistant Jung. This proved to be the beginning of the first spread of psychoanalysis. An international meeting of psycho-analysts gathered at Salzburg in 1908, and in 1909 Freud and Jung were invited to give a number of lectures in the United States. Freud's writings began to be translated into many languages, and groups of practising analysts sprang up all over the world. But the progress of psychoanalysis was not without its set-backs: the currents which its subject-matter stirred up in the mind ran too deep for its easy acceptance. In 1911 one of Freud's prominent Viennese supporters, Alfred Adler, broke away from him, and two or three years later Jung's differences from Freud led to their separation. Almost immediately after this came the First World War and an interruption of the international spread of psychoanalysis. Soon afterwards, too, came the gravest personal tragedies – the death of a daughter and of a favourite grandchild, and the onset of the malignant illness which was to pursue him relentlessly for the last sixteen years of his life. None of these troubles, however, brought any interruption to the development of Freud's observations and inferences. The structure of his ideas continued to expand and to find ever wider applications – particularly in the sociological field. By now he had become generally recognized as a figure of world celebrity, and no honour pleased him more than his election in 1936, the year of his eightieth birthday, as a Corresponding Member of the Royal Society. It was no doubt this fame, supported by the efforts of influential admirers, including, it is said, President Roosevelt, that protected him from the worst excesses of the National Socialists when Hitler invaded Austria in 1938, though they seized and destroyed his publications. Freud's departure from Vienna was nevertheless essential, and in June of that year, accompanied by some of his family, he made the journey to London, and it was there, a year later, on 23 September 1939, that he died.

It has become a journalistic cliché to speak of Freud as one of the revolutionary founders of modern thought and to couple his name with that of Einstein. Most people would, however, find it almost as hard to summarize the changes introduced by the one as by the other.

Freud's discoveries may be grouped under three headings – an instrument of research, the findings produced by the instrument, and the theoretical hypotheses inferred from the findings – though the three groups were of course mutually interrelated. Behind all of Freud's work, however, we should posit his belief in the universal validity of the law of determinism. As regards physical phenomena this belief was perhaps derived from his experience in Brücke's laboratory and so, ultimately, from the school of Helmholtz; but Freud extended the belief uncompromisingly to the field of mental phenomena, and here he may have been influenced by his teacher, the psychiatrist Meynert, and indirectly by the philosophy of Herbart.

First and foremost, Freud was the discoverer of the first instrument for the scientific examination of the human mind. Creative writers of genius had had fragmentary insight into mental processes, but no systematic method of investigation existed before Freud. It was only gradually that he perfected the instrument, since it was only gradually that the difficulties in the way of such an investigation became apparent. The forgotten trauma in Breuer's explanation of hysteria provided the earliest problem and perhaps the most fundamental of all, for it showed conclusively that there were active parts of the mind not immediately open to inspection either by an on-looker or by the subject himself. These parts of the mind were described by Freud, without regard for metaphysical or terminological disputes, as the unconscious. Their existence was equally demonstrated by the fact of post-hypnotic suggestion, where a person in a fully waking state performs an action which had been suggested to him some time earlier, though he had totally forgotten the suggestion itself. No examination of the mind could thus be considered complete unless it included this unconscious part of it in its scope. How was this to be accomplished? The obvious answer seemed to be: by means of hypnotic suggestion, and this was the instrument used by Breuer and, to begin with, by Freud. But it soon turned out to be an imperfect one, acting irregularly and un-certainly and sometimes not at all. Little by little, accordingly, Freud abandoned the use of suggestion and replaced it by an entirely fresh instrument, which was later known as 'free association'. He adopted the unheard-of plan of simply asking the person whose mind he was investigating to say whatever came into his head. This crucial decision led at once to the most startling results; even in this primitive form Freud's instru-ment produced fresh insight. For, though things went along swimmingly for a while, sooner or later the flow of associa-tions dried up: the subject would not or could not think of anything more to say. There thus came to light the fact of 'resistance', of a force, separate from the subject's conscious will, which was refusing to collaborate with the investigation. Here was one basis for a very fundamental piece of theory, for a hypothesis of the mind as something dynamic, as consisting in a number of mental forces, some conscious and some unconscious, operating now in harmony now in opposition with one another.

Though these phenomena eventually turned out to be of universal occurrence, they were first observed and studied in neurotic patients, and the earlier years of Freud's work were largely concerned with discovering means by which the 'resistance' of these patients could be overcome and what lay behind it could be brought to light. The solution was only made possible by an extraordinary piece of self-observation on Freud's part – what we should now describe as his self-analysis. We are fortunate in having a contemporary first-hand description of this event in his letters to Fliess which have already been mentioned. This analysis enabled him to discover the nature of the unconscious processes at work in the mind and to understand why there is such a strong resistance to their becoming conscious; it enabled him to devise techniques for overcoming or evading the resistance in his patients; and, most important of all, it enabled him to realize the very great difference between the mode of functioning of these unconscious processes and that of our familiar conscious ones. A word may be said on each of these three points, for in fact they constitute the core of Freud's contributions to our knowledge of the mind.

The unconscious contents of the mind were found to consist wholly in the activity of conative trends – desires or wishes – which derive their energy directly from the primary physical instincts. They function quite regardless of any consideration other than that of obtaining immediate satisfaction, and are thus liable to be out of step with those more conscious elements in the mind which are concerned with adaptation to reality and the avoidance of external dangers. Since, moreover, these primitive trends are to a great extent of a sexual or of a destructive nature, they are bound to come in conflict with the more social and civilized mental forces. Investigations along this path were what led Freud to his discoveries of the long-disguised secrets of the sexual life of children and of the Oedipus complex.

In the second place, his self-analysis led him to an inquiry into the nature of dreams. These turned out to be, like neurotic symptoms, the product of a conflict and a compromise between the primary unconscious impulses and the secondary conscious ones. By analysing them into their elements it was therefore possible to infer their hidden unconscious contents; and, since dreams are common phenomena of almost universal occurrence, their interpretation turned out to be one of the most useful technical contrivances for penetrating the resistances of neurotic patients.

Finally, the painstaking examination of dreams enabled Freud to classify the remarkable differences between what he termed the primary and secondary processes of thought, between events in the unconscious and conscious regions of the mind. In the unconscious, it was found, there is no sort of organization or coordination: each separate impulse seeks satisfaction independently of all the rest; they proceed uninfluenced by one another; contradictions are completely inoperative, and the most opposite impulses flourish side by side. So, too, in the unconscious, associations of ideas proceed along lines without any regard to logic: similarities are treated as identities, negatives are equated with positives. Again, the objects to which the conative trends are attached in the unconscious are extraordinarily changeable – one may be replaced by another along a whole chain of associations that have no rational basis. Freud perceived that the intrusion into conscious thinking of mechanisms that belong properly to the primary process accounts for the oddity not only of dreams but of many other normal and pathological mental events.

It is not much of an exaggeration to say that all the later part of Freud's work lay in an immense extension and elaboration of these early ideas. They were applied to an elucidation of the mechanisms not only of the psychoneuroses and psychoses but also of such normal processes as slips of the tongue, making jokes, artistic creation, political institutions, and religions; they played a part in throwing fresh light on many applied sciences – archaeology, anthropology, criminology, education; they also served to account for the effectiveness of psychoanalytic therapy. Lastly, too, Freud erected on the basis of these elementary observations a theoretical superstructure, what he named a 'metapsychology', of more general concepts. These, however, fascinating as many people will find them, he always insisted were in the nature of provisional hypotheses. Quite late in his life, indeed, influenced by the ambiguity of the term 'unconscious' and its many conflicting uses, he proposed a new structural account of the mind in which the unco-ordinated instinctual trends were called the 'id', the organized realistic part the 'ego', and the critical and moralizing function the 'super-ego' – a new account which has certainly made for a clarification of many issues.

This, then, will have given the reader an outline of the external events of Freud's life and some notion of the scope of his discoveries. Is it legitimate to ask for more? to try to penetrate a little further and to inquire what sort of person Freud was? Possibly not. But human curiosity about great men is insatiable, and if it is not gratified with true accounts it will inevitably clutch at mythological ones. In two of Freud's early books (*The Interpretation of Dreams* and *The Psychopathology of Everyday Life*) the presentation of his thesis had forced on him the necessity of bringing up an unusual amount of personal material. Nevertheless, or perhaps for that very reason, he intensely objected to any intrusion into his private life, and he was correspondingly the subject of a wealth of myths. According to the first and most naïve rumours, for instance, he was an abandoned profligate, devoted to the corruption of public morals. Later fantasies have tended in the opposite direction: he has been represented as a harsh moralist, a ruthless disciplinarian, an autocrat, egocentric and unsmiling, and an essentially unhappy man. To anyone who was acquainted with him, even slightly, both these pictures must seem equally preposterous. The second of them was no doubt partly derived from a knowledge of his physical sufferings during his last years; but partly too it may have been due to the unfortunate impression produced by some of his most widespread portraits. He disliked being photographed, at least by professional photographers, and his features on occasion expressed the fact; artists too seem always to have been overwhelmed by the necessity for representing the inventor of psychoanalysis as a ferocious and terrifying figure. Fortunately, however, alternative versions exist of a more amiable and truer kind – snapshots, for instance, taken on a holiday or with his children, such as will be found in his eldest son's memoir of his father (*Glory Reflected*, by Martin Freud [1957]). In many ways, indeed, this delightful and amusing book serves to redress the balance from more official biographies, invaluable as they are, and reveals something of Freud as he was in ordinary life. Some of these portraits show us that in his earlier days he had well-filled features, but in later life, at any rate after the First World War and even before his illness, this was no longer so, and his features, as well as his whole figure (which was of medium height), were chiefly remarkable for the impression they gave of tense energy and alert observation. He was serious but kindly and considerate in his more formal manners, but in other circumstances could be an entertaining talker with a pleasantly ironical sense of humour. It was easy to discover his devoted fondness for his family and to recognize a man who would inspire affection. He had many miscellaneous interests – he was fond of travelling abroad, of country holidays, of mountain walks – and there were other, more engrossing subjects, art, archaeology, literature. Freud was a very well-read man in many languages, not only in German. He read English and French fluently, besides having a fair knowledge of Spanish and Italian. It must be remembered, too, that though the later phases of his education were chiefly scientific (it is true that at the University he studied philosophy for a short time) at school he had learnt the classics and never lost his affection for them. We happen to have a letter written by him at the age of seventeen to a school friend.[1] In it he describes his varying success in the different papers of his school-leaving examination: in Latin a passage from Virgil, and in Greek thirty-three lines from, of all things, *Oedipus Rex*.

In short, we might regard Freud as what in England we should consider the best kind of product of a Victorian upbringing. His tastes in literature and art would obviously differ from ours, his views on ethics, though decidedly liberal, would not belong to the post-Freudian age. But we should see in him a man who lived a life of full emotion and of much suffering without embitterment. Complete honesty and directness were qualities that stood out in him, and so too did his intellectual readiness to take in and consider any fact, however new or extraordinary, that was presented to him. It was perhaps an inevitable corollary and extension of these qualities, combined with a general benevolence which a surface misanthropy failed to disguise, that led to some features of a surprising kind. In spite of his subtlety of mind he was essentially unsophisticated, and there were sometimes unexpected lapses in his critical faculty – a failure, for instance, to perceive an untrustworthy authority in some subject that was off his own beat such as Egyptology or philology, and, strangest of all in someone whose powers of perception had to be experienced to be believed, an occasional blindness to defects in his acquaintances. But though it may flatter our vanity to declare that Freud was a human being of a kind like our own, that satisfaction can easily be carried too far. There must in fact have been something very extraordinary in the

1. [Emil Fluss. The letter is included in the volume of Freud's correspondence (1960a).]

man who was first able to recognize a whole field of mental facts which had hitherto been excluded from normal consciousness, the man who first interpreted dreams, who first accepted the facts of infantile sexuality, who first made the distinction between the primary and secondary processes of thinking – the man who first made the unconscious mind real to us.

JAMES STRACHEY

[Those in search of further information will find it in the three-volume biography of Freud by Ernest Jones, an abridged version of which was published in Pelican in 1964 (reissued 1974), in the important volume of Freud's letters edited by his son and daughter-in-law, Ernst and Lucie Freud (1960a), in several further volumes of his correspondence, with Wilhelm Fliess (1950a), Karl Abraham (1965a), C. G. Jung (1974a), Oskar Pfister (1963a), Lou Andreas-Salomé (1966a), Edoardo Weiss (1970a) and Arnold Zweig (1968a), and above all in the many volumes of Freud's own works.]

CHRONOLOGICAL TABLE

This table traces very roughly some of the main turning-points in Freud's intellectual development and opinions. A few of the chief events in his external life are also included in it.

1856. 6 May. Birth at Freiberg in Moravia.

1860. Family settles in Vienna.

1865. Enters Gymnasium (secondary school).

1873. Enters Vienna University as medical student.

1876–82. Works under Brücke at the Institute of Physiology in Vienna.

1877. First publications: papers on anatomy and physiology.

1881. Graduates as Doctor of Medicine.

1882. Engagement to Martha Bernays.

1882–5. Works in Vienna General Hospital, concentrating on cerebral anatomy: numerous publications.

1884–7. Researches into the clinical uses of cocaine.

1885. Appointed *Privatdozent* (University Lecturer) in Neuro-pathology.

1885 (October)–1886 (February). Studies under Charcot at the Salpêtrière (hospital for nervous diseases) in Paris. Interest first turns to hysteria and hypnosis.

1886. Marriage to Martha Bernays. Sets up private practice in nervous diseases in Vienna.

1886–93. Continues work on neurology, especially on the cerebral palsies of children at the Kassowitz Institute in Vienna, with numerous publications. Gradual shift of interest from neurology to psychopathology.

1887. Birth of eldest child (Mathilde).

1887–1902. Friendship and correspondence with Wilhelm Fliess in Berlin. Freud's letters to him during this period, published posthumously in 1950, throw much light on the development of his views.

1887. Begins the use of hypnotic suggestion in his practice.

c. 1888. Begins to follow Breuer in using hypnosis for cathartic treatment of hysteria. Gradually drops hypnosis and substitutes free association.

1889. Visits Bernheim at Nancy to study his suggestion technique.
Birth of eldest son (Martin).

1891. Monograph on aphasia.
Birth of second son (Oliver).

1892. Birth of youngest son (Ernst).

1893. Publication of Breuer and Freud 'Preliminary Communication': exposition of trauma theory of hysteria and of cathartic treatment.
Birth of second daughter (Sophie).

1893-8. Researches and short papers on hysteria, obsessions, and anxiety.

1895. Jointly with Breuer, *Studies on Hysteria*: case histories and description by Freud of his technique, including first account of transference.

1893-6. Gradual divergence of views between Freud and Breuer. Freud introduces concepts of defence and repression and of neurosis being a result of a conflict between the ego and the libido.

1895. *Project for a Scientific Psychology*: included in Freud's letters to Fliess and first published in 1950. An abortive attempt to state psychology in neurological terms; but foreshadows much of Freud's later theories.
Birth of youngest child (Anna).

1896. Introduces the term 'psychoanalysis'.
Death of father (aged 80).

1897. Freud's self-analysis, leading to the abandonment of the trauma theory and the recognition of infantile sexuality and the Oedipus complex.

1900. *The Interpretation of Dreams*, with final chapter giving first full account of Freud's dynamic view of mental processes, of the unconscious, and of the dominance of the 'pleasure principle'.

1901. *The Psychopathology of Everyday Life*. This, together with the book on dreams, made it plain that Freud's theories applied not only to pathological states but also to normal mental life.

1902. Appointed Professor Extraordinarius.

1905. *Three Essays on the Theory of Sexuality*: tracing for the first time the course of development of the sexual instinct in human beings from infancy to maturity.

c. 1906. Jung becomes an adherent of psychoanalysis.

1908. First international meeting of psychoanalysts (at Salzburg).

1909. Freud and Jung invited to the USA to lecture.

Case history of the first analysis of a child (Little Hans, aged five): confirming inferences previously made from adult analyses, especially as to infantile sexuality and the Oedipus and castration complexes.

c. 1910. First emergence of the theory of 'narcissism'.

1911–15. Papers on the technique of psychoanalysis.

1911. Secession of Adler.

Application of psychoanalytic theories to a psychotic case: the autobiography of Dr Schreber.

1912–13. *Totem and Taboo*: application of psychoanalysis to anthropological material.

1914. Secession of Jung.

'On the History of the Psycho-Analytic Movement'. Includes a polemical section on Adler and Jung.

Writes his last major case history, of the 'Wolf Man' (not published till 1918).

1915. Writes a series of twelve 'metapsychological' papers on basic theoretical questions, of which only five have survived.

1915–17. *Introductory Lectures*: giving an extensive general account of the state of Freud's views up to the time of the First World War.

1919. Application of the theory of narcissism to the war neuroses.

1920. Death of second daughter.

Beyond the Pleasure Principle: the first explicit introduction of the concept of the 'compulsion to repeat' and of the theory of the 'death instinct'.

1921. *Group Psychology*. Beginnings of a systematic analytic study of the ego.

1923. *The Ego and the Id*. Largely revised account of the structure and functioning of the mind with the division into an id, an ego, and a super-ego.

First onset of cancer.

1925. Revised views on the sexual development of women.

1926. *Inhibitions, Symptoms and Anxiety*. Revised views on the problem of anxiety.

1927. *The Future of an Illusion*. A discussion of religion: the first of a number of sociological works to which Freud devoted most of his remaining years.

1930. *Civilization and its Discontents.* This includes Freud's first extensive study of the destructive instinct (regarded as a manifestation of the 'death instinct').

Freud awarded the Goethe Prize by the City of Frankfurt.

Death of mother (aged 95).

1933. Hitler seizes power in Germany: Freud's books publicly burned in Berlin.

1934–8. *Moses and Monotheism*: the last of Freud's works to appear during his lifetime.

1936. Eightieth birthday. Election as Corresponding Member of Royal Society.

1938. Hitler's invasion of Austria. Freud leaves Vienna for London. *An Outline of Psycho-Analysis.* A final, unfinished, but profound, exposition of psychoanalysis.

1939. 23 September. Death in London.

JAMES STRACHEY

THREE ESSAYS ON
THE THEORY OF SEXUALITY
(1905)

EDITOR'S INTRODUCTION

DREI ABHANDLUNGEN ZUR
SEXUALTHEORIE

(A) German Editions:

(B) English Translations:

Three Contributions to the Sexual Theory

Three Contributions to the Theory of Sex

Three Essays on the Theory of Sexuality

1949   London: Imago Publishing Co. Pp. 133. (Tr. James Strachey.)

1953   *Standard Edition*, **7**, 123–245. (Revised and expanded version of the one published in 1949.) (Reprinted with corrections, 1956.)

The present edition is a corrected reprint of the *Standard Edition* translation, with several editorial modifications.

Freud's *Three Essays on the Theory of Sexuality* stand, there can be no doubt, beside his *Interpretation of Dreams* as his most momentous and original contributions to human knowledge. Nevertheless, until the publication of the *Standard Edition* in 1953, it had been difficult to estimate the precise nature of their impact when they were first published. For they were submitted by their author, in the course of a succession of editions over a period of twenty years, to more modifications and additions than any other of his writings, with the exception of, perhaps, *The Interpretation of Dreams* itself.[1] These changes were not pointed out in the editions published during Freud's lifetime, nor in the *Gesammelte Werke*. In the second (1910) edition only, Freud himself distinguished his new footnotes by an asterisk, though alterations to the text itself were not indicated. (See his Preface to the Second Edition, p. 39 below.) The present edition, though based on the German sixth edition of 1925, the last published in Freud's lifetime (in which the text is identical with that in both the *Gesammelte Schriften* and the *Gesammelte Werke*), indicates with dates every significant addition that has been introduced into the work since its first issue. And as well as that, wherever material

1. Freud himself commented at some length on this circumstance, and the possible inconsistencies it might have introduced into the text, in the second paragraph of his paper on the 'phallic phase' (1923e), see below, p. 307.

of particular interest has been dropped or greatly modified in later editions, the cancelled passage or earlier version is given in an Editor's footnote. This will enable the reader to arrive at a clearer notion of how these essays were altered in accordance with the development of Freud's knowledge and opinions.

It will probably come as a surprise to learn, for instance, that the entire sections on the sexual theories of children and on the pregenital organizations of the libido (both in the second essay) were only added in 1915, ten years after the book was first published. The same year, too, brought the addition of the section on the libido theory to the third essay. Less surprisingly, the advances of biochemistry made it necessary (in 1920) to rewrite the paragraph on the chemical basis of sexuality. Here, indeed, the surprise works the other way. For the original version of this paragraph, here printed in a footnote, shows Freud's remarkable foresight in this connection and how little modification was required in his views (p. 137f.).

But in spite of the considerable additions made to the book after its first appearance, its essence was already there in 1905 and can, indeed, be traced back to still earlier dates. The whole history of Freud's concern with the subject can now, thanks to the publication of the Fliess correspondence (1950a), be followed in detail; but here it will be enough to indicate its outlines. Clinical observations of the importance of sexual factors in the causation, first, of anxiety neurosis and neurasthenia, and later, of the psychoneuroses, were what first led Freud into a general investigation of the subject of sexuality. His first approaches, during the early nineties, were from the physiological and chemical standpoints. A hypothesis on neuro-physiological lines, for instance, of the processes of sexual excitation and discharge will be found in Section III of his first paper on anxiety neurosis (1895b). His insistence on the chemical basis of sexuality goes back at least as far as this. In this case Freud believed that he owed much to suggestions from Fliess, as is shown in, among other places, his associations to the famous dream of Irma's injection in the summer of

1895 (*The Interpretation of Dreams*, Chapter II). He was also indebted to Fliess for hints on the kindred subject of bisexuality (see below, pp. 54–5n.), which he later came to regard as a 'decisive factor' (p. 142), though his ultimate opinion on the operation of that factor brought him into disagreement with Fliess. In his communications to Fliess in which we find the first mention of erotogenic zones (liable to stimulation in childhood but later suppressed) and their connections with perversions, as well as – and here we can see indications of a more psychological approach – a discussion of the repressive forces, disgust, shame and morality.

But though so many elements of Freud's theory of sexuality were already present in his mind by 1896, its keystone was still to be discovered. There had from the very first been a suspicion that the causative factors of hysteria went back to childhood; by 1895 Freud had a complete explanation of hysteria based on the traumatic effects of sexual seduction in early childhood. But during all these years before 1897 infantile sexuality was regarded as no more than a dormant factor, only liable to be brought into the open, with disastrous results, by the intervention of an adult. It was not until the summer of 1897 that Freud found himself obliged to abandon his seduction theory. He announced the event in a latter to Fliess of September 21 (Letter 69),[1] and his almost simultaneous discovery of the Oedipus complex in his self-analysis (Letters 70 and 71 of October 3 and 15) led inevitably to the realization that sexual impulses operated normally in the youngest children without any need for outside stimulation (see, e.g., Letter 75 of November 14). With this realization Freud's sexual theory was in fact completed.

It took some years, however, for him to become entirely

---

1. His abandonment of the seduction theory was first publicly announced in a brief passage and footnote in the present work (p. 108). He later described his own reactions to the event in his 'History of the Psycho-Analytic Movement' (1914d) and in his *Autobiographical Study* 1925d).

reconciled to his own discovery. In a passage, for instance, in his paper on 'Sexuality in the Aetiology of the Neuroses' (1898a) he blows hot and cold on it. On the one hand he says that children are 'capable of every psychical sexual function and of many somatic ones' and that it is wrong to suppose that their sexual life begins only at puberty. But on the other hand he declares that 'the organization and evolution of the human species seek to avoid any considerable sexual activity in childhood', that the sexual motive forces in human beings should be stored up and only released at puberty and that this explains why sexual experiences in childhood are bound to be pathogenic. It is, he goes on, the *after-effects* produced by such experiences in maturity that are important, owing to the development of the somatic and psychical sexual apparatus that has taken place in the meantime. Even in the first edition of *The Interpretation of Dreams* (1900a), there is a curious passage towards the end of Chapter III (P.F.L., 4 209–10), in which Freud remarks that 'we think highly of the happiness of childhood because it is still innocent of sexual desires'. (A corrective footnote was added to this passage in 1911.) This was no doubt a relic from an early draft of the book, for elsewhere (e.g. in his discussion of the Oedipus complex in Chapter V) he writes quite unambiguously of the existence of sexual wishes even in normal children. And it is evident that by the time he drew up his case history of 'Dora' (at the beginning of 1901) the main lines of his theory of sexuality were firmly laid down.

Even so, however, he was in no hurry to publish his results. When *The Interpretation of Dreams* was finished and on the point of appearing, on October 11, 1899 (Letter 121), he wrote to Fliess: 'A theory of sexuality might well be the dream book's immediate successor'; and three months later, on January 26, 1900 (Letter 128): 'I am putting together material for the theory of sexuality and waiting till some spark can set what I have collected ablaze.' But the spark was a long time in coming. Apart from the little essay *On Dreams* and

The Psychopathology of Everyday Life, both of which appeared before the autumn of 1901, Freud published nothing of importance for another five years.

Then, suddenly, in 1905 he brought out three major works: his book on *Jokes*, his *Three Essays* and his case history of 'Dora'. It is certain that the last-named of these had for the most part been written four years earlier in 1901; it was published in October and November 1905. Freud worked on the other two simultaneously: Ernest Jones (1955, 13) tells us that Freud kept the two manuscripts on adjoining tables and added to one or the other according to his mood. The two books were published almost simultaneously; the exact dates are not certain, but they were at least four months before the appearance of the 'Dora' case history.

In the German editions up to *Gesammelte Werke* (1942), the sections are numbered only in the first essay; and indeed before 1924 they were numbered only half-way through the first essay. For convenience of reference, the numbering of the sections has here been extended to the second and third essays.

PREFACE TO THE SECOND EDITION[1]

THE author is under no illusion as to the deficiencies and obscurities of this little work. Nevertheless he has resisted the temptation of introducing into it the results of the researches of the last five years, since this would have destroyed its unity and documentary character. He is, therefore, reprinting the original text with only slight alterations, and has contented himself with adding a few footnotes which are distinguished from the older ones by an asterisk.[2] It is, moreover, his earnest wish that the book may age rapidly – that what was once new in it may become generally accepted, and that what is imperfect in it may be replaced by something better.

VIENNA, *December* 1909

PREFACE TO THE THIRD EDITION

I HAVE now been watching for more than ten years the effects produced by this work and the reception accorded to it; and I take the opportunity offered by the publication of its third edition to preface it with a few remarks intended to prevent misunderstandings and expectations that cannot be fulfilled. It must above all be emphasized that the exposition to be found in the following pages is based entirely upon everyday medical observation, to which the findings of psychoanalytic research should lend additional depth and scientific significance. It is impossible that these *Three Essays on the Theory of*

1. [This preface was omitted from 1920 onwards.]
2. [The distinction was dropped in all subsequent editions; cf. the Editor's Introduction, p. 34 above.]

Sexuality should contain anything but what psychoanalysis makes it necessary to assume or possible to establish. It is, therefore, out of the question that they could ever be extended into a complete 'theory of sexuality', and it is natural that there should be a number of important problems of sexual life with which they do not deal at all. But the reader should not conclude from this that the branches of this large subject which have been thus passed over are unknown to the author or have been neglected by him as of small importance.

The fact that this book is based upon the psychoanalytic observations which led to its composition is shown, however, not only in the choice of the topics dealt with, but also in their arrangement. Throughout the entire work the various factors are placed in a particular order of precedence: preference is given to the accidental factors, while disposition is left in the background, and more weight is attached to ontogenesis than to phylogenesis. For it is the accidental factors that play the principal part in analysis: they are almost entirely subject to its influence. The dispositional ones only come to light after them, as something stirred into activity by experience: adequate consideration of them would lead far beyond the sphere of psychoanalysis.

The relation between ontogenesis and phylogenesis is a similar one. Ontogenesis may be regarded as a recapitulation of phylogenesis, in so far as the latter has not been modified by more recent experience. The phylogenetic disposition can be seen at work behind the ontogenetic process. But disposition is ultimately the precipitate of earlier experience of the species to which the more recent experience of the individual, as the sum of the accidental factors, is super-added.

I must, however, emphasize that the present work is characterized not only by being completely based upon psychoanalytic research, but also by being deliberately independent of the findings of biology. I have carefully avoided introducing any preconceptions, whether derived from general sexual biology or from that of particular animal species, into this study – a study which is concerned with the sexual functions of human beings and which is made possible through the technique of psychoanalysis. Indeed, my aim has rather been to discover how far psychological investigation can throw light upon the biology of the sexual life of man. It was legitimate for me to indicate points of contact and agreement which came to light during my investigation, but there was no need for me to be diverted from my course if the psychoanalytic method led in a number of important respects to opinions and findings which differed largely from those based on biological considerations.

In this third edition I have introduced a considerable amount of fresh matter, but have not indicated it in any special way, as I did in the previous edition. Progress in our field of scientific work is at present less rapid; nevertheless it was essential to make a certain number of additions to this volume if it was to be kept in touch with recent psychoanalytic literature.[1]

VIENNA, *October* 1914

1. [The following footnote appeared at this point in 1915 only:] In 1910, after the publication of the second edition, an English translation by A. A. Brill was published in New York; and in 1911 a Russian one by N. Ossipow in Moscow. [Translations also appeared during Freud's lifetime in Hungarian (1915), Italian (1921), Spanish (1922), French 1923), Polish (1924), Czech (1926) and Japanese (1931).]

PREFACE TO THE FOURTH EDITION

Now that the flood-waters of war have subsided, it is satis-factory to be able to record the fact that interest in psycho-analytic research remains unimpaired in the world at large. But the different parts of the theory have not all had the same history. The purely psychological theses and findings of psychoanalysis on the unconscious, repression, conflict as a cause of illness, the advantage accruing from illness, the mechanisms of the formation of symptoms, etc., have come to enjoy increasing recognition and have won notice even from those who are in general opposed to our views. That part of the theory, however, which lies on the frontiers of biology and the foundations of which are contained in this little work is still faced with undiminished contradiction. It has even led some who for a time took a very active interest in psycho-analysis to abandon it and to adopt fresh views which were intended to restrict once more the part played by the factor of sexuality in normal and pathological mental life.

Nevertheless I cannot bring myself to accept the idea that this part of psychoanalytic theory can be very much more dis-tant than the rest from the reality which it is its business to discover. My recollections, as well as a constant re-examina-tion of the material, assure me that this part of the theory is based upon equally careful and impartial observation. There is, moreover, no difficulty in finding an explanation of this dis-crepancy in the general acceptance of my views. In the first place, the beginnings of human sexual life which are here described can only be confirmed by investigators who have enough patience and technical skill to trace back an analysis to the first years of a patient's childhood. And there is often no possibility of doing this, since medical treatment demands that an illness should, at least in appearance, be dealt with more rapidly. None, however, but physicians who practise psychoanalysis can have any access whatever to this sphere of knowledge or any possibility of forming a judgement that is uninfluenced by their own dislikes and prejudices. If mankind had been able to learn from a direct observation of children, these three essays could have remained unwritten.

It must also be remembered, however, that some of what this book contains – its insistence on the importance of sexuality in all human achievements and the attempt that it makes at enlarging the concept of sexuality – has from the first provided the strongest motives for the resistance against psychoanalysis. People have gone so far in their search for high-sounding catchwords as to talk of the 'pan-sexualism' of psychoanalysis and to raise the senseless charge against it of explaining 'everything' by sex. We might be astonished at this, if we ourselves could forget the way in which emotional factors make people confused and forgetful. For it is some time since Arthur Schopenhauer, the philosopher, showed mankind the extent to which their activities are determined by sexual impulses – in the ordinary sense of the word. It should surely have been impossible for a whole world of readers to banish such a startling piece of information so completely from their minds. And as for the 'stretching' of the concept of sexuality which has been necessitated by the analysis of children and what are called perverts, anyone who looks down with contempt upon psychoanalysis from a superior vantage-point should remember how closely the enlarged sexuality of psychoanalysis coincides with the Eros of the divine Plato. (Cf. Nachmansohn, 1915.)

VIENNA, *May* 1920

I

THE SEXUAL ABERRATIONS[1]

THE fact of the existence of sexual needs in human beings and animals is expressed in biology by the assumption of a 'sexual instinct', on the analogy of the instinct of nutrition, that is of hunger. Everyday language possesses no counterpart to the word 'hunger', but science makes use of the word 'libido' for that purpose.[2]

Popular opinion has quite definite ideas about the nature and characteristics of this sexual instinct. It is generally understood to be absent in childhood, to set in at the time of puberty in connection with the process of coming to maturity and to be revealed in the manifestations of an irresistible attraction exercised by one sex upon the other; while its aim is presumed to be sexual union, or at all events actions leading in that direction. We have every reason to believe, however, that these views give a very false picture of the true situation. If we look into them more closely we shall find that they contain a number of errors, inaccuracies and hasty conclusions.

I shall at this point introduce two technical terms. Let us call the person from whom sexual attraction proceeds the

1. The information contained in this first essay is derived from the well-known writings of Krafft-Ebing, Moll, Moebius, Havelock Ellis, Schrenck-Notzing, Löwenfeld, Eulenburg, Bloch and Hirschfeld, and from the works in the *Jahrbuch für sexuelle Zwischenstufen*, published under the direction of the last-named author. Since full bibliographies of the remaining literature of the subject will be found in the works of these writers, I have been able to spare myself the necessity for giving detailed references. [*Added* 1910:] The data obtained from the psychoanalytic investigation of inverts are based upon material supplied to me by I. Sadger and upon my own findings.

2. [*Footnote added* 1910:] The only appropriate word in the German language, '*Lust*', is unfortunately ambiguous, and is used to denote the experience both of a need and of a gratification. [Unlike the English 'lust' it can mean either 'desire' or 'pleasure'. See footnote, page 133.]

sexual object and the act towards which the instinct tends the *sexual aim*. Scientifically sifted observation, then, shows that numerous deviations occur in respect of both of these – the sexual object and the sexual aim. The relation between these deviations and what is assumed to be normal requires thorough investigation.

(1) DEVIATIONS IN RESPECT OF THE SEXUAL OBJECT

The popular view of the sexual instinct is beautifully reflected in the poetic fable which tells how the original human beings were cut up into two halves – man and woman – and how these are always striving to unite again in love.[1] It comes as a great surprise therefore to learn that there are men whose sexual object is a man and not a woman, and women whose sexual object is a woman and not a man. People of this kind are described as having 'contrary sexual feelings', or better, as being 'inverts', and the fact is described as 'inversion'. The number of such people is very considerable, though there are difficulties in establishing it precisely.[2]

(A) INVERSION

Behaviour of Inverts

Such people vary greatly in their behaviour in several respects.

(a) They may be *absolute* inverts. In that case their sexual objects are exclusively of their own sex. Persons of the opposite sex are never the object of their sexual desire, but leave them cold, or even arouse sexual aversion in them. As a

1. [This is no doubt an allusion to the theory expounded by Aristophanes in Plato's *Symposium*. Freud recurred to this much later, at the end of Chapter VI of *Beyond the Pleasure Principle* (1920g).]

2. On these difficulties and on the attempts which have been made to arrive at the proportional number of inverts, see Hirschfeld (1904).

consequence of this aversion, they are incapable, if they are men, of carrying out the sexual act, or else they derive no enjoyment from it.

(b) They may be *amphigenic* inverts, that is psychosexual hermaphrodites. In that case their sexual objects may equally well be of their own or of the opposite sex. This kind of inversion thus lacks the characteristic of exclusiveness.

(c) They may be *contingent* inverts. In that case, under certain external conditions – of which inaccessibility of any normal sexual object and imitation are the chief – they are capable of taking as their sexual object someone of their own sex and of deriving satisfaction from sexual intercourse with him.

Again, inverts vary in their views as to the peculiarity of their sexual instinct. Some of them accept their inversion as something in the natural course of things, just as a normal person accepts the direction of *his* libido, and insist energetically that inversion is as legitimate as the normal attitude; others rebel against their inversion and feel it as a pathological compulsion.[1]

Other variations occur which relate to questions of time. The trait of inversion may either date back to the very beginning, as far back as the subject's memory reaches, or it may not have become noticeable till some particular time before or after puberty.[2] It may either persist throughout life, or it may

1. The fact of a person struggling in this way against a compulsion towards inversion may perhaps determine the possibility of his being influenced by suggestion [*added* 1910:] or psychoanalysis.

2. Many writers have insisted with justice that the dates assigned by inverts themselves for the appearance of their tendency to inversion are untrustworthy, since they may have repressed the evidence of their heterosexual feelings from their memory. [*Added* 1910:] These suspicions have been confirmed by psychoanalysis in those cases of inversion to which it has had access; it has produced decisive alterations in their anamnesis by filling in their infantile amnesia. – [In the first edition (1905) the place of this last sentence was taken by the following one: 'A decision on this point could be arrived at only by a psychoanalytic investigation of inverts.']

go into temporary abeyance, or again it may constitute an episode on the way to a normal development. It may even make its first appearance late in life after a long period of normal sexual activity. A periodic oscillation between a normal and an inverted sexual object has also sometimes been observed. Those cases are of particular interest in which the libido changes over to an inverted sexual object after a distressing experience with a normal one.

As a rule these different kinds of variations are found side by side independently of one another. It is, however, safe to assume that the most extreme form of inversion will have been present from a very early age and that the person concerned will feel at one with his peculiarity.

Many authorities would be unwilling to class together all the various cases which I have enumerated and would prefer to lay stress upon their differences rather than their resemblances, in accordance with their own preferred view of inversion. Nevertheless, though the distinctions cannot be disputed, it is impossible to overlook the existence of numerous intermediate examples of every type, so that we are driven to conclude that we are dealing with a connected series.

Nature of Inversion

The earliest assessments regarded inversion as an innate indication of nervous degeneracy. This corresponded to the fact that medical observers first came across it in persons suffering, or appearing to suffer, from nervous diseases. This characterization of inversion involves two suppositions, which must be considered separately: that it is innate and that it is degenerate.

Degeneracy

The attribution of degeneracy in this connection is open to the objections which can be raised against the indiscriminate use of the word in general. It has become the fashion to regard any symptom which is not obviously due to trauma or infection as a sign of degeneracy. Magnan's classification of degenerates is indeed of such a kind as not to exclude the possibility of the concept of degeneracy being applied to a nervous system whose general functioning is excellent. This being so, it may well be asked whether an attribution of 'degeneracy' is of any value or adds anything to our knowledge. It seems wiser only to speak of it where

(1) several serious deviations from the normal are found together, and

(2) the capacity for efficient functioning and survival seem to be severely impaired.[1]

Several facts go to show that in this legitimate sense of the word inverts cannot be regarded as degenerate:

(1) Inversion is found in people who exhibit no other serious deviations from the normal.

(2) It is similarly found in people whose efficiency is unimpaired, and who are indeed distinguished by specially high intellectual development and ethical culture.[2]

(3) If we disregard the patients we come across in our medical practice, and cast our eyes round a wider horizon, we shall come in two directions upon facts which make it impossible to regard inversion as a sign of degeneracy:

(a) Account must be taken of the fact that inversion was a frequent phenomenon – one might almost say an institution charged with important functions – among the peoples of antiquity at the height of their civilization.

(b) It is remarkably widespread among many savage and

1. Moebius (1900) confirms the view that we should be chary in making a diagnosis of degeneracy and that it has very little practical value: 'If we survey the wide field of degeneracy upon which some glimpses of revealing light have been thrown in these pages, it will at once be clear that there is small value in ever making a diagnosis of degeneracy.'

2. It must be allowed that the spokesmen of 'Uranism' are justified in asserting that some of the most prominent men in all recorded history were inverts and perhaps even absolute inverts. [The term 'Uranism' (derived from Uranos in Plato's *Symposium*) was coined by Karl Heinrich Ulrichs, who used it as early as 1862. See also p. 54 and *n.* 1 below.]

primitive races, whereas the concept of degeneracy is usually restricted to states of high civilization (cf. Bloch); and, even amongst the civilized peoples of Europe, climate and race exercise the most powerful influence on the prevalence of inversion and upon the attitude adopted towards it.[1]

Innate Character

As may be supposed, innateness is only attributed to the first, most extreme, class of inverts, and the evidence for it rests upon assurances given by them that at no time in their lives has their sexual instinct shown any sign of taking another course. The very existence of the two other classes, and especially the third [the 'contingent' inverts], is difficult to reconcile with the hypothesis of the innateness of inversion. This explains why those who support this view tend to separate out the group of absolute inverts from all the rest, thus abandoning any attempt at giving an account of inversion which shall have universal application. In the view of these authorities inversion is innate in one group of cases, while in others it may have come about in other ways.

The reverse of this view is represented by the alternative one that inversion is an acquired character of the sexual instinct. This second view is based on the following considerations:

(1) In the case of many inverts, even absolute ones, it is possible to show that very early in their lives a sexual impression occurred which left a permanent after-effect in the shape of a tendency to homosexuality.

(2) In the case of many others, it is possible to point to external influences in their lives, whether of a favourable or inhibiting character, which have led sooner or later to a fixation of their inversion. (Such influences are exclusive relations

1. The pathological approach to the study of inversion has been displaced by the anthropological. The merit for bringing about this change is due to Bloch (1902–3), who has also laid stress on the occurrence of inversion among the civilizations of antiquity.

with persons of their own sex, comradeship in war, detention in prison, the dangers of heterosexual intercourse, celibacy, sexual weakness, etc.)

(3) Inversion can be removed by hypnotic suggestion, which would be astonishing in an innate characteristic.

In view of these considerations it is even possible to doubt the very existence of such a thing as innate inversion. It can be argued (cf. Havelock Ellis [1897]) that, if the cases of allegedly innate inversion were more closely examined, some experience of their early childhood would probably come to light which had a determining effect upon the direction taken by their libido. This experience would simply have passed out of the subject's conscious recollection, but could be recalled to his memory under appropriate influence. In the opinion of these writers inversion can only be described as a frequent variation of the sexual instinct, which can be determined by a number of external circumstances in the subject's life.

The apparent certainty of this conclusion is, however, completely countered by the reflection that many people are subjected to the same sexual influences (e.g. to seduction or mutual masturbation, which may occur in early youth) without becoming inverted or without remaining so permanently. We are therefore forced to a suspicion that the choice between 'innate' and 'acquired' is not an exclusive one or that it does not cover all the issues involved in inversion.

Explanation of Inversion

The nature of inversion is explained neither by the hypothesis that it is innate nor by the alternative hypothesis that it is acquired. In the former case we must ask in what respect it is innate, unless we are to accept the crude explanation that everyone is born with his sexual instinct attached to a particular sexual object. In the latter case it may be questioned whether the various accidental influences would be sufficient to explain the acquisition of inversion without the co-operation of something in the subject himself. As we have already shown, the existence of this last factor is not to be denied.

Bisexuality

A fresh contradiction of popular views is involved in the considerations put forward by Lydston [1889], Kiernan [1888] and Chevalier [1893] in an endeavour to account for the possibility of sexual inversion. It is popularly believed that a human being is either a man or a woman. Science, however, knows of cases in which the sexual characters are obscured, and in which it is consequently difficult to determine the sex. This arises in the first instance in the field of anatomy. The genitals of the individuals concerned combine male and female characteristics. (This condition is known as hermaphroditism.) In rare cases both kinds of sexual apparatus are found side by side fully developed (true hermaphroditism); but far more frequently both sets of organs are found in an atrophied condition.[1]

The importance of these abnormalities lies in the unexpected fact that they facilitate our understanding of normal development. For it appears that a certain degree of anatomical hermaphroditism occurs normally. In every normal male or female individual, traces are found of the apparatus of the opposite sex. These either persist without function as rudimentary organs or become modified and take on other functions.

These long-familiar facts of anatomy lead us to suppose that an originally bisexual physical disposition has, in the course of evolution, become modified into a unisexual one, leaving behind only a few traces of the sex that has become atrophied.

It was tempting to extend this hypothesis to the mental sphere and to explain inversion in all its varieties as the expression of a psychical hermaphroditism. All that was required

1. For the most recent descriptions of somatic hermaphroditism, see Taruffi (1903), and numerous papers by Neugebauer in various volumes of the *Jahrbuch für sexuelle Zwischenstufen.*

further in order to settle the question was that inversion should be regularly accompanied by the mental and somatic signs of hermaphroditism.

But this expectation was disappointed. It is impossible to demonstrate so close a connection between the hypothetical psychical hermaphroditism and the established anatomical one. A general lowering of the sexual instinct and a slight anatomical atrophy of the organs is found frequently in inverts (cf. Havelock Ellis [1897]). Frequently, but by no means regularly or even usually. The truth must therefore be recognized that inversion and somatic hermaphroditism are on the whole independent of each other.

A great deal of importance, too, has been attached to what are called the secondary and tertiary sexual characters and to the great frequency of the occurrence of those of the opposite sex in inverts (cf. Havelock Ellis [1897]). Much of this, again, is correct; but it should never be forgotten that in general the secondary and tertiary sexual characters of one sex occur very frequently in the opposite one. They are indications of hermaphroditism, but are not attended by any change of sexual object in the direction of inversion.

Psychical hermaphroditism would gain substance if the inversion of the sexual object were at least accompanied by a parallel change-over of the subject's other mental qualities, instincts and character traits into those marking the opposite sex. But it is only in inverted women that character-inversion of this kind can be looked for with any regularity. In men the most complete mental masculinity can be combined with inversion. If the belief in psychical hermaphroditism is to be persisted in, it will be necessary to add that its manifestations in various spheres show only slight signs of being mutually determined. Moreover the same is true of somatic hermaphroditism: according to Halban (1903),[1] occurrences of individual atrophied organs and of secondary sexual characters are to a considerable extent independent of one another.

1. His paper includes a bibliography of the subject.

The theory of bisexuality has been expressed in its crudest form by a spokesman of the male inverts: 'a feminine brain in a masculine body'.[1] But we are ignorant of what characterizes a feminine brain. There is neither need nor justification for replacing the psychological problem by the anatomical one. Krafft-Ebing's attempted explanation seems to be more exactly framed than that of Ulrichs but does not differ from it in essentials. According to Krafft-Ebing [1895, 5], every individual's bisexual disposition endows him with masculine and feminine brain centres as well as with somatic organs of sex; these centres develop only at puberty, for the most part under the influence of the sex-gland, which is independent of them in the original disposition. But what has just been said of masculine and feminine brains applies equally to masculine and feminine 'centres'; and incidentally we have not even any grounds for assuming that certain areas of the brain ('centres') are set aside for the functions of sex, as is the case, for instance, with those of speech.[2]

1. [The description was Ulrichs': '*Anima muliebris in corpore virili inclusa.*' Cf. also p. 49 *n.* 2 above.]

2. It appears (from a bibliography given in the sixth volume of the *Jahrbuch für sexuelle Zwischenstufen*) that E. Gley was the first writer to suggest bisexuality as an explanation of inversion. As long ago as in January, 1884, he published a paper, 'Les aberrations de l'instinct sexuel', in the *Revue philosophique*. It is, moreover, noteworthy that the majority of authors who derive inversion from bisexuality bring forward that factor not only in the case of inverts, but also for all those who have grown up to be normal, and that, as a logical consequence, they regard inversion as the result of a disturbance in development. Chevalier (1893) already writes in this sense. Krafft-Ebing (1895, [10]) remarks that there are a great number of observations 'which prove at least the virtual persistence of this second centre (that of the subordinated sex)'. A Dr Arduin (1900) asserts that 'there are masculine and feminine elements in every human being (cf. Hirschfeld, 1899); but one set of these – according to the sex of the person in question – is incomparably more strongly developed than the other, so far as heterosexual individuals are concerned. . . .' Herman (1903) is convinced that 'masculine elements and characteristics are present in every woman and feminine ones in every man', etc. [*Added* 1910:] Fliess (1906) subsequently claimed

Nevertheless, two things emerge from these discussions. In the first place, a bisexual disposition is somehow concerned in inversion, though we do not know in what that disposition consists, beyond anatomical structure. And secondly, we have to deal with disturbances that affect the sexual instinct in the course of its development.

Sexual Object of Inverts

The theory of psychical hermaphroditism presupposes that the sexual object of an invert is the opposite of that of a normal person. An inverted man, it holds, is like a woman in being subject to the charm that proceeds from masculine attributes both physical and mental: he feels he is a woman in search of a man.

But however well this applies to quite a number of inverts, it is, nevertheless, far from revealing a universal characteristic of inversion. There can be no doubt that a large proportion of male inverts retain the mental quality of masculinity, that they possess relatively few of the secondary characters of the opposite sex and that what they look for in their sexual object are in fact feminine mental traits. If this were not so, how would it be possible to explain the fact that male prostitutes who offer themselves to inverts – today just as they did in ancient times – imitate women in all the externals of their clothing and behaviour? Such imitation would otherwise inevitably clash with the ideal of the inverts. It is clear that in Greece, where the

---

the idea of bisexuality (in the sense of *duality of sex*) as his own. [*Added* 1924:] In lay circles the hypothesis of human bisexuality is regarded as being due to O. Weininger, the philosopher, who died at an early age, and who made the idea the basis of a somewhat unbalanced book (1903). The particulars which I have enumerated above will be sufficient to show how little justification there is for the claim.

[Freud's own realization of the importance of bisexuality owed much to Fliess (cf. p. 142 *n*.1). He did not, however, accept Fliess's view that bisexuality provided the explanation of repression. See Freud's discussion of this in 'A Child is Being Beaten' (1919*e*, half-way through Section VI, *P.F.L.*, 10, 188–91).]

most masculine men were numbered among the inverts, what excited a man's love was not the *masculine* character of a boy, but his physical resemblance to a woman as well as his feminine mental qualities – his shyness, his modesty and his need for instruction and assistance. As soon as the boy became a man he ceased to be a sexual object for men and himself, perhaps, became a lover of boys. In this instance, therefore, as in many others, the sexual object is not someone of the same sex but someone who combines the characters of both sexes; there is, as it were, a compromise between an impulse that seeks for a man and one that seeks for a woman, while it remains a paramount condition that the object's body (i.e. genitals) shall be masculine. Thus the sexual object is a kind of reflection of the subject's own bisexual nature.[1]

1. [This last sentence was added in 1915. – *Footnote added* 1910:] It is true that psychoanalysis has not yet produced a complete explanation of the origin of inversion; nevertheless, it has discovered the psychical mechanism of its development, and has made essential contributions to the statement of the problems involved. In all the cases we have examined we have established the fact that the future inverts, in the earliest years of their childhood, pass through a phase of very intense but short-lived fixation to a woman (usually their mother), and that, after leaving this behind, they identify themselves with a woman and take *themselves* as their sexual object. That is to say, proceeding from a basis of narcissim, they look for a young man who resembles themselves and whom *they* may love as their mother loved *them*. Moreover, we have frequently found that alleged inverts have been by no means insusceptible to the charms of women, but have continually transposed the excitation aroused by women on to a male object. They have thus repeated all through their lives the mechanism by which their inversion arose. Their compulsive longing for men has turned out to be determined by their ceaseless flight from women.

[*Added* 1915:] Psychoanalytic research is most decidedly opposed to any attempt at separating off homosexuals from the rest of mankind as a group of a special character. By studying sexual excitations other than those that are manifestly displayed, it has found that all human beings are capable of making a homosexual object-choice and have in fact made one in their unconscious. Indeed, libidinal attachments to persons of the same sex play no less a part as factors in normal mental life, and a greater part as a motive force for illness, than do similar attachments

The position in the case of women is less ambiguous; for among them the active inverts exhibit masculine characteristics, both physical and mental, with peculiar frequency and look for femininity in their sexual objects – though here again a closer knowledge of the facts might reveal greater variety.

---

to the opposite sex. On the contrary, psychoanalysis considers that a choice of an object independently of its sex – freedom to range equally over male and female objects – as it is found in childhood, in primitive states of society and early periods of history, is the original basis from which, as a result of restriction in one direction or the other, both the normal and the inverted types develop. Thus from the point of view of psychoanalysis the exclusive sexual interest felt by men for women is also a problem that needs elucidating and is not a self-evident fact based upon an attraction that is ultimately of a chemical nature. A person's final sexual attitude is not decided until after puberty and is the result of a number of factors, not all of which are yet known; some are of a constitutional nature but others are accidental. No doubt a few of these factors may happen to carry so much weight that they influence the result in their sense. But in general the multiplicity of determining factors is reflected in the variety of manifest sexual attitudes in which they find their issue in mankind. In inverted types, a predominance of archaic constitutions and primitive psychical mechanisms is regularly to be found. Their most essential characteristics seem to be a coming into operation of *narcissistic object-choice* and a *retention* of the erotic significance of the *anal zone*. There is nothing to be gained, however, by separating the most extreme types of inversion from the rest on the basis of constitutional peculiarities of that kind. What we find as an apparently sufficient explanation of these types can be equally shown to be present, though less strongly, in the constitution of transitional types and of those whose manifest attitude is normal. The differences in the end-products may be of a qualitative nature, but analysis shows that the differences between their determinants are only quantitative. Among the accidental factors that influence object-choice we have found that frustration (in the form of an early deterrence, by fear, from sexual activity) deserves attention, and we have observed that the presence of both parents plays an important part. The absence of a strong father in childhood not infrequently favours the occurrence of inversion. Finally, it may be insisted that the concept of inversion in respect of the sexual object should be sharply distinguished from that of the occurrence in the subject of a mixture of sexual characters. In the

Sexual Aim of Inverts

The important fact to bear in mind is that no one single aim can be laid down as applying in cases of inversion. Among men, intercourse *per anum* by no means coincides with inversion; masturbation is quite as frequently their exclusive aim,

---

relation between these two factors, too, a certain degree of reciprocal independence is unmistakably present.

[*Added* 1920:] Ferenczi (1914) has brought forward a number of interesting points on the subject of inversion. He rightly protests that, because they have in common the symptom of inversion, a large number of conditions, which are very different from one another and which are of unequal importance both in organic and psychical respects, have been thrown together under the name of 'homosexuality' (or, to follow him in giving it a better name, 'homo-erotism'). He insists that a sharp distinction should at least be made between two types: 'subject homo-erotics', who feel and behave like women, and 'object homo-erotics', who are completely masculine and who have merely exchanged a female for a male object. The first of these two types he recognizes as true 'sexual intermediates' in Hirschfeld's sense of the word; the second he describes, less happily, as obsessional neurotics. According to him, it is only in the case of object homo-erotics that there is any question of their struggling against their inclination to inversion or of the possibility of their being influenced psychologically. While granting the existence of these two types, we may add that there are many people in whom a certain quantity of subject homo-erotism is found in combination with a proportion of object homo-erotism.

During the last few years work carried out by biologists, notably by Steinach, has thrown a strong light on the organic determinants of homo-erotism and of sexual characters in general. By carrying out experimental castration and subsequently grafting the sex-glands of the opposite sex, it was possible in the case of various species of mammals to transform a male into a female and vice versa. The transformation affected more or less completely both the somatic sexual characters and the psychosexual attitude (that is, both subject and object erotism). It appeared that the vehicle of the force which thus acted as a sex-determinant was not the part of the sex-gland which forms the sex-cells but what is known as its interstitial tissue (the 'puberty-gland'). In one case this transformation of sex was actually effected in a man who had lost his testes owing to tuberculosis. In his sexual life he behaved in a feminine manner, as a passive homosexual, and exhibited very clearly-

and it is even true that restrictions of sexual aim – to the point of its being limited to simple outpourings of emotion – are commoner among them than among heterosexual lovers. Among women, too, the sexual aims of inverts are various; there seems to be a special preference for contact with the mucous membrane of the mouth.

Conclusion

It will be seen that we are not in a position to base a satisfactory explanation of the origin of inversion upon the material at present before us. Nevertheless our investigation has put us in possession of a piece of knowledge which may turn out to be of greater importance to us than the solution of that problem. It has been brought to our notice that we have been in the habit of regarding the connection between the sexual instinct and the sexual object as more intimate than it in fact is. Experience of the cases that are considered abnormal has shown us that in them the sexual instinct and the sexual object are merely soldered together – a fact which we have been in danger of overlooking in consequence of the uniformity of the normal picture, where the object appears to form part and parcel of the instinct. We are thus warned to loosen the bond that exists in our thoughts between instinct and object. It

---

marked feminine sexual characters of a secondary kind (e.g. in regard to growth of hair and beard and deposits of fat on the breasts and hips). After an undescended testis from another male patient had been grafted into him, he began to behave in a masculine manner and to direct his libido towards women in a normal way. Simultaneously his somatic feminine characters disappeared (Lipschütz, 1919, 356–7).

It would be unjustifiable to assert that these interesting experiments put the theory of inversion on a new basis, and it would be hasty to expect them to offer a universal means of 'curing' homosexuality. Fliess has rightly insisted that these experimental findings do not invalidate the theory of the general bisexual disposition of the higher animals. On the contrary, it seems to me probable that further research of a similar kind will produce a direct confirmation of this presumption of bi-sexuality.

seems probable that the sexual instinct is in the first instance independent of its object; nor is its origin likely to be due to its object's attractions.

(B) SEXUALLY IMMATURE PERSONS AND ANIMALS AS SEXUAL OBJECTS

People whose sexual objects belong to the normally inappropriate sex – that is, inverts – strike the observer as a collection of individuals who may be quite sound in other respects. On the other hand, cases in which sexually immature persons (children) are chosen as sexual objects are instantly judged as sporadic aberrations. It is only exceptionally that children are the exclusive sexual objects in such a case. They usually come to play that part when someone who is cowardly or has become impotent adopts them as a substitute, or when an urgent instinct (one which will not allow of postponement) cannot at the moment get possession of any more appropriate object. Nevertheless, a light is thrown on the nature of the sexual instinct by the fact that it permits of so much variation in its objects and such a cheapening of them – which hunger, with its far more energetic retention of its objects, would only permit in the most extreme instances. A similar consideration applies to sexual intercourse with animals, which is by no means rare, especially among country people, and in which sexual attraction seems to override the barriers of species.

One would be glad on aesthetic grounds to be able to ascribe these and other severe aberrations of the sexual instinct to insanity; but that cannot be done. Experience shows that disturbances of the sexual instinct among the insane do not differ from those that occur among the healthy and in whole races or occupations. Thus the sexual abuse of children is found with uncanny frequency among school teachers and child attendants, simply because they have the best opportunity for it. The insane merely exhibit any such aberration to an intensified degree; or, what is particularly significant, it may become exclusive and replace normal sexual satisfaction entirely.

The very remarkable relation which thus holds between sexual variations and the descending scale from health to insanity gives us plenty of material for thought. I am inclined to believe that it may be explained by the fact that the impulses of sexual life are among those which, even normally, are the least controlled by the higher activities of the mind. In my experience anyone who is in any way, whether socially or ethically, abnormal mentally is invariably abnormal also in his sexual life. But many people are abnormal in their sexual life who in every other respect approximate to the average, and have, along with the rest, passed through the process of human cultural development, in which sexuality remains the weak spot.

The most general conclusion that follows from all these discussions seems, however, to be this. Under a great number of conditions and in surprisingly numerous individuals, the nature and importance of the sexual object recedes into the background. What is essential and constant in the sexual instinct is something else.[1]

(2) DEVIATIONS IN RESPECT OF THE SEXUAL AIM

The normal sexual aim is regarded as being the union of the genitals in the act known as copulation, which leads to a release of the sexual tension and a temporary extinction of the sexual instinct – a satisfaction analogous to the sating of hunger. But even in the most normal sexual process we may detect

1. [*Footnote added* 1910:] The most striking distinction between the erotic life of antiquity and our own no doubt lies in the fact that the ancients laid the stress upon the instinct itself, whereas we emphasize its object. The ancients glorified the instinct and were prepared on its account to honour even an inferior object; while we despise the instinctual activity in itself, and find excuses for it only in the merits of the object.

rudiments which, if they had developed, would have led to the deviations described as 'perversions'. For there are certain intermediate relations to the sexual object, such as touching and looking at it, which lie on the road towards copulation and are recognized as being preliminary sexual aims. On the one hand these activities are themselves accompanied by pleasure, and on the other hand they intensify the excitation, which should persist until the final sexual aim is attained. Moreover, the kiss, one particular contact of this kind, between the mucous membrane of the lips of the two people concerned, is held in high sexual esteem among many nations (including the most highly civilized ones), in spite of the fact that the parts of the body involved do not form part of the sexual apparatus but constitute the entrance to the digestive tract. Here, then, are factors which provide a point of contact between the perversions and normal sexual life and which can also serve as a basis for their classification. Perversions are sexual activities which either (a) *extend*, in an anatomical sense, beyond the regions of the body that are designed for sexual union, or (b) *linger* over the intermediate relations to the sexual object which should normally be traversed rapidly on the path towards the final sexual aim.

(A) ANATOMICAL EXTENSIONS

Overvaluation of the Sexual Object

It is only in the rarest instances that the psychical valuation that is set on the sexual object, as being the goal of the sexual instinct, stops short at its genitals. The appreciation extends to the whole body of the sexual object and tends to involve every sensation derived from it. The same overvaluation spreads over into the psychological sphere: the subject becomes, as it were, intellectually infatuated (that is, his powers of judgement are weakened) by the mental achievements and perfections of the sexual object and he submits to the latter's judgements with credulity. Thus the credulity of love becomes an important, if not the most fundamental, source of *authority*.[1]

This sexual overvaluation is something that cannot be easily reconciled with a restriction of the sexual aim to union of the actual genitals and it helps to turn activities connected with other parts of the body into sexual aims.[2]

The significance of the factor of sexual overvaluation can be best studied in men, for their erotic life alone has become accessible to research. That of women – partly owing to the stunting effect of civilized conditions and partly owing to their conventional secretiveness and insincerity – is still veiled in an impenetrable obscurity.[3]

Sexual Use of the Mucous Membrane of the Lips and Mouth

The use of the mouth as a sexual organ is regarded as a perversion if the lips (or tongue) of one person are brought into

1. In this connection I cannot help recalling the credulous submissiveness shown by a hypnotized subject towards his hypnotist. This leads me to suspect that the essence of hypnosis lies in an unconscious fixation of the subject's libido to the figure of the hypnotist, through the medium of the masochistic components of the sexual instinct. [*Added* 1910:] Ferenczi (1909) has brought this characteristic of suggestibility into relation with the 'parental complex'. – [The relation of the subject to the hypnotist was discussed by Freud much later, in Chapter VIII of his *Group Psychology* (1921c).]

2. [The following footnote (the last sentence of which was new) and the paragraph in the text above, to which it is attached, were recast in 1920 in their present, slightly modified form:] It must be pointed out, however, that sexual overvaluation is not developed in the case of *every* mechanism of object-choice. We shall become acquainted later on with another and more direct explanation of the sexual role assumed by the other parts of the body. The factor of 'craving for stimulation' has been put forward by Hoche and Bloch as an explanation of the extension of sexual interest to parts of the body other than the genitals; but it does not seem to me to deserve such an important place. The various channels along which the libido passes are related to each other from the very first like inter-communicating pipes, and we must take the phenomenon of collateral flow into account. [See p. 85.]

3. [*Footnote added* 1920:] In typical cases women fail to exhibit any sexual overvaluation towards men; but they scarcely ever fail to do so towards their own children.

contact with the genitals of another, but not if the mucous membranes of the lips of both of them come together. This exception is the point of contact with what is normal. Those who condemn the other practices (which have no doubt been common among mankind from primaeval times) as being perversions, are giving way to an unmistakable feeling of *disgust*, which protects them from accepting sexual aims of the kind. The limits of such disgust are, however, often purely conventional: a man who will kiss a pretty girl's lips passionately, may perhaps be disgusted at the idea of using her toothbrush, though there are no grounds for supposing that his own oral cavity, for which he feels no disgust, is any cleaner than the girl's. Here, then, our attention is drawn to the factor of disgust, which interferes with the libidinal overvaluation of the sexual object but can in turn be overridden by libido. Disgust seems to be one of the forces which have led to a restriction of the sexual aim. These forces do not as a rule extend to the genitals themselves. But there is no doubt that the genitals of the opposite sex can in themselves be an object of disgust and that such an attitude is one of the characteristics of all hysterics, and especially of hysterical women. The sexual instinct in its strength enjoys overriding this disgust. (See below [p. 69 f.].)

Sexual Use of the Anal Orifice

Where the anus is concerned it becomes still clearer that it is disgust which stamps that sexual aim as a perversion. I hope, however, I shall not be accused of partisanship when I assert that people who try to account for this disgust by saying that the organ in question serves the function of excretion and comes in contact with excrement – a thing which is disgusting in itself – are not much more to the point than hysterical girls who account for their disgust at the male genital by saying that it serves to void urine.

The playing of a sexual part by the mucous membrane of the anus is by no means limited to intercourse between men:

preference for it is in no way characteristic of inverted feeling. On the contrary, it seems that *paedicatio* with a male owes its origin to an analogy with a similar act performed with a woman; while mutual masturbation is the sexual aim most often found in intercourse between inverts.

Significance of other Regions of the Body

The extension of sexual interest to other regions of the body, with all its variations, offers us nothing that is new in principle; it adds nothing to our knowledge of the sexual instinct, which merely proclaims its intention in this way of getting possession of the sexual object in every possible direction. But these anatomical extensions inform us that, besides sexual overvaluation, there is a second factor at work which is strange to popular knowledge. Certain regions of the body, such as the mucous membrane of the mouth and anus, which are constantly appearing in these practices, seem, as it were, to be claiming that they should themselves be regarded and treated as genitals. We shall learn later that this claim is justified by the history of the development of the sexual instinct and that it is fulfilled in the symptomatology of certain pathological states.

Unsuitable Substitutes for the Sexual Object – Fetishism

There are some cases which are quite specially remarkable – those in which the normal sexual object is replaced by another which bears some relation to it, but is entirely unsuited to serve the normal sexual aim. From the point of view of classification, we should no doubt have done better to have mentioned this highly interesting group of aberrations of the sexual instinct among the deviations in respect of the sexual *object*. But we have postponed their mention till we could become acquainted with the factor of sexual overvaluation, on which these phenomena, being connected with an abandonment of the sexual aim, are dependent.

What is substituted for the sexual object is some part of the body (such as the foot or hair) which is in general very inappropriate for sexual purposes, or some inanimate object which bears an assignable relation to the person whom it replaces and preferably to that person's sexuality (e.g. a piece of clothing or underlinen). Such substitutes are with some justice likened to the fetishes in which savages believe that their gods are embodied.

A transition to those cases of fetishism in which the sexual aim, whether normal or perverse, is entirely abandoned is afforded by other cases in which the sexual object is required to fulfil a fetishistic condition – such as the possession of some particular hair-colouring or clothing, or even some bodily defect – if the sexual aim is to be attained. No other variation of the sexual instinct that borders on the pathological can lay so much claim to our interest as this one, such is the peculiarity of the phenomena to which it gives rise. Some degree of diminution in the urge towards the normal sexual aim (an executive weakness of the sexual apparatus) seems to be a necessary precondition in every case.[1] The point of contact with the normal is provided by the psychologically essential overvaluation of the sexual object, which inevitably extends to everything that is associated with it. A certain degree of fetishism is thus habitually present in normal love, especially in those stages of it in which the normal sexual aim seems unattainable or its fulfilment prevented:

> Schaff' mir ein Halstuch von ihrer Brust,
> Ein Strumpfband meiner Liebeslust![2]

The situation only becomes pathological when the longing

1. [*Footnote added* 1915:] This weakness would represent the *constitutional* precondition. Psychoanalysis has found that the phenomenon can also be *accidentally* determined, by the occurrence of an early deterrence from sexual activity owing to fear, which may divert the subject from the normal sexual aim and encourage him to seek a substitute for it.

2. [Get me a kerchief from her breast,
   A garter that her knee has pressed.
           Goethe, *Faust*, Part I, Scene 7. (*Trans.* Bayard Taylor.)]

for the fetish passes beyond the point of being merely a necessary condition attached to the sexual object and actually *takes the place* of the normal aim, and, further, when the fetish becomes detached from a particular individual and becomes the *sole* sexual object. These are, indeed, the general conditions under which mere variations of the sexual instinct pass over into pathological aberrations.

Binet [1888] was the first to maintain (what has since been confirmed by a quantity of evidence) that the choice of a fetish is an after-effect of some sexual impression, received as a rule in early childhood. (This may be brought into line with the proverbial durability of first loves: *on revient toujours à ses premiers amours.*) This derivation is particularly obvious in cases where there is merely a fetishistic condition attached to the sexual object. We shall come across the importance of early sexual impressions again in another connection [p. 167].[1]

In other cases the replacement of the object by a fetish is determined by a symbolic connection of thought, of which the person concerned is usually not conscious. It is not always possible to trace the course of these connections with certainty. (The foot, for instance, is an age-old sexual symbol which occurs even in mythology;[2] no doubt the part played by fur as

1. [*Footnote added* 1920:] Deeper-going psychoanalytic research has raised a just criticism of Binet's assertion. All the observations dealing with this point have recorded a first meeting with the fetish at which it already aroused sexual interest without there being anything in the accompanying circumstances to explain the fact. Moreover, all of these 'early' sexual impressions relate to a time after the age of five or six, whereas psychoanalysis makes it doubtful whether fresh pathological fixations can occur so late as this. The true explanation is that behind the first recollection of the fetish's appearance there lies a submerged and forgotten phase of sexual development. The fetish, like a 'screen-memory', represents this phase and is thus a remnant and precipitate of it. The fact that this early infantile phase turns in the direction of fetishism, as well as the choice of the fetish itself, are constitutionally determined.

2. [*Footnote added* 1910:] The shoe or slipper is a corresponding symbol of the *female* genitals.

a fetish owes its origin to an association with the hair of the *mons Veneris*.) None the less even symbolism such as this is not always unrelated to sexual experiences in childhood.[1]

(B) FIXATIONS OF PRELIMINARY SEXUAL AIMS

Appearance of New Aims

Every external or internal factor that hinders or postpones the attainment of the normal sexual aim (such as impotence, the high price of the sexual object or the danger of the sexual act) will evidently lend support to the tendency to linger over the preparatory activities and to turn them into new sexual aims that can take the place of the normal one. Attentive examination always shows that even what seem to be the strangest of these new aims are already hinted at in the normal sexual process.

1. [*Footnote added* 1910:] Psychoanalysis has cleared up one of the remaining gaps in our understanding of fetishism. It has shown the importance, as regards the choice of a fetish, of a coprophilic pleasure in smelling which has disappeared owing to repression. Both the feet and the hair are objects with a strong smell which have been exalted into fetishes after the olfactory sensation has become unpleasurable and been abandoned. Accordingly, in the perversion that corresponds to foot-fetishism, it is only dirty and evil-smelling feet that become sexual objects. Another factor that helps towards explaining the fetishistic preference for the foot is to be found among the sexual theories of children (see below [p. 113f.]): the foot represents a woman's penis, the absence of which is deeply felt. [*Added* 1915:] In a number of cases of foot-fetishism it has been possible to show that the scopophilic instinct, seeking to reach its object (originally the genitals) from underneath, was brought to a halt in its pathway by prohibition and repression. For that reason it became attached to a fetish in the form of a foot or shoe, the female genitals (in accordance with the expectations of childhood) being imagined as male ones. – [The importance of the repression of pleasure in smell was mentioned at the end of his analysis of the 'Rat Man' (1909*d*), and discussed at considerable length in two long footnotes to Chapter IV of *Civilization and its Discontents* (1930*a*). The topic of fetishism was further considered in Freud's paper on that subject (1927*e*); cf. the Editor's introductory note, pp. 347–9 below.]

Touching and Looking

A certain amount of touching is indispensable (at all events among human beings) before the normal sexual aim can be attained. And everyone knows what a source of pleasure on the one hand and what an influx of fresh excitation on the other is afforded by tactile sensations of the skin of the sexual object. So that lingering over the stage of touching can scarcely be counted a perversion, provided that in the long run the sexual act is carried further.

The same holds true of seeing – an activity that is ultimately derived from touching. Visual impressions remain the most frequent pathway along which libidinal excitation is aroused; indeed, natural selection counts upon the accessibility of this pathway – if such a teleological form of statement is permissible[1] – when it encourages the development of beauty in the sexual object. The progressive concealment of the body which goes along with civilization keeps sexual curiosity awake. This curiosity seeks to complete the sexual object by revealing its hidden parts. It can, however, be diverted ('sublimated') in the direction of art, if its interest can be shifted away from the genitals on to the shape of the body as a whole.[2] It is usual for most normal people to linger to some extent over the intermediate sexual aim of a looking that has a sexual tinge to it;

1. [The words in this parenthesis were added in 1915. Cf. footnote, p. 105.]

2. [This seems to be Freud's first published use of the term 'sublimate'. It also appears twice in the 'Dora' case history, (1905e), *P.F.L.*, **8**, 84 and 158, actually published later than the present work though drafted in 1901. The concept is further discussed below on pp. 93–4. – *Footnote added* 1915:] There is to my mind no doubt that the concept of 'beautiful' has its roots in sexual excitation and that its original meaning was 'sexually stimulating'. [There is an allusion in the original to the fact that the German word '*Reiz*' is commonly used both as the technical term for 'stimulus' and, in ordinary language, as an equivalent to the English 'charm' or 'attraction'.] This is related to the fact that we never regard the genitals themselves, the sight of which produces the strongest sexual excitation, as really 'beautiful'.

indeed, this offers them a possibility of directing some proportion of their libido on to higher artistic aims. On the other hand, this pleasure in looking [scopophilia] becomes a perversion (a) if it is restricted exclusively to the genitals, or (b) if it is connected with the overriding of disgust (as in the case of *voyeurs* or people who look on at excretory functions), or (c) if, instead of being *preparatory* to the normal sexual aim, it supplants it. This last is markedly true of exhibitionists, who, if I may trust the findings of several analyses,[1] exhibit their own genitals in order to obtain a reciprocal view of the genitals of the other person.[2]

In the perversions which are directed towards looking and being looked at, we come across a very remarkable characteristic with which we shall be still more intensely concerned in the aberration that we shall consider next: in these perversions the sexual aim occurs in two forms, an *active* and a *passive* one.

The force which opposes scopophilia, but which may be overridden by it (in a manner parallel to what we have previously seen in the case of disgust), is *shame*.

Sadism and Masochism

The most common and the most significant of all the perversions – the desire to inflict pain upon the sexual object, and its reverse – received from Krafft-Ebing the names of 'sadism' and 'masochism' for its active and passive forms respectively. Other writers [e.g. Schrenck-Notzing (1899)] have preferred the narrower term 'algolagnia'. This emphasizes the pleasure in

---

1. [In the editions before 1924 this read 'of a single analysis'.]

2. [*Footnote added* 1920:] Under analysis, these perversions – and indeed most others – reveal a surprising variety of motives and determinants. The compulsion to exhibit, for instance, is also closely dependent on the castration complex: it is a means of constantly insisting upon the integrity of the subject's own (male) genitals and it reiterates his infantile satisfaction at the absence of a penis in those of women. [Cf. p. 113f.]

pain, the cruelty; whereas the names chosen by Krafft-Ebing bring into prominence the pleasure in any form of humiliation or subjection.

As regards active algolagnia, sadism, the roots are easy to detect in the normal. The sexuality of most male human beings contains an element of *aggressiveness* – a desire to subjugate; the biological significance of it seems to lie in the need for overcoming the resistance of the sexual object by means other than the process of wooing. Thus sadism would correspond to an aggressive component of the sexual instinct which has become independent and exaggerated and, by displacement, has usurped the leading position.[1]

In ordinary speech the connotation of sadism oscillates between, on the one hand, cases merely characterized by an active or violent attitude to the sexual object, and, on the other hand, cases in which satisfaction is entirely conditional on the humiliation and maltreatment of the object. Strictly speaking, it is only this last extreme instance which deserves to be described as a perversion.

Similarly, the term masochism comprises any passive attitude towards sexual life and the sexual object, the extreme instance of which appears to be that in which satisfaction is conditional upon suffering physical or mental pain at the hands of the sexual object. Masochism, in the form of a perversion, seems to be further removed from the normal sexual aim than its counterpart; it may be doubted at first whether it can ever occur as a primary phenomenon or whether, on the contrary, it may not invariably arise from a transformation of sadism.[2] It can often be shown that masochism is nothing more

1. [In the editions of 1905 and 1910 the following two sentences appeared in the text at this point: 'One at least of the roots of masochism can be inferred with equal certainty. It arises from sexual over-valuation as a necessary psychical consequence of the choice of a sexual object.' From 1915 onwards these sentences were omitted and the next two paragraphs were inserted in their place.]

2. [*Footnote added* 1924:] My opinion of masochism has been to a large extent altered by later reflection, based upon certain hypotheses as

than an extension of sadism turned round upon the subject's own self, which thus, to begin with, takes the place of the sexual object. Clinical analysis of extreme cases of masochistic perversion show that a great number of factors (such as the castration complex and the sense of guilt) have combined to exaggerate and fixate the original passive sexual attitude.

Pain, which is overridden in such cases, thus falls into line with disgust and shame as a force that stands in opposition and resistance to the libido.[1]

Sadism and masochism occupy a special position among the perversions, since the contrast between activity and passivity which lies behind them is among the universal characteristics of sexual life.

The history of human civilization shows beyond any doubt that there is an intimate connection between cruelty and the sexual instinct; but nothing has been done towards explaining the connection, apart from laying emphasis on the aggressive factor in the libido. According to some authorities this aggressive element of the sexual instinct is in reality a relic of canni-balistic desires – that is, it is a contribution derived from the apparatus for obtaining mastery, which is concerned with the satisfaction of the other and, ontogenetically, the older of the great instinctual needs.[2] It has also been maintained that every pain contains in itself the possibility of a feeling of pleasure. All that need be said is that no satisfactory explanation of this perversion has been put forward and that it seems possible that

---

to the structure of the apparatus of the mind and the classes of instincts operating in it. I have been led to distinguish a *primary* or *erotogenic* masochism, out of which two later forms, *feminine* and *moral* masochism, have developed. Sadism which cannot find employment in actual life is turned round upon the subject's own self and so produces a *secondary* masochism, which is superadded to the primary kind. (Cf. 'The Economic Problem of Masochism', 1924*c*.)

1. [This short paragraph was in the first edition (1905), but the last two, as well as the next one, were only added in 1915.]

2. [*Footnote added* 1915:] Cf. my remarks below [p. 116f.] on the pre-genital phases of sexual development, which confirm this view.

a number of mental impulses are combined in it to produce a single resultant.[1]

But the most remarkable feature of this perversion is that its active and passive forms are habitually found to occur together in the same individual. A person who feels pleasure in producing pain in someone else in a sexual relationship is also capable of enjoying as pleasure any pain which he may himself derive from sexual relations. A sadist is always at the same time a masochist, although the active or the passive aspect of the perversion may be the more strongly developed in him and may represent his predominant sexual activity.[2]

We find, then, that certain among the impulses to perversion occur regularly as *pairs of opposites*; and this, taken in conjunction with material which will be brought forward later, has a high theoretical significance.[3] It is, moreover, a suggestive fact that the existence of the pair of opposites formed by sadism and masochism cannot be attributed merely to the element of aggressiveness. We should rather be inclined to connect the simultaneous presence of these opposites with the opposing masculinity and femininity which are combined in bisexuality – a contrast which often has to be replaced in psychoanalysis by that between activity and passivity.[4]

1. [*Footnote added* 1924:] The inquiry mentioned above [in footnote 2 on p. 71f.] has led me to assign a peculiar position, based upon the origin of the instincts, to the pair of opposites constituted by sadism and masochism, and to place them outside the class of the remaining 'perversions'.

2. Instead of multiplying the evidence for this statement, I will quote a passage from Havelock Ellis ([1913, 119; 1st ed.:] 1903): 'The investigation of histories of sadism and masochism, even those given by Krafft-Ebing (as indeed Colin Scott and Féré have already pointed out), constantly reveals traces of both groups of phenomena in the same individual.'

3. [*Footnote added* 1915:] Cf. my discussion of 'ambivalence' below [pp. 117–18].

4. [The last clause did not occur in the 1905 or 1910 editions. In 1915 the following clause was added: 'a contrast whose significance is re-

(3) THE PERVERSIONS IN GENERAL

Variation and Disease

It is natural that medical men, who first studied perversions in outstanding examples and under special conditions, should have been inclined to regard them, like inversion, as indications of degeneracy or disease. Nevertheless, it is even easier to dispose of that view in this case than in that of inversion. Everyday experience has shown that most of these extensions, or at any rate the less severe of them, are constituents which are rarely absent from the sexual life of healthy people, and are judged by them no differently from other intimate events. If circumstances favour such an occurrence, normal people too can substitute a perversion of this kind for the normal sexual aim for quite a time, or can find place for the one alongside the other. No healthy person, it appears, can fail to make some addition that might be called perverse to the normal sexual aim; and the universality of this finding is in itself enough to show how inappropriate it is to use the word perversion as a term of reproach. In the sphere of sexual life we are brought up against peculiar and, indeed, insoluble difficulties as soon as we try to draw a sharp line to distinguish mere variations within the range of what is physiological from pathological symptoms.

Nevertheless, in some of these perversions the quality of the new sexual aim is of a kind to demand special examination. Certain of them are so far removed from the normal in their content that we cannot avoid pronouncing them 'pathological'. This is especially so where (as, for instance, in cases of licking excrement or of intercourse with dead bodies) the sexual instinct goes to astonishing lengths in successfully overriding the resistances of shame, disgust, horror or pain. But

---

duced in psychoanalysis to that between activity and passivity.' This was replaced in 1924 by the words now appearing in the text.]

even in such cases we should not be too ready to assume that people who act in this way will necessarily turn out to be insane or subject to grave abnormalities of other kinds. Here again we cannot escape from the fact that people whose behaviour is in other respects normal can, under the domination of the most unruly of all the instincts, put themselves in the category of sick persons in the single sphere of sexual life. On the other hand, manifest abnormality in the other relations of life can invariably be shown to have a background of abnormal sexual conduct.

In the majority of instances the pathological character in a perversion is found to lie not in the *content* of the new sexual aim but in its relation to the normal. If a perversion, instead of appearing merely *alongside* the normal sexual aim and object, and only when circumstances are unfavourable to *them* and favourable to *it* – if, instead of this, it ousts them completely and takes their place in *all* circumstances – if, in short, a perversion has the characteristics of *exclusiveness* and *fixation* – then we shall usually be justified in regarding it as a pathological symptom.

The Mental Factor in the Perversions

It is perhaps in connection precisely with the most repulsive perversions that the mental factor must be regarded as playing its largest part in the transformation of the sexual instinct. It is impossible to deny that in their case a piece of mental work has been performed which, in spite of its horrifying result, is the equivalent of an idealization of the instinct. The omnipotence of love is perhaps never more strongly proved than in such of its aberrations as these. The highest and the lowest are always closest to each other in the sphere of sexuality: 'vom Himmel durch die Welt zur Hölle.'[1]

1. ['From Heaven, across the world, to Hell.'
   Goethe, *Faust*, Prelude in the Theatre. (*Trans.* Bayard Taylor.)]

Two Conclusions

Our study of the perversions has shown us that the sexual instinct has to struggle against certain mental forces which act as resistances, and of which shame and disgust are the most prominent. It is permissible to suppose that these forces play a part in restraining that instinct within the limits that are regarded as normal; and if they develop in the individual before the sexual instinct has reached its full strength, it is no doubt they that will determine the course of its development.[1]

In the second place we have found that some of the perversions which we have examined are only made intelligible if we assume the convergence of several motive forces. If such perversions admit of analysis, that is, if they can be taken to pieces, then they must be of a composite nature. This gives us a hint that perhaps the sexual instinct itself may be no simple thing, but put together from components which have come apart again in the perversions. If this is so, the clinical observation of these abnormalities will have drawn our attention to *amalgamations* which have been lost to view in the uniform behaviour of normal people.[2]

1. [*Footnote added* 1915:] On the other hand, these forces which act like dams upon sexual development – disgust, shame and morality – must also be regarded as historical precipitates of the external inhibitions to which the sexual instinct has been subjected during the psychogenesis of the human race. We can observe the way in which, in the development of individuals, they arise at the appropriate moment, as though spontaneously, when upbringing and external influence give the signal.

2. [*Footnote added* 1920:] As regards the origin of the perversions, I will add a word in anticipation of what is to come. There is reason to suppose that, just as in the case of fetishism, abortive beginnings of normal sexual development occur before the perversions become fixated. Analytic investigation has already been able to show in a few cases that perversions are a residue of development towards the Oedipus complex and that after the repression of that complex the components of the sexual instinct which are strongest in the disposition of the individual concerned emerge once more.

(4) THE SEXUAL INSTINCT IN NEUROTICS

Psychoanalysis

An important addition to our knowledge of the sexual instinct in certain people who at least approximate to the normal can be obtained from a source which can only be reached in one particular way. There is only one means of obtaining exhaustive information that will not be misleading about the sexual life of the persons known as 'psychoneurotics' – sufferers from hysteria, from obsessional neurosis, from what is wrongly described as neurasthenia, and, undoubtedly, from dementia praecox and paranoia as well.[1] They must be subjected to psychoanalytic investigation, which is employed in the therapeutic procedure introduced by Josef Breuer and myself in 1893 and known at that time as 'catharsis'.

I must first explain – as I have already done in other writings – that all my experience shows that these psychoneuroses are based on sexual instinctual forces. By this I do not merely mean that the energy of the sexual instinct makes a contribution to the forces that maintain the pathological manifestations (the symptoms). I mean expressly to assert that that contribution is the most important and only constant source of energy of the neurosis and that in consequence the sexual life of the persons in question is expressed – whether exclusively or principally or only partly – in these symptoms. As I have put it elsewhere,[2] the symptoms constitute the sexual activity of the patient. The evidence for this assertion is derived from the ever-increasing number of psychoanalyses of hysterical and other neurotics which I have carried out during the last 25 years[3] and of whose findings I have given (and shall continue to give) a detailed account in other publications.[4]

1. [Before 1915 the words 'probably from paranoia as well' take the place of the last eight words of this sentence.]

2. [Cf. the 'Dora' case history (1905e), Postscript, *P.F.L.*, **8**, 156.]

3. [In 1905 '10 years', the figure being increased with each edition up to and including 1920.]

4. [*Footnote added* 1920:] It implies no qualification of the above

The removal of the symptoms of hysterical patients by psychoanalysis proceeds on the supposition that those symptoms are substitutes – transcriptions as it were – for a number of emotionally cathected mental processes, wishes and desires, which, by the operation of a special psychical procedure (*repression*), have been prevented from obtaining discharge in psychical activity that is admissible to consciousness. These mental processes, therefore, being held back in a state of unconsciousness, strive to obtain an expression that shall be appropriate to their emotional importance – to obtain *discharge*; and in the case of hysteria they find such an expression (by means of the process of 'conversion') in somatic phenomena, that is, in hysterical symptoms. By systematically turning these symptoms back (with the help of a special technique) into emotionally cathected ideas – ideas that will now have become conscious – is it possible to obtain the most accurate knowledge of the nature and origin of these formerly unconscious psychical structures.

Findings of Psychoanalysis

In this manner the fact has emerged that symptoms represent a substitute for impulses the source of whose strength is derived from the sexual instinct. What we know about the nature of hysterics before they fall ill – and they may be regarded as typical of all psychoneurotics – and about the occasions which precipitate their falling ill, is in complete harmony with this view. The character of hysterics shows a degree of *sexual repression* in excess of the normal quantity, an intensification of resistance against the sexual instinct (which we have already met with in the form of shame, disgust and morality), and what seems like an instinctive aversion on their part to any intellectual consideration of sexual problems. As a result of

assertion, but rather an amplification of it, if I restate it as follows: neurotic symptoms are based on the one hand on the demands of the libidinal instincts and on the other hand on those made by the ego by way of reaction to them.

this, in especially marked cases, the patients remain in complete ignorance of sexual matters right into the period of sexual maturity.[1]

On a cursory view, this trait, which is so characteristic of hysteria, is not uncommonly screened by the existence of a second constitutional character present in hysteria, namely the predominant development of the sexual instinct. Psychoanalysis, however, can invariably bring the first of these factors to light and clear up the enigmatic contradiction which hysteria presents, by revealing the pair of opposites by which it is characterized – exaggerated sexual craving and excessive aversion to sexuality.

In the case of anyone who is predisposed to hysteria, the onset of his illness is precipitated when, either as a result of his own progressive maturity or of the external circumstances of his life, he finds himself faced by the demands of a real sexual situation. Between the pressure of the instinct and his antagonism to sexuality, illness offers him a way of escape. It does not solve his conflict, but seeks to evade it by transforming his libidinal impulses into symptoms.[2] The exception is only an *apparent* one when a hysteric – a male patient it may be – falls ill as a result of some trivial emotion, some conflict which does not centre around any sexual interest. In such cases psychoanalysis is regularly able to show that the illness has been made possible by the sexual component of the conflict, which has prevented the mental processes from reaching a normal issue.

Neurosis and Perversion

There is no doubt that a large part of the opposition to these views of mine is due to the fact that sexuality, to which I trace

1. Breuer (Breuer and Freud, 1895) writes of the patient in connection with whom he first adopted the cathartic method: 'The factor of sexuality was astonishingly undeveloped in her.' [The reference is to the case of Anna O.; cf. *Studies on Hysteria*, P.F.L., 3, 73.]

2. [This theme was elaborated by Freud in his paper on the different types of onset of neurosis (1912c).]

back psychoneurotic symptoms, is regarded as though it coincided with the normal sexual instinct. But psychoanalytic teaching goes further than this. It shows that it is by no means only at the cost of the so-called *normal* sexual instinct that these symptoms originate – at any rate such is not exclusively or mainly the case; they also give expression (by conversion) to instincts which would be described as *perverse* in the widest sense of the word if they could be expressed directly in phantasy and action without being diverted from consciousness. Thus symptoms are formed in part at the cost of *abnormal* sexuality; *neuroses are, so to say, the negative of perversions.*[1]

The sexual instinct of psychoneurotics exhibits all the aberrations which we have studied as variations of normal, and as manifestations of abnormal, sexual life.

(*a*) The unconscious mental life of all neurotics (without exception) shows inverted impulses, fixation of their libido upon persons of their own sex. It would be impossible without deep discussion to give any adequate appreciation of the importance of this factor in determining the form taken by the symptoms of the illness. I can only insist that an unconscious tendency to inversion is never absent and is of particular value in throwing light upon hysteria in men.[2]

(*b*) It is possible to trace in the unconscious of psycho-

1. [This idea also appears in the 'Dora' case history (1905*e*), *P.F.L.*, **8**, 84.] The contents of the clearly conscious phantasies of perverts (which in favourable circumstances can be transformed into manifest behaviour), of the delusional fears of paranoics (which are projected in a hostile sense on to other people) and of the unconscious phantasies of hysterics (which psychoanalysis reveals behind their symptoms) – all of these coincide with one another even down to their details.

2. Psychoneuroses are also very often associated with *manifest* inversion. In such cases the heterosexual current of feeling has undergone complete suppression. It is only fair to say that my attention was first drawn to the necessary universality of the tendency to inversion in psychoneurotics by Wilhelm Fliess of Berlin, after I had discussed its presence in individual cases. – [*Added* 1920:] This fact, which has not been sufficiently appreciated, cannot fail to have a decisive influence on any theory of homosexuality.

neurotics tendencies to every kind of anatomical extension of sexual activity and to show that those tendencies are factors in the formation of symptoms. Among them we find occurring with particular frequency those in which the mucous membrane of the mouth and anus are assigned the role of genitals.

(c) An especially prominent part is played as factors in the formation of symptoms in psychoneuroses by the component instincts,[1] which emerge for the most part as pairs of opposites and which we have met with as introducing new sexual aims – the scopophilic instinct and exhibitionism and the active and passive forms of the instinct for cruelty. The contribution made by the last of these is essential to the understanding of the fact that symptoms involve *suffering*, and it almost invariably dominates a part of the patient's social behaviour. It is also through the medium of this connection between libido and cruelty that the transformation of love into hate takes place, the transformation of affectionate into hostile impulses, which is characteristic of a great number of cases of neurosis, and indeed, it would seem, of paranoia in general.

The interest of these findings is still further increased by certain special facts.[2]

(α) Whenever we find in the unconscious an instinct of this sort which is capable of being paired off with an opposite one, this second instinct will regularly be found in operation as well. Every active perversion is thus accompanied by its passive counterpart: anyone who is an exhibitionist in his unconscious is at the same time a *voyeur*; in anyone who suffers from the consequences of repressed sadistic impulses there is

1. [The term 'component instinct' here makes its first appearance in Freud's published works, though the *concept* has already been introduced above on p. 76.]

2. [In the editions before 1920 *three* such 'special facts' were enumerated. The first, which was subsequently omitted, ran as follows: 'Among the unconscious trains of thought found in neuroses there is nothing corresponding to a tendency to fetishism – a circumstance which throws light on the psychological peculiarity of this well-understood perversion.']

sure to be another determinant of his symptoms which has its source in masochistic inclinations. The complete agreement which is here shown with what we have found to exist in the corresponding 'positive' perversions is most remarkable, though in the actual symptoms one or other of the opposing tendencies plays the predominant part.

(β) In any fairly marked case of psychoneurosis it is unusual for only a single one of these perverse instincts to be developed. We usually find a considerable number and as a rule traces of them all. The degree of development of each particular instinct is, however, independent of that of the others. Here, too, the study of the 'positive' perversions provides an exact counterpart.

(5) COMPONENT INSTINCTS AND EROTOGENIC ZONES[1]

If we put together what we have learned from our investigation of positive and negative perversions, it seems plausible to trace them back to a number of 'component instincts', which, however, are not of a primary nature, but are susceptible to further analysis.[2] By an 'instinct' is provisionally to be under-

1. [This appears to be the first published occurrence of the term 'erotogenic zone'. It also occurs in a passage in Section I of the case history of 'Dora' (1905e), P.F.L., 8, 86, presumably written in 1901. It was evidently constructed on the analogy of the term 'hysterogenic zone' which was already in common use.]

2. [The passage from this point till the end of the paragraph dates from 1915. In the first two editions (1905 and 1910) the following sentences appeared instead: 'We can distinguish in them [the component instincts] (in addition to an "instinct" which is not itself sexual and which has its source in motor impulses) a contribution from an organ capable of receiving stimuli (e.g. the skin, the mucous membrane or a sense organ). An organ of this kind will be described in this connection as an "erotogenic zone" – as being the organ whose excitation lends the instinct a sexual character.' – The revised version dates from the period of Freud's paper on 'Instincts and their Vicissitudes' (1915c), where the whole topic is examined at length.]

stood the psychical representative of an endosomatic, continuously flowing source of stimulation, as contrasted with a 'stimulus', which is set up by *single* excitations coming from *without*. The concept of instinct is thus one of those lying on the frontier between the mental and the physical. The simplest and likeliest assumption as to the nature of instincts would seem to be that in itself an instinct is without quality, and, so far as mental life is concerned, is only to be regarded as a measure of the demand made upon the mind for work. What distinguishes the instincts from one another and endows them with specific qualities is their relation to their somatic *sources* and to their *aims*. The source of an instinct is a process of excitation occurring in an organ and the immediate aim of the instinct lies in the removal of this organic stimulus.[1]

There is a further provisional assumption that we cannot escape in the theory of the instincts. It is to the effect that excitations of two kinds arise from the somatic organs, based upon differences of a chemical nature. One of these kinds of excitation we describe as being specifically sexual, and we speak of the organ concerned as the 'erotogenic zone' of the sexual component instinct arising from it.[2]

The part played by the erotogenic zones is immediately obvious in the case of those perversions which assign a sexual significance to the oral and anal orifices. These behave in every respect like a portion of the sexual apparatus. In hysteria these parts of the body and the neighbouring tracts of mucous membrane become the seat of new sensations and of changes in innervation – indeed, of processes that can be compared to

1. [*Footnote added* 1924:] The theory of the instincts is the most important but at the same time the least complete portion of psychoanalytic theory. I have made further contributions to it in my later works *Beyond the Pleasure Principle* (1920g) and *The Ego and the Id* (1923b).

2. [*Footnote added* 1915:] It is not easy in the present place to justify these assumptions, derived as they are from the study of a particular class of neurotic illness. But on the other hand, if I omitted all mention of them, it would be impossible to say anything of substance about the instincts.

erection[1] – in just the same way as do the actual genitalia under the excitations of the normal sexual processes.

The significance of the erotogenic zones as apparatuses subordinate to the genitals and as substitutes for them is, among all the psychoneuroses, most clearly to be seen in hysteria; but this does not imply that that significance is any the less in the other forms of illness. It is only that in them it is less recognizable, because in their case (obsessional neurosis and paranoia) the formation of the symptoms takes place in regions of the mental apparatus which are more remote from the particular centres concerned with somatic control. In obsessional neurosis what is more striking is the significance of those impulses which create new sexual aims and seem independent of erotogenic zones. Nevertheless, in scopophilia and exhibitionism the eye corresponds to an erotogenic zone; while in the case of those components of the sexual instinct which involve pain and cruelty the same role is assumed by the skin – the skin, which in particular parts of the body has become differentiated into sense organs or modified into mucous membrane, and is thus the erotogenic zone *par excellence*.[2]

(6) Reasons for the Apparent Preponderance of Perverse Sexuality in the Psychoneuroses

The preceding discussion may perhaps have placed the sexuality of psychoneurotics in a false light. It may have given

1. [The phrase in parentheses was added in 1920.]
2. We are reminded at this point of Moll's analysis of the sexual instinct into an instinct of 'contrectation' and an instinct of 'detumescence'. Contrectation represents a need for contact with the skin. [The instinct of detumescence was described by Moll (1898) as an impulse for the spasmodic relief of tension of the sexual organs, and the instinct of contrectation as an impulse to come into contact with another person. He believed that the latter impulse arose later than the first in the individual's development. (See also below, p. 96 *n.* 2.)]

the impression that, owing to their disposition, psychoneur-otics approximate closely to perverts in their sexual behaviour and are proportionately remote from normal people. It may indeed very well be that the constitutional disposition of these patients (apart from their exaggerated degree of sexual repres-sion and the excessive intensity of their sexual instinct) includes an unusual tendency to perversion, using that word in its widest sense. Nevertheless, investigation of compara-tively slight cases shows that this last assumption is not abso-lutely necessary, or at least that in forming a judgement on these pathological developments there is a factor to be con-sidered which weighs in the other direction. Most psycho-neurotics only fall ill after the age of puberty as a result of the demands made upon them by normal sexual life. (It is most particularly against the latter that repression is directed.) Or else illnesses of this kind set in later, when the libido fails to obtain satisfaction along normal lines. In both these cases the libido behaves like a stream whose main bed has become blocked. It proceeds to fill up collateral channels which may hitherto have been empty. Thus, in the same way, what appears to be the strong tendency (though, it is true, a negative one) of psychoneurotics to perversion may be collaterally determined, and must, in any case, be collaterally intensified. The fact is that we must put sexual repression as an internal factor alongside such external factors as limitation of freedom, inaccessibility of a normal sexual object, the dangers of the normal sexual act, etc., which bring about perversions in persons who might perhaps otherwise have remained normal.

In this respect different cases of neurosis may behave differ-ently: in one case the preponderating factor may be the innate strength of the tendency to perversion, in another it may be the collateral increase of that tendency owing to the libido being forced away from a normal sexual aim and sexual object. It would be wrong to represent as opposition what is in fact a co-operative relation. Neurosis will always produce its greatest effects when constitution and experience work together in the same direction. Where the constitution is a marked one it will perhaps not require the support of actual experiences; while a great shock in real life will perhaps bring about a neurosis even in an average constitution. (Incidentally, this view of the relative aetiological importance of what is innate and what is accidentally experienced applies equally in other fields.)

If we prefer to suppose, nevertheless, that a particularly strongly developed tendency to perversion is among the characteristics of psychoneurotic constitutions, we have before us the prospect of being able to distinguish a number of such constitutions according to the innate preponderance of one or the other of the erotogenic zones or of one or the other of the component instincts. The question whether a special relation holds between the perverse disposition and the particular form of illness adopted, has, like so much else in this field, not yet been investigated.

(7) Intimation of the Infantile Character of Sexuality

By demonstrating the part played by perverse impulses in the formation of symptoms in the psychoneuroses, we have quite remarkably increased the number of people who might be regarded as perverts. It is not only that neurotics in themselves constitute a very numerous class, but it must also be considered that an unbroken chain bridges the gap between the neuroses in all their manifestations and normality. After all, Moebius could say with justice that we are all to some extent hysterics. Thus the extraordinarily wide dissemination of the perversions forces us to suppose that the disposition to perversions is itself of no great rarity but must form a part of what passes as the normal constitution.

It is, as we have seen, debatable whether the perversions go back to innate determinants or arise, as Binet assumed was the case with fetishism [p. 67], owing to chance experiences. The conclusion now presents itself to us that there is indeed something innate lying behind the perversions but that it is something *innate in everyone*, though as a disposition it may vary in its intensity and may be increased by the influences of actual life. What is in question are the innate constitutional roots of the sexual instinct. In one class of cases (the perversions) these roots may grow into the actual vehicles of sexual activity; in others they may be submitted to an insufficient suppression (repression) and thus be able in a roundabout way to attract a considerable proportion of sexual energy to themselves as symptoms; while in the most favourable cases, which lie between these two extremes, they may by means of effective restriction and other kinds of modification bring about what is known as normal sexual life.

We have, however, a further reflection to make. This postulated constitution, containing the germs of all the perversions, will only be demonstrable in *children*, even though in them it is only with modest degrees of intensity that any of the instincts can emerge. A formula begins to take shape which lays it down that the sexuality of neurotics has remained in, or been brought back to, an infantile state. Thus our interest turns to the sexual life of children, and we will now proceed to trace the play of influences which govern the evolution of infantile sexuality till its outcome in perversion, neurosis or normal sexual life.

INFANTILE SEXUALITY

Neglect of the Infantile Factor

One feature of the popular view of the sexual instinct is that it is absent in childhood and only awakens in the period of life described as puberty. This, however, is not merely a simple error but one that has had grave consequences, for it is mainly to this idea that we owe our present ignorance of the fundamental conditions of sexual life. A thorough study of the sexual manifestations of childhood would probably reveal the essential characters of the sexual instinct and would show us the course of its development and the way in which it is put together from various sources.

It is noticeable that writers who concern themselves with explaining the characteristics and reactions of the adult have devoted much more attention to the primaeval period which is comprised in the life of the individual's ancestors – have, that is, ascribed much more influence to heredity – than to the other primaeval period, which falls within the lifetime of the individual himself – that is, to childhood. One would surely have supposed that the influence of this latter period would be easier to understand and could claim to be considered before that of heredity.[1] It is true that in the literature of the subject one occasionally comes across remarks upon precocious sexual activity in small children – upon erections, masturbation and even activities resembling coitus. But these are always quoted only as exceptional events, as oddities or as horrifying instances of precocious depravity. So far as I know, not a single author has clearly recognized the regular existence of a sexual instinct in childhood; and in the writings that have become so

1. [*Footnote added* 1915:] Nor is it possible to estimate correctly the part played by heredity until the part played by childhood has been assessed.

numerous on the development of children, the chapter on 'Sexual Development' is as a rule omitted.[1]

Infantile Amnesia

The reason for this strange neglect is to be sought, I think, partly in considerations of propriety, which the authors obey as a result of their own upbringing, and partly in a psychological phenomenon which has itself hitherto eluded explanation. What I have in mind is the peculiar *amnesia* which, in the case of most people, though by no means all, hides the earliest

1. The assertion made in the text has since struck me myself as being so bold that I have undertaken the task of testing its validity by looking through the literature once more. The outcome of this is that I have allowed my statement to stand unaltered. The scientific examination of both the physical and mental phenomena of sexuality in childhood is still in its earliest beginnings. One writer, Bell (1902, [327]), remarks: 'I know of no scientist who has given a careful analysis of the emotion as it is seen in the adolescent.' Somatic sexual manifestations from the period before puberty have only attracted attention in connection with phenomena of degeneracy and as indications of degeneracy. In none of the accounts which I have read of the psychology of this period of life is a chapter to be found on the erotic life of children; and this applies to the well-known works of Preyer [1882], Baldwin (1895), Pérez (1886), Strümpell (1899), Groos (1904), Heller (1904), Sully (1895) and others. We can obtain the clearest impression of the state of things in this field today from the periodical *Die Kinderfehler* from 1896 onwards. Nevertheless the conviction is borne in upon us that the existence of love in childhood stands in no need of discovery. Pérez (1886, [272 ff.]) argues in favour of its existence. Groos (1899, 326) mentions as a generally recognized fact that 'some children are already accessible to sexual impulses at a very early age and feel an urge to have contact with the opposite sex'. The earliest instance of the appearance of 'sex-love' recorded by Bell (1902, [330]) concerns a child in the middle of his third year. On this point compare further Havelock Ellis (1903, Appendix B).

[*Added* 1910:] This judgement upon the literature of infantile sexuality need no longer be maintained since the appearance of Stanley Hall's exhaustive work (1904). No such modification is necessitated by Moll's recent book (1909). See, on the other hand, Bleuler (1908). [*Added* 1915:] Since this was written, a book by Hug-Hellmuth (1913) has taken the neglected sexual factor fully into account.

beginnings of their childhood up to their sixth or eighth year. Hitherto it has not occurred to us to feel any astonishment at the fact of this amnesia, though we might have had good grounds for doing so. For we learn from other people that during these years, of which at a later date we retain nothing in our memory but a few unintelligible and fragmentary recollections, we reacted in a lively manner to impressions, that we were capable of expressing pain and joy in a human fashion, that we gave evidence of love, jealousy and other passionate feelings by which we were strongly moved at the time, and even that we gave utterance to remarks which were regarded by adults as good evidence of our possessing insight and the beginnings of a capacity for judgement. And of all this we, when we are grown up, have no knowledge of our own! Why should our memory lag so far behind the other activities of our minds? We have, on the contrary, good reason to believe that there is no period at which the capacity for receiving and reproducing impressions is greater than precisely during the years of childhood.[1]

On the other hand we must assume, or we can convince ourselves by a psychological examination of other people, that the very same impressions that we have forgotten have none the less left the deepest traces on our minds and have had a determining effect upon the whole of our later development. There can, therefore, be no question of any real abolition of the impressions of childhood, but rather of an amnesia similar to that which neurotics exhibit for later events, and of which the essence consists in a simple withholding of these impressions from consciousness, viz., in their repression. But what are the forces which bring about this repression of the impressions of childhood? Whoever could solve this riddle would, I think, have explained *hysterical* amnesia as well.

1. I have attempted to solve one of the problems connected with the earliest memories of childhood in a paper on 'Screen Memories' (1899*a*). [*Added* 1924:] See also Chapter IV of my *Psychopathology of Everyday Life* (1901*b*).

Meanwhile we must not fail to observe that the existence of infantile amnesia provides a new point of comparison between the mental states of children and psychoneurotics. We have already [p. 87] come across another such point in the formula to which we were led, to the effect that the sexuality of psychoneurotics has remained at, or been carried back to, an infantile stage. Can it be, after all, that infantile amnesia, too, is to be brought into relation with the sexual impulses of childhood?

Moreover, the connection between infantile and hysterical amnesia is more than a mere play upon words. Hysterical amnesia, which occurs at the bidding of repression, is only explicable by the fact that the subject is already in possession of a store of memory-traces which have been withdrawn from conscious disposal, and which are now, by an associative link, attracting to themselves the material which the forces of repression are engaged in repelling from consciousness.[1] It may be said that without infantile amnesia there would be no hysterical amnesia.

I believe, then, that infantile amnesia, which turns everyone's childhood into something like a *prehistoric* epoch and conceals from him the beginnings of his own sexual life, is responsible for the fact that in general no importance is attached to childhood in the development of sexual life. The gaps in our knowledge which have arisen in this way cannot be bridged by a single observer. As long ago as in the year 1896[2] I insisted on the significance of the years of childhood in the origin of certain important phenomena connected with sexual life, and since then I have never ceased to emphasize the part played in sexuality by the infantile factor.

1. [*Footnote added* 1915:] The mechanism of repression cannot be understood unless account is taken of *both* of these two concurrent processes. They may be compared with the manner in which tourists are conducted to the top of the Great Pyramid of Giza by being pushed from one direction and pulled from the other. [Cf. Freud's paper on 'Repression' (1915*d*).]

2. [E.g. in the last paragraph of Section I of his paper on the aetiology of hysteria (1896*c*).]

[1] THE PERIOD OF SEXUAL LATENCY IN CHILDHOOD AND ITS INTERRUPTIONS

The remarkably frequent reports of what are described as irregular and exceptional sexual impulses in childhood, as well as the uncovering in neurotics of what have hitherto been unconscious memories of childhood, allow us to sketch out the sexual occurrences of that period in some such way as this.[1]

There seems no doubt that germs of sexual impulses are already present in the new-born child and that these continue to develop for a time, but are then overtaken by a progressive process of suppression; this in turn is itself interrupted by periodical advances in sexual development or may be held up by individual peculiarities. Nothing is known for certain concerning the regularity and periodicity of this oscillating course of development. It seems, however, that the sexual life of children usually emerges in a form accessible to observation round about the third or fourth year of life.[2]

1. We are able to make use of the second of these two sources of material since we are justified in expecting that the early years of children who are later to become neurotic are not likely in this respect to differ *essentially* from those of children who are to grow up into normal adults, [*added* 1915:] but only in the intensity and clarity of the phenomena involved.

2. There is a possible anatomical analogy to what I believe to be the course of development of the infantile sexual function in Bayer's discovery (1902) that the internal sexual organs (i.e. the uterus) are as a rule larger in new-born children than in older ones. It is not certain, however, what view we should take of this involution that occurs after birth (which has been shown by Halban to apply also to other portions of the genital apparatus). According to Halban (1904) the proceess of involution comes to an end after a few weeks of extra-uterine life. [*Added* 1920:] Those authorities who regard the interstitial portion of the sex-gland as the organ that determines sex have on their side been led by anatomical researches to speak of infantile sexuality and a period of sexual latency. I quote a passage from Lipschütz's book (1919, 168), which I mentioned on p. 59 *n*.: 'We shall be doing more justice to the acts if we say that the maturation of the sexual characters which is

Sexual Inhibitions

It is during this period of total or only partial latency that are built up the mental forces which are later to impede the course of the sexual instinct and, like dams, restrict its flow – disgust, feelings of shame and the claims of aesthetic and moral ideals. One gets an impression from civilized children that the construction of these dams is a product of education, and no doubt education has much to do with it. But in reality this development is organically determined and fixed by heredity, and it can occasionally occur without any help at all from education. Education will not be trespassing beyond its appropriate domain if it limits itself to following the lines which have already been laid down organically and to impressing them somewhat more clearly and deeply.

Reaction-formation and Sublimation

What is it that goes to the making of these constructions which are so important for the growth of a civilized and

---

accomplished at puberty is only due to a great acceleration which occurs at that time of processes which began much earlier – in my view as early as during intra-uterine life.' ' *What has hitherto been described in a summary way as puberty is probably only a second major phase of puberty which sets in about the middle of the second decade of life* . . . Childhood, from birth until the beginning of this second major phase, might be described as the "*intermediate phase of puberty*"' (ibid., 170). Attention was drawn to this coincidence between anatomical findings and psychological observation in a review [of Lipschütz's book] by Ferenczi (1920). The agreement is marred only by the fact that the '*first peak*' in the development of the sexual organ occurs during the early intra-uterine period, whereas the early efflorescence of infantile sexual life must be ascribed to the third and fourth years of life. There is, of course, no need to expect that anatomical growth and psychical development must be exactly simultaneous. The researches in question were made on the sex-glands of human beings. Since a period of latency in the psychological sense does not occur in animals, it would be very interesting to know whether anatomical findings which have led these writers to assume the occurrence of two peaks in sexual development are also demonstrable in the higher animals.

normal individual? They probably emerge at the cost of the infantile sexual impulses themselves. Thus the activity of those impulses does not cease even during this period of latency, though their energy is diverted, wholly or in great part, from their sexual use and directed to other ends. Historians of civilization appear to be at one in assuming that powerful components are acquired for every kind of cultural achievement by this diversion of sexual instinctual forces from sexual aims and their direction to new ones – a process which deserves the name of 'sublimation'. To this we would add, accordingly, that the same process plays a part in the development of the individual and we would place its beginning in the period of sexual latency of childhood.[1]

It is possible further to form some idea of the mechanism of this process of sublimation. On the one hand, it would seem, the sexual impulses cannot be utilized during these years of childhood, since the reproductive functions have been deferred – a fact which constitutes the main feature of the period of latency. On the other hand, these impulses would seem in themselves to be perverse – that is, to arise from erotogenic zones and to derive their activity from instincts which, in view of the direction of the subject's development, can only arouse unpleasurable feelings. They consequently evoke opposing mental forces (reacting impulses) which, in order to suppress this unpleasure effectively, build up the mental dams that I have already mentioned – disgust, shame and morality.[2]

1. Once again, it is from Fliess that I have borrowed the term 'period of sexual latency'.

2. [Footnote added 1915:] In the case which I am here discussing, the sublimation of sexual instinctual forces takes place along the path of reaction-formation. But in general it is possible to distinguish the concepts of sublimation and reaction-formation from each other as two different processes. Sublimation can also take place by other and simpler mechanisms. [Further theoretical discussions of sublimation will be found in Section III of Freud's paper on narcissism (1914c) and at several points in The Ego and the Id (1923b, Chapters III, IV and V).]

Interruptions of the Latency Period

We must not deceive ourselves as to the hypothetical nature and insufficient clarity of our knowledge concerning the processes of the infantile period of latency or deferment; but we shall be on firmer ground in pointing out that such an application of infantile sexuality represents an educational idea from which individual development usually diverges at some point and often to a considerable degree. From time to time a fragmentary manifestation of sexuality which has evaded sublimation may break through; or some sexual activity may persist through the whole duration of the latency period until the sexual instinct emerges with greater intensity at puberty. In so far as educators pay any attention at all to infantile sexuality, they behave exactly as though they shared our views as to the construction of the moral defensive forces at the cost of sexuality, and as though they knew that sexual activity makes a child ineducable: for they stigmatize every sexual manifestation by children as a 'vice', without being able to do much against it. We, on the other hand, have every reason for turning our attention to these phenomena which are so much dreaded by education, for we may expect them to help us to discover the original configuration of the sexual instincts.

[2] THE MANIFESTATIONS OF INFANTILE SEXUALITY

Thumb-sucking

For reasons which will appear later, I shall take thumb-sucking (or sensual sucking) as a sample of the sexual manifestations of childhood. (An excellent study of this subject has been made by the Hungarian paediatrician, Lindner, 1879.)[1]

1. [There seems to be no nursery word in English equivalent to the German 'lutschen' and 'ludeln', used by Freud alongside '*wonnesaugen*'

Thumb-sucking appears already in early infancy and may continue into maturity, or even persist all through life. It consists in the rhythmic repetition of a sucking contact by the mouth (or lips). There is no question of the purpose of this procedure being the taking of nourishment. A portion of the lip itself, the tongue, or any other part of the skin within reach – even the big toe – may be taken as the object upon which this sucking is carried out. In this connection a grasping-instinct may appear and may manifest itself as a simultaneous rhythmic tugging at the lobes of the ears or a catching hold of some part of another person (as a rule the ear) for the same purpose. Sensual sucking involves a complete absorption of the attention and leads either to sleep or even to a motor reaction in the nature of an orgasm.[1] It is not infrequently combined with rubbing some sensitive part of the body such as the breast or the external genitalia. Many children proceed by this path from sucking to masturbation.

Lindner himself[2] clearly recognized the sexual nature of this activity and emphasized it without qualification. In the nursery, sucking is often classed along with the other kinds of sexual 'naughtiness' of children. This view has been most energetically repudiated by numbers of paediatricians and nerve-specialists, though this is no doubt partly due to a confusion between 'sexual' and 'genital'. Their objection raises a difficult question and one which cannot be evaded: what is the general characteristic which enables us to recognize the sexual

('sensual sucking'). Conrad in *Struwwelpeter* was a '*Lutscher*'; but, as will be seen from the context, 'suck-a-thumbs' and 'thumb-sucking' have in fact too narrow a connotation for the present purpose.]

1. Thus we find at this early stage, what holds good all through life, that sexual satisfaction is the best soporific. Most cases of nervous insomnia can be traced back to lack of sexual satisfaction. It is well known that unscrupulous nurses put crying children to sleep by stroking their genitals.

2. [This paragraph was added in 1915, replacing one (in the 1905 and 1910 editions) criticizing the views of Moll on this example of the sexual behaviour of children. Cf. above, p. 84 *n.* 2.]

manifestations of children? The concatenation of phenomena
into which we have been given an insight by psychoanalytic
investigation justifies us, in my opinion, in regarding thumb-
sucking as a sexual manifestation and in choosing it for our
study of the essential features of infantile sexual activity.[1]

Auto-erotism

We are in duty bound to make a thorough examination of this
example. It must be insisted that the most striking feature of
this sexual activity is that the instinct is not directed towards
other people, but obtains satisfaction from the subject's own
body. It is 'auto-erotic', to call it by a happily chosen term
introduced by Havelock Ellis [1898].[2]

Furthermore, it is clear that the behaviour of a child who
indulges in thumb-sucking is determined by a search for some
pleasure which has already been experienced and is now remembered. In the simplest case he proceeds to find this satisfaction by sucking rhythmically at some part of the skin or

1. [*Footnote added* 1920:] In 1919, a Dr Galant published, under the
title of 'Das Lutscherli', the confession of a grown-up girl who had
never given up this infantile sexual activity and who represents the
satisfaction to be gained from sucking as something completely analogous to sexual satisfaction, particularly when this is obtained from a
lover's kiss: 'Not every kiss is equal to a "*Lutscherli*" – no, no, not by
any means! It is impossible to describe what a lovely feeling goes
through your whole body when you suck; you are right away from
this world. You are absolutely satisfied, and happy beyond desire. It is a
wonderful feeling; you long for nothing but peace – uninterrupted
peace. It is just unspeakably lovely: you feel no pain and no sorrow, and
ah! you are carried into another world.'

2. [*Footnote added* 1920:] Havelock Ellis, it is true, uses the word
'auto-erotic' in a somewhat different sense, to describe an excitation
which is not provoked from outside but arises internally. What psychoanalysis regards as the essential point is not the genesis of the excitation,
but the question of its relation to an object. – [In all editions before 1920
this footnote read as follows: 'Havelock Ellis, however, has spoilt the
meaning of the term he invented by including the whole of hysteria and
all the manifestations of masturbation among the phenomena of auto-
erotism.']

mucous membrane. It is also easy to guess the occasions on which the child had his first experiences of the pleasure which he is now striving to renew. It was the child's first and most vital activity, his sucking at his mother's breast, or at substitutes for it, that must have familiarized him with this pleasure. The child's lips, in our view, behave like an *erotogenic zone*, and no doubt stimulation by the warm flow of milk is the cause of the pleasurable sensation. The satisfaction of the erotogenic zone is associated, in the first instance, with the satisfaction of the need for nourishment. To begin with, sexual activity attaches itself to one of the functions serving the purpose of self-preservation and does not become independent of them until later.[1] No one who has seen a baby sinking back satiated from the breast and falling asleep with flushed cheeks and a blissful smile can escape the reflection that this picture persists as a prototype of the expression of sexual satisfaction in later life. The need for repeating the sexual satisfaction now becomes detached from the need for taking nourishment – a separation which becomes inevitable when the teeth appear and food is no longer taken in only by sucking, but is also chewed up. The child does not make use of an extraneous body for his sucking, but prefers a part of his own skin because it is more convenient, because it makes him independent of the external world, which he is not yet able to control, and because in that way he provides himself, as it were, with a second erotogenic zone, though one of an inferior kind. The inferiority of this second region is among the reasons why at a later date he seeks the corresponding part – the lips – of another person. ('It's a pity I can't kiss myself', he seems to be saying.)

It is not every child who sucks in this way. It may be assumed that those children do so in whom there is a constitutional intensification of the erotogenic significance of the labial region. If that significance persists, these same children

1. [This sentence was added in 1915. Cf. Section II of Freud's paper on narcissism (1914c).]

when they are grown up will become epicures in kissing, will be inclined to perverse kissing, or, if males, will have a powerful motive for drinking and smoking. If, however, repression ensues, they will feel disgust at food and will produce hysterical vomiting. The repression extends to the nutritional instinct owing to the dual purpose served by the labial zone. Many[1] of my women patients who suffer from disturbances of eating, *globus hystericus*, constriction of the throat and vomiting, have indulged energetically in sucking during their childhood.

Our study of thumb-sucking or sensual sucking has already given us the three essential characteristics of an infantile sexual manifestation. At its origin it *attaches* itself to one of the vital somatic functions;[2] it has as yet no sexual object, and is thus *auto-erotic*; and its sexual aim is dominated by an *erotogenic zone*. It is to be anticipated that these characteristics will be found to apply equally to most of the other activities of the infantile sexual instincts.

[3] THE SEXUAL AIM OF INFANTILE SEXUALITY

Characteristics of Erotogenic Zones

The example of thumb-sucking shows us still more about what constitutes an erotogenic zone. It is a part of the skin or mucous membrane in which stimuli of a certain sort evoke a feeling of pleasure possessing a particular quality. There can be no doubt that the stimuli which produce the pleasure are governed by special conditions, though we do not know what those are. A rhythmic character must play a part among them and the analogy of tickling is forced upon our notice. It seems less certain whether the character of the pleasurable feeling evoked by the stimulus should be described as a 'specific'

1. [In the first edition only this reads 'all'.]
2. [This clause was added in 1915; and in the earlier editions the word 'three' in the last sentence is replaced by 'two'.]

one – a 'specific' quality in which the sexual factor would precisely lie. Psychology is still so much in the dark in questions of pleasure and unpleasure that the most cautious assumption is the one most to be recommended. We may later come upon reasons which seem to support the idea that the pleasurable feeling does in fact possess a specific quality.

The character of erotogenicity can be attached to some parts of the body in a particularly marked way. There are predestined erotogenic zones, as is shown by the example of sucking. The same example, however, also shows us that any other part of the skin or mucous membrane can take over the functions of an erotogenic zone, and must therefore have some aptitude in that direction. Thus the quality of the stimulus has more to do with producing the pleasurable feeling than has the nature of the part of the body concerned. A child who is indulging in sensual sucking searches about his body and chooses some part of it to suck – a part which is afterwards preferred by him from force of habit; if he happens to hit upon one of the predestined regions (such as the nipples or genitals) no doubt it retains the preference. A precisely analogous tendency to displacement is also found in the symptomatology of hysteria. In that neurosis repression affects most of all the actual genital zones and these transmit their susceptibility to stimulation to other erotogenic zones (normally neglected in adult life), which then behave exactly like genitals. But besides this, precisely as in the case of sucking, any other part of the body can acquire the same susceptibility to stimulation as is possessed by the genitals and can become an erotogenic zone. Erotogenic and hysterogenic zones show the same characteristics.[1]

1. [*Footnote added* 1915:] After further reflection and after taking other observations into account, I have been led to ascribe the quality of erotogenicity to all parts of the body and to all the internal organs. Cf. also in this connection what is said below on narcissism [p. 138f.]. [In the 1910 edition only, the following footnote appeared at this point: 'The biological problems relating to the hypothesis of erotogenic zones have been discussed by Alfred Adler (1907).']

The Infantile Sexual Aim

The sexual aim of the infantile instinct consists in obtaining satisfaction by means of an appropriate stimulation of the erotogenic zone which has been selected in one way or another. This satisfaction must have been previously experienced in order to have left behind a need for its repetition; and we may expect that Nature will have made safe provisions so that this experience of satisfaction shall not be left to chance.[1] We have already learnt what the contrivance is that fulfils this purpose in the case of the labial zone: it is the simultaneous connection which links this part of the body with the taking in of food. We shall come across other, similar contrivances as sources of sexuality. The state of being in need of a repetition of the satisfaction reveals itself in two ways: by a peculiar feeling of tension, possessing, rather, the character of unpleasure, and by a sensation of itching or stimulation which is *centrally conditioned* and projected on to the peripheral erotogenic zone. We can therefore formulate a sexual aim in another way: it consists in replacing the projected sensation of stimulation in the erotogenic zone by an external stimulus which removes that sensation by producing a feeling of satisfaction. This external stimulus will usually consist in some kind of manipulation that is analogous to the sucking.[2]

The fact that the need can also be evoked peripherally, by a real modification of the erotogenic zone, is in complete harmony with our physiological knowledge. This strikes us as

1. [*Footnote added* 1920:] In biological discussions it is scarcely possible to avoid a teleological way of thinking, even though one is aware that in any particular instance one is not secure against error. [Cf. footnote, p. 105.]

2. [This account of the way in which a particular sexual desire becomes established on the basis of an 'experience of satisfaction' is only a special application of Freud's general theory of the mechanism of wishes, as explained in Section C of Chapter VII of *The Interpretation of Dreams* (1900a, *P.F.L.*, **4**, 718–20). The whole topic links up with Freud's views on 'reality-testing', as discussed, for instance, in his paper on 'Negation' (1925h), ibid., **11**, 439–40.]

somewhat strange only because, in order to remove one stimulus, it seems necessary to adduce a second one at the same spot.

[4] MASTURBATORY SEXUAL MANIFESTATIONS[1]

It must come as a great relief to find that, when once we have understood the nature of the instinct arising from a single one of the erotogenic zones, we shall have very little more to learn of the sexual activity of children. The clearest distinctions as between one zone and another concern the nature of the contrivance necessary for satisfying the instinct; in the case of the labial zone it consisted of sucking, and this has to be replaced by other muscular actions according to the position and nature of the other zones.

Activity of the Anal Zone

Like the labial zone, the anal zone is well suited by its position to act as a medium through which sexuality may *attach* itself to other somatic functions. It is to be presumed that the erotogenic significance of this part of the body is very great from the first. We learn with some astonishment from psychoanalysis of the transmutations normally undergone by the sexual excitations arising from this zone and of the frequency with which it retains a considerable amount of susceptibility to genital stimulation throughout life.[2] The intestinal disturbances which are so common in childhood see to it that the

1. Cf. the very copious literature on the subject of masturbation, which for the most part, however, is at sea upon the main issues, e.g. Rohleder (1899). [*Added* 1915:] See also the report of the discussion on the subject in the Vienna Psycho-Analytical Society (*Diskussionen*, 1912) – [and especially Freud's own contributions to it (1912*f*)].

2. [*Footnote added* 1910:] Cf. my papers on 'Character and Anal Erotism' (1908*b*) [*added* 1920:] and 'On Transformations of Instinct as Exemplified in Anal Erotism' (1917*c*) [both in the present volume, pp. 205ff. and 293ff. below].

zone shall not lack intense excitations. Intestinal catarrhs at the tenderest age make children 'nervy', as people say, and in cases of later neurotic illness they have a determining influence on the symptoms in which the neurosis is expressed, and they put at its disposal the whole range of intestinal disturbances. If we bear in mind the erotogenic significance of the outlet of the intestinal canal, which persists, at all events in a modified form, we shall not be inclined to scoff at the influence of haemorrhoids, to which old-fashioned medicine used to attach so much importance in explaining neurotic conditions.

Children who are making use of the susceptibility to erotogenic stimulation of the anal zone betray themselves by holding back their stool till its accumulation brings about violent muscular contractions and, as it passes through the anus, is able to produce powerful stimulation of the mucous membrane. In so doing it must no doubt cause not only painful but also highly pleasurable sensations. One of the clearest signs of subsequent eccentricity or nervousness is to be seen when a baby obstinately refuses to empty his bowels when he is put on the pot – that is, when his nurse wants him to – and holds back that function till he himself chooses to exercise it. He is naturally not concerned with dirtying the bed, he is only anxious not to miss the subsidiary pleasure attached to defaecating. Educators are once more right when they describe children who keep the process back as 'naughty'.

The contents of the bowels,[1] which act as a stimulating mass upon a sexually sensitive portion of mucous membrane, behave like forerunners of another organ, which is destined to come into action after the phase of childhood. But they have other important meanings for the infant. They are clearly treated as a part of the infant's own body and represent his first 'gift': by producing them he can express his active

1. [This paragraph was added in 1915. Its contents were expanded in one of the papers (1917c) mentioned in the last footnote. See p. 295ff. below.]

compliance with his environment and, by withholding them, his disobedience. From being a 'gift' they later come to acquire the meaning of 'baby' – for babies, according to one of the sexual theories of children [see below, p. 114], are acquired by eating and are born through the bowels.

The retention of the faecal mass, which is thus carried out intentionally by the child to begin with, in order to serve, as it were, as a masturbatory stimulus upon the anal zone or to be employed in his relation to the people looking after him, is also one of the roots of the constipation which is so common among neuropaths. Further, the whole significance of the anal zone is reflected in the fact that few neurotics are to be found without their special scatological practices, ceremonies, and so on, which they carefully keep secret.[1]

Actual masturbatory stimulation of the anal zone by means of the finger, provoked by a centrally determined or peripherally maintained sensation of itching, is by no means rare among older children.

Activity of the Genital Zones

Among the erotogenic zones that form part of the child's body there is one which certainly does not play the opening

---

1. [Footnote added 1920:] Lou Andreas-Salomé (1916), in a paper which has given us a very much deeper understanding of the significance of anal erotism, has shown how the history of the first prohibition which a child comes across – the prohibition against getting pleasure from anal activity and its products – has a decisive effect on his whole development. This must be the first occasion on which the infant has a glimpse of an environment hostile to his instinctual impulses, on which he learns to separate his own entity from this alien one and on which he carries out the first 'repression' of his possibilities for pleasure. From that time on, what is 'anal' remains the symbol of everything that is to be repudiated and excluded from life. The clear-cut distinction between anal and genital processes which is later insisted upon is contradicted by the close anatomical and functional analogies and relations which hold between them. The genital apparatus remains the neighbour of the cloaca, and actually [to quote Lou Andreas-Salomé] 'in the case of women is only taken from it on lease'.

part, and which cannot be the vehicle of the oldest sexual impulses, but which is destined to great things in the future. In both male and female children it is brought into connection with micturition (in the glans and clitoris) and in the former is enclosed in a pouch of mucous membrane, so that there can be no lack of stimulation of it by secretions which may give an early start to sexual excitation. The sexual activities of this erotogenic zone, which forms part of the sexual organs proper, are the beginning of what is later to become 'normal' sexual life. The anatomical situation of this region, the secretions in which it is bathed, the washing and rubbing to which it is subjected in the course of a child's toilet, as well as accidental stimulation (such as the movement of intestinal worms in the case of girls), make it inevitable that the pleasurable feeling which this part of the body is capable of producing should be noticed by children even during their earliest infancy, and should give rise to a need for its repetition. If we consider this whole range of contrivances and bear in mind that both making a mess and measures for keeping clean are bound to operate in much the same way, it is scarcely possible to avoid the conclusion that the foundations for the future primacy over sexual activity exercised by this erotogenic zone are established by early infantile masturbation, which scarcely a single individual escapes.[1] The action which disposes of the stimulus and brings about satisfaction consists in a rubbing movement

1. [In the editions of 1905 and 1910 the last part of this sentence read 'it is difficult to overlook Nature's purpose of establishing the future primacy over sexual activity exercised by this erotogenic zone by means of early infantile masturbation, which scarcely a single individual escapes'. The teleological nature of this argument in favour of the universality of infantile masturbation was sharply criticized by Rudolf Reitler in the course of the discussions on that topic in the Vienna Psycho-Analytical Society in 1912 (Diskussionen, 1912, 92f.). In his own contribution to the discussion (ibid., 134; – Freud, 1912f), Freud agreed that the phrasing he had used was unfortunate, and undertook to alter it in later reprints. The present version of the sentence was accordingly substituted in 1915. Cf. pp. 69 and n. 1 and 101 and n. 1.]

with the hand or in the application of pressure (no doubt on the lines of a pre-existing reflex) either from the hand or by bringing the thighs together. This last method is by far the more common in the case of girls. The preference for the hand which is shown by boys is already evidence of the important contribution which the instinct for mastery is destined to make to masculine sexual activity.[1]

It will be in the interests of clarity[2] if I say at once that three phases of infantile masturbation are to be distinguished. The first of these belongs to early infancy, and the second to the brief efflorescence of sexual activity about the fourth year of life; only the third phase corresponds to pubertal masturbation, which is often the only kind taken into account.

Second Phase of Infantile Masturbation

The masturbation of early infancy seems to disappear after a short time; but it may persist uninterruptedly until puberty, and this would constitute the first great deviation from the course of development laid down for civilized men. At some point of childhood after early infancy, as a rule before the fourth year, the sexual instinct belonging to the genital zone usually revives and persists again for a time until it is once

1. [*Footnote added* 1915:] Unusual techniques in carrying out masturbation in later years seem to point to the influence of a prohibition against masturbation which has been overcome.

2. [This paragraph was added in 1915. In the edition of that year there were also added the title of the next paragraph and the parenthesis 'as a rule before the fourth year' in its second sentence. Moreover, in the first sentence of the same paragraph the words 'after a short time' were substituted for the words 'at the onset of the latency period' which had appeared in 1905 and 1910. Finally, in those first two editions, the *following* paragraph began with the words 'During the years of childhood (it has not yet been possible to generalize as to the chronology) the sexual excitation of early infancy returns . . .' The motive for all these changes made in 1915 was evidently to distinguish more sharply between the second and first phases of infantile sexual activity and to assign a more precise data – 'about the fourth year' – to the second phase.]

more suppressed, or it may continue without interruption. This *second* phase of infantile sexual activity may assume a variety of different forms which can only be determined by a precise analysis of individual cases. But all its details leave behind the deepest (unconscious) impressions in the subject's memory, determine the development of his character, if he is to remain healthy, and the symptomatology of his neurosis, if he is to fall ill after puberty.[1] In the latter case we find that this sexual period has been forgotten and that the conscious memories that bear witness to it have been displaced. (I have already mentioned that I am also inclined to relate normal infantile amnesia to this infantile sexual activity.) Psychoanalytic investigation enables us to make what has been forgotten conscious and thus do away with a compulsion that arises from the unconscious psychical material.

Return of Early Infantile Masturbation

During the years of childhood with which I am now dealing, the sexual excitation of early infancy returns, either as a centrally determined tickling stimulus which seeks satisfaction in masturbation, or as a process in the nature of a nocturnal emission which, like the nocturnal emissions of adult years, achieves satisfaction without the help of any action by the subject. The latter case is the more frequent with girls and in the second half of childhood; its determinants are not entirely intelligible and often, though not invariably, it seems to be conditioned by a period of earlier *active* masturbation. The symptoms of these sexual manifestations are scanty; they are mostly displayed on behalf of the still undeveloped sexual

1. [*Footnote added* 1915:] The problem of why the sense of guilt of neurotics is, as Bleuler [1913] recently recognized, regularly attached to the memory of some masturbatory activity, usually at puberty, still awaits an exhaustive analytic explanation. [*Added* 1920:] The most general and most important factor concerned must no doubt be that masturbation represents the executive agency of the whole of infantile sexuality and is, therefore, able to take over the sense of guilt attaching to it.

apparatus by the *urinary* apparatus, which thus acts, as it were, as the former's trustee. Most of the so-called bladder disorders of this period are sexual disturbances: *enuresis nocturna*, unless it represents an epileptic fit, corresponds to a nocturnal emission.

The reappearance of sexual activity is determined by internal causes and external contingencies, both of which can be guessed in cases of neurotic illness from the form taken by their symptoms and can be discovered with certainty by psychoanalytic investigation. I shall have to speak presently of the internal causes; great and lasting importance attaches at this period to the accidental *external* contingencies. In the foreground we find the effects of seduction, which treats a child as a sexual object prematurely and teaches him, in highly emotional circumstances, how to obtain satisfaction from his genital zones, a satisfaction which he is then usually obliged to repeat again and again by masturbation. An influence of this kind may originate either from adults or from other children. I cannot admit that in my paper on 'The Aetiology of Hysteria' (1896c) I exaggerated the frequency or importance of that influence, though I did not then know that persons who remain normal may have had the same experiences in their childhood, and though I consequently overrated the importance of seduction in comparison with the factors of sexual constitution and development.[1] Obviously seduction is not

1. [See Freud's detailed discussion of this in his paper on the role of sexuality in the neuroses (1906a: *P.F.L.*, **10**, 74–5).] Havelock Ellis [1903, Appendix B] has published a number of autobiographical narratives written by people who remained predominantly normal in later life and describing the first sexual impulses of their childhood and the occasions which gave rise to them. These reports naturally suffer from the fact that they omit the prehistoric period of the writers' sexual lives, which is veiled by infantile amnesia and which can only be filled in by psychoanalysis in the case of an individual who has developed a neurosis. In more than one respect, nevertheless, the statements are valuable, and similar narratives were what led me to make the modification in my aetiological hypotheses which I have mentioned in the text. [These narratives were mentioned again in the paper on infantile sexual theories (1908c); cf. p. 189 below.]

required in order to arouse a child's sexual life; that can also come about spontaneously from internal causes.

Polymorphously Perverse Disposition

It is an instructive fact that under the influence of seduction children can become polymorphously perverse, and can be led into all possible kinds of sexual irregularities. This shows that an aptitude for them is innately present in their disposition. There is consequently little resistance towards carrying them out, since the mental dams against sexual excesses – shame, disgust and morality – have either not yet been constructed at all or are only in course of construction, according to the age of the child. In this respect children behave in the same kind of way as an average uncultivated woman in whom the same polymorphously perverse disposition persists. Under ordinary conditions she may remain normal sexually, but if she is led on by a clever seducer she will find every sort of perversion to her taste, and will retain them as part of her own sexual activities. Prostitutes exploit the same polymorphous, that is, infantile, disposition for the purposes of their profession; and, considering the immense number of women who are prostitutes or who must be supposed to have an aptitude for prostitution without becoming engaged in it, it becomes impossible not to recognize that this same disposition to perversions of every kind is a general and fundamental human characteristic.

Component Instincts

Moreover, the effects of seduction do not help to reveal the early history of the sexual instinct; they rather confuse our view of it by presenting children prematurely with a sexual object for which the infantile sexual instinct at first shows no need. It must, however, be admitted that infantile sexual life, in spite of the preponderating dominance of erotogenic zones, exhibits components which from the very first involve other people as sexual objects. Such are the instincts of scopophilia, exhibitionism and cruelty, which appear in a sense independently of erotogenic zones; these instincts do not enter into intimate relations with genital[1] life until later, but are already to be observed in childhood as independent impulses, distinct in the first instance from erotogenic sexual activity. Small children are essentially without shame, and at some periods of their earliest years show an unmistakable satisfaction in exposing their bodies, with especial emphasis on the sexual parts. The counterpart of this supposedly perverse inclination, curiosity to see other people's genitals, probably does not become manifest until somewhat later in childhood, when the obstacle set up by a sense of shame has already reached a certain degree of development.[2] Under the influence of seduction the scopophilic perversion can attain great importance in the sexual life of a child. But my researches into the early years of normal people, as well as of neurotic patients, force me to the conclusion that scopophilia can also appear in children as a spontaneous manifestation. Small children whose attention has once been drawn – as a rule by masturbation – to their own genitals usually take the further step without help from outside and develop a lively interest in the genitals of their playmates. Since opportunities for satisfying curiosity of this kind usually occur only in the course of satisfying the two kinds of need for excretion, children of this kind turn into *voyeurs*, eager spectators of the processes of micturition and defaecation. When repression of these inclinations sets in, the desire to see other people's genitals (whether of their own or the opposite sex) persists as a tormenting compulsion, which in some cases of neurosis later afford the strongest motive force for the formation of symptoms.

The cruel component of the sexual instinct develops in childhood even more independently of the sexual activities that are attached to erotogenic zones. Cruelty in general comes

1. ['Sexual' in 1905 and 1910.]

2. [This sentence in its present form dates from 1920. In earlier editions the statement was more emphatic. The subject of exhibitionism in young children had been discussed at some length by Freud in his *Interpretation of Dreams*, Chapter V, Section D (α) (*P.F.L.*, 4, 342-4).]

easily to the childish nature, since the obstacle that brings the instinct for mastery to a halt at another person's pain – namely a capacity for pity – is developed relatively late. The fundamental psychological analysis of this instinct has, as we know, not yet been satisfactorily achieved. It may be assumed that the impulse of cruelty arises from the instinct for mastery and appears at a period of sexual life at which the genitals have not yet taken over their later role. It then dominates a phase of sexual life which we shall later describe as pregenital organization.[1] Children who distinguish themselves by special cruelty towards animals and playmates usually give rise to a just suspicion of an intense and precocious sexual activity arising from erotogenic zones; and, though all the sexual instincts may display simultaneous precocity, *erotogenic* sexual activity seems, nevertheless, to be the primary one. The absence of the barrier of pity brings with it a danger that the connection between the cruel and the erotogenic instincts, thus established in childhood, may prove unbreakable in later life. Ever since Jean Jacques Rousseau's *Confessions*, it has been well known to all educationists that the painful stimulation of the skin of the buttocks is one of the erotogenic roots of the *passive* instinct of cruelty (masochism). The conclusion has rightly been drawn by them that corporal punishment, which is usually applied to this part of the body, should not be inflicted upon any children whose libido is liable to be forced into collateral channels by the later demands of cultural education.[2]

1. [The last two sentences were given their present form in 1915. In 1905 and 1910 they read as follows: 'It may be assumed that the impulses of cruelty arise from sources which are in fact independent of sexuality, but may become united with it at an early stage owing to an anastomosis [cross-connection] near their points of origin. Observation teaches us, however, that sexual development and the development of the instinct of scopophilia and cruelty are subject to mutual influences which limit this presumed independence of the two sets of instincts.']

2. [*Footnote added* 1910:] When the account which I have given above of infantile sexuality was first published in 1905, it was founded for the most part on the results of psychoanalytic research upon adults.

[5] THE SEXUAL RESEARCHES OF CHILDHOOD[1]

The Instinct for Knowledge

At about the same time as the sexual life of children reaches its first peak, between the ages of three and five, they also begin to show signs of the activity which may be ascribed to the instinct for knowledge or research. This instinct cannot be counted among the elementary instinctual components, nor can it be classed as exclusively belonging to sexuality. Its activity corresponds on the one hand to a sublimated manner of obtaining mastery, while on the other hand it makes use of the energy of scopophilia. Its relations to sexual life, however, are of particular importance, since we have learnt from psychoanalysis that the instinct for knowledge in children is

---

At that time it was impossible to make full use of direct observation on children: only isolated hints and some valuable pieces of confirmation came from that source. Since then it has become possible to gain direct insight into infantile psychosexuality by the analysis of some cases of neurotic illness during the early years of childhood. It is gratifying to be able to report that direct observation has fully confirmed the conclusions arrived at by psychoanalysis – which is incidentally good evidence of the trustworthiness of that method of research. In addition to this, the 'Analysis of a Phobia in a Five-Year-Old Boy' (1909b) has taught us much that is new for which we have not been prepared by psychoanalysis: for instance, the fact that sexual symbolism – the representation of what is sexual by non-sexual objects and relations – extends back into the first years of possession of the power of speech. I was further made aware of a defect in the account I have given in the text, which, in the interests of lucidity, describes the conceptual distinction between the two phases of *auto-erotism* and *object-love* as though it were also a separation in time. But the analyses that I have just mentioned, as well as the findings of Bell quoted in the footnote, p. 89, above, show that children between the ages of three and five are capable of very clear *object-choice*, accompanied by strong affects. – [In 1910 only, this footnote ended with an allusion to the sexual researches and theories of children and to Freud's paper on the subject (1908c); see below, p. 183ff.]

1. [The whole of this section on the sexual researches of children first appeared in 1915.]

attracted unexpectedly early and intensively to sexual problems and is in fact possibly first aroused by them.

The Riddle of the Sphinx

It is not by theoretical interests but by practical ones that
activities of research are set going in children. The threat to the
bases of a child's existence offered by the discovery or the
suspicion of the arrival of a new baby and the fear that he may,
as a result of it, cease to be cared for and loved, make him
thoughtful and clear-sighted. And this history of the instinct's
origin is in line with the fact that the first problem with which
it deals is not the question of the distinction between the sexes
but the riddle of where babies come from.[1] (This, in a distorted form which can easily be rectified, is the same riddle
that was propounded by the Theban Sphinx.) On the contrary,
the existence of two sexes does not to begin with arouse any
difficulties or doubts in children. It is self-evident to a male
child that a genital like his own is to be attributed to everyone
he knows, and he cannot make its absence tally with his picture of these other people.

Castration Complex and Penis Envy

This conviction is energetically maintained by boys, is
obstinately defended against the contradictions which soon
result from observation, and is only abandoned after severe
internal struggles (the castration complex). The substitutes for
this penis which they feel is missing in women play a great
part in determining the form taken by many perversions.[2]

1. [In a later work (1925j, see below, p. 336 n. 2), Freud corrected
this statement, saying that it is not true of girls, and not always true of
boys.]

2. [*Footnote added* 1920:] We are justified in speaking of a castration
complex in women as well. Both male and female children form a
theory that women no less than men originally had a penis, but that
they have lost it by castration. The conviction which is finally reached
by males that women have no penis often leads them to an enduringly
low opinion of the other sex.

The assumption that all human beings have the same (male) form of genital is the first of the many remarkable and momentous sexual theories of children. It is of little use to a child that the science of biology justifies his prejudice and has been obliged to recognize the female clitoris as a true substitute for the penis.

Little girls do not resort to denial of this kind when they see that boys' genitals are formed differently from their own. They are ready to recognize them immediately and are overcome by envy for the penis – an envy culminating in the wish, which is so important in its consequences, to be boys themselves.

Theories of Birth

Many people can remember clearly what an intense interest they took during the prepubertal period in the question of where babies come from. The anatomical answers to the question were at the time very various: babies come out of the breast, or are cut out of the body, or the navel opens to let them through.[1] Outside analysis, there are very seldom memories of any similar researches having been carried out in the *early* years of childhood. These earlier researches fell a victim to repression long since, but all their findings were of a uniform nature: people get babies by eating some particular thing (as they do in fairy tales) and babies are born through the bowel like a discharge of faeces. These infantile theories remind us of conditions that exist in the animal kingdom – and especially of the cloaca in types of animals lower than mammals.

Sadistic View of Sexual Intercourse

If children at this early age witness sexual intercourse between adults – for which an opportunity is provided by the conviction

1. [*Footnote added* 1924:] In these later years of childhood there is a great wealth of sexual theories, of which only a few examples are given in the text.

of grown-up people that small children cannot understand anything sexual – they inevitably regard the sexual act as a sort of ill-treatment or act of subjugation: they view it, that is, in a sadistic sense. Psychoanalysis also shows us that an impression of this kind in early childhood contributes a great deal towards a predisposition to a subsequent sadistic displacement of the sexual aim. Furthermore, children are much concerned with the problem of what sexual intercourse – or, as they put it, being married – consists in: and they usually seek a solution of the mystery in some common activity concerned with the function of micturition or defaecation.

Typical Failure of Infantile Sexual Researches

We can say in general of the sexual theories of children that they are reflections of their own sexual constitution, and that in spite of their grotesque errors the theories show more understanding of sexual processes than one would have given their creators credit for. Children also perceive the alterations that take place in their mother owing to pregnancy and are able to interpret them correctly. The fable of the stork is often told to an audience that receives it with deep, though mostly silent, mistrust. There are, however, two elements that remain undiscovered by the sexual researches of children: the fertilizing role of semen and the existence of the female sexual orifice – the same elements, incidentally, in which the infantile organization is itself undeveloped. It therefore follows that the efforts of the childish investigator are habitually fruitless, and end in a renunciation which not infrequently leaves behind it a permanent injury to the instinct for knowledge. The sexual researches of these early years of childhood are always carried out in solitude. They constitute a first step towards taking an independent attitude in the world, and imply a high degree of alienation of the child from the people in his environment who formerly enjoyed his complete confidence.

[6] THE PHASES OF DEVELOPMENT OF THE SEXUAL ORGANIZATION[1]

The characteristics of infantile sexual life which we have hitherto emphasized are the facts that it is essentially auto-erotic (i.e. that it finds its object in the infant's own body) and that its individual component instincts are upon the whole disconnected and independent of one another in their search for pleasure. The final outcome of sexual development lies in what is known as the normal sexual life of the adult, in which the pursuit of pleasure comes under the sway of the reproductive function and in which the component instincts, under the primacy of a single erotogenic zone, form a firm organization directed towards a sexual aim attached to some extraneous sexual object.

Pregenital Organizations

The study, with the help of psychoanalysis, of the inhibitions and disturbances of this process of development enables us to recognize abortive beginnings and preliminary stages of a firm organization of the component instincts such as this – preliminary stages which themselves constitute a sexual régime of a sort. These phases of sexual organization are normally passed through smoothly, without giving more than a hint of their existence. It is only in pathological cases that they become active and recognizable to superficial observation.

We shall give the name of 'pregenital' to organizations of sexual life in which the genital zones have not yet taken over their predominant part. We have hitherto identified two such organizations, which almost seem as though they were harking back to early animal forms of life.

The first of these is the *oral* or, as it might be called, *cannibalistic* pregenital sexual organization. Here sexual activity

1. [The whole of this section, too, first appeared in 1915. The oral organization was apparently recognized as such for the first time in the present passage.]

has not yet been separated from the ingestion of food; nor are opposite currents within the activity differentiated. The *object* of both activities is the same; the sexual *aim* consists in the *incorporation* of the object – the prototype of a process which, in the form of *identification*, is later to play such an important psychological part. A relic of this constructed phase of organization, which is forced upon our notice by pathology, may be seen in thumb-sucking, in which the sexual activity, detached from the nutritive activity, has substituted for the extraneous object one situated in the subject's own body.[1]

A second pregenital phase is that of the *sadistic-anal* organization. Here the opposition between two currents, which runs through all sexual life, is already developed: they cannot yet, however, be described as 'masculine' and 'feminine', but only as 'active' and 'passive'. The *activity* is put into operation by the instinct for mastery through the agency of the somatic musculature; the organ which, more than any other, represents the *passive* sexual aim is the erotogenic mucous membrane of the anus. Both of these currents have objects, which, however, are not identical. Alongside these, other component instincts operate in an auto-erotic manner. In this phase, therefore, sexual polarity and an extraneous object are already observable. But organization and subordination to the reproductive function are still absent.[2]

Ambivalence

This form of sexual organization can persist throughout life and can permanently attract a large portion of sexual activity

1. [*Footnote added* 1920:] For remnants of this phase in adult neurotics, cf. Ábraham (1916). [*Added* 1924:] In another, later work (1924) the same writer has divided both this oral phase, and also the later sadistic-anal one, into two sub-divisions, which are characterized by differing attitudes towards the object.

2. [*Footnote added* 1924:] Abraham, in the paper last quoted (1924), points out that the anus is developed from the embryonic blastopore – a fact which seems like a biological prototype of psychosexual development.

to itself. The predominance in it of sadism and the cloacal part played by the anal zone give it a quite peculiarly archaic colouring. It is further characterized by the fact that in it the opposing pairs of instincts are developed to an approximately equal extent, a state of affairs described by Bleuler's happily chosen term 'ambivalence'.

The assumption of the existence of pregenital organizations of sexual life is based on the analysis of the neuroses, and without a knowledge of them can scarcely be appreciated. Further analytic investigation may be expected to provide us with far more information on the structure and development of the normal sexual function.

In order to complete our picture of infantile sexual life, we must also suppose that the choice of an object, such as we have shown to be characteristic of the pubertal phase of development, has already frequently or habitually been effected during the years of childhood: that is to say, the whole of the sexual currents have become directed towards a single person in relation to whom they seek to achieve their aims. This then is the closest approximation possible in childhood to the final form taken by sexual life after puberty. The only difference lies in the fact that in childhood the combination of the component instincts and their subordination under the primacy of the genitals have been effected only very incompletely or not at all. Thus the establishment of that primacy in the service of reproduction is the last phase through which the organization of sexuality passes.[1]

1. [*Footnote added* 1924:] At a later date (1923), I myself modified this account by inserting a third phase in the development of childhood, subsequent to the two pregenital organizations. This phase, which already deserves to be described as genital, presents a sexual object and some degree of convergence of the sexual impulses upon that object; but it is differentiated from the final organization of sexual maturity in one essential respect. For it knows only one kind of genital: the male one. For that reason I have named it the 'phallic' stage of organization ('The Infantile Genital Organization' [1923e; see below, p. 303ff.]). According to Abraham [1924], it has a biological prototype in the

Diphasic Choice of Object

It may be regarded as typical of the choice of an object that the process is diphasic, that is, that it occurs in two waves. The first of these begins between the ages of two[1] and five, and is brought to a halt or to a retreat by the latency period; it is characterized by the infantile nature of the sexual aims. The second wave sets in with puberty and determines the final outcome of sexual life.

Although the diphasic nature of object-choice comes down in essentials to no more than the operation of the latency period, it is of the highest importance in regard to disturbances of that final outcome. The resultants of infantile object-choice are carried over into the later period. They either persist as such or are revived at the actual time of puberty. But as a consequence of the repression which has developed between the two phases they prove unutilizable. Their sexual aims have become mitigated and they now represent what may be described as the 'affectionate current' of sexual life. Only psychoanalytic investigation can show that behind this affection, admiration and respect there lie concealed the old sexual longings of the infantile component instincts which have now become unserviceable. The object-choice of the pubertal period is obliged to dispense with the objects of childhood and to start afresh as a 'sensual current'. Should these two currents fail to converge, the result is often that one of the ideals of sexual life, the focusing of all desires upon a single object, will be unattainable.[2]

---

embryo's undifferentiated genital disposition, which is the same for both sexes.

1. [In 1915 this figure was 'three'; it was altered to 'two' in 1920. Cf. also the end of footnote 1 on p. 145.]

2. [The two currents had been discussed at length in the second of Freud's 'Contributions to the Psychology of Love' (1912*d*); see below pp. 248-56.]

[7] The Sources of Infantile Sexuality

Our efforts to trace the origins of the sexual instinct have shown us so far that sexual excitation arises (*a*) as a reproduction of a satisfaction experienced in connection with other organic processes, (*b*) through appropriate peripheral stimulation of erotogenic zones and (*c*) as an expression of certain 'instincts' (such as the scopophilic instinct and the instinct of cruelty) of which the origin is not yet completely intelligible. Psychoanalytic investigation, reaching back into childhood from a later time, and contemporary observation of children combine to indicate to us still other regularly active sources of sexual excitation. The direct observation of children has the disadvantage of working upon data which are easily misunderstandable; psychoanalysis is made difficult by the fact that it can only reach its data, as well as its conclusions, after long détours. But by co-operation the two methods can attain a satisfactory degree of certainty in their findings.

We have already discovered in examining the erotogenic zones that these regions of the skin merely show a special intensification of a kind of susceptibility to stimulus which is possessed in a certain degree by the whole cutaneous surface. We shall therefore not be surprised to find that very definite erotogenic effects are to be ascribed to certain kinds of general stimulation of the skin. Among these we may especially mention thermal stimuli, whose importance may help us to understand the therapeutic effects of warm baths.

Mechanical Excitations

At this point we must also mention the production of sexual excitation by rhythmic mechanical agitation of the body. Stimuli of this kind operate in three different ways: on the sensory apparatus of the vestibular nerves, on the skin, and on the deeper parts (e.g. the muscles and articular structures). The existence of these pleasurable sensations – and it is worth emphasizing the fact that in this connection the concepts of 'sexual excitation' and 'satisfaction' can to a great extent be used without distinction, a circumstance which we must later endeavour to explain [p. 132f.] – the existence, then, of these pleasurable sensations, caused by forms of mechanical agitation of the body, is confirmed by the fact that children are so fond of games of passive movement, such as swinging and being thrown up into the air, and insist on such games being incessantly repeated.[1] It is well known that rocking is habitually used to induce sleep in restless children. The shaking produced by driving in carriages and later by railway-travel exercises such a fascinating effect upon older children that every boy, at any rate, has at one time or other in his life wanted to be an engine driver or a coachman. It is a puzzling fact that boys take such an extraordinarily intense interest in things connected with railways, and, at the age at which the production of phantasies is most active (shortly before puberty), use those things as the nucleus of a symbolism that is peculiarly sexual. A compulsive link of this kind between railway-travel and sexuality is clearly derived from the pleasurable character of the sensations of movement. In the event of repression, which turns so many childish preferences into their opposite, these same individuals, when they are adolescents or adults, will react to rocking or swinging with a feeling of nausea, will be terribly exhausted by a railway journey, or will be subject to attacks of anxiety on the journey and will protect themselves against a repetition of the painful experience by *railway anxiety*.

Here again we must mention the fact, which is not yet understood, that the combination of fright and mechanical agitation produces the severe, hysteriform, traumatic neurosis. It may at least be assumed that these influences, which, when

---

1. Some people can remember that in swinging they felt the impact of moving air upon their genitals as an immediate sexual pleasure. [A specific instance of this is quoted in a footnote to a passage in *The Interpretation of Dreams* (1900a, near the end of Chapter V) in which this whole topic is discussed (*P.F.L.*, 4, 375–6).]

they are of small intensity, become sources of sexual excitation, lead to a profound disorder in the sexual mechanism or chemistry[1] if they operate with exaggerated force.

Muscular Activity

We are all familiar with the fact that children feel a need for a large amount of active muscular exercise and derive extraordinary pleasure from satisfying it. Whether this pleasure has any connection with sexuality, whether it itself comprises sexual satisfaction or whether it can become the occasion of sexual excitation – all of this is open to critical questioning, which may indeed also be directed against the view maintained in the previous paragraphs that the pleasure derived from sensations of *passive* movement is of a sexual nature or may produce sexual excitation. It is, however, a fact that a number of people report that they experienced the first signs of excitement in their genitals while they were romping or wrestling with playmates – a situation in which, apart from general muscular exertion, there is a large amount of contact with the skin of the opponent. An inclination to physical struggles with some one particular person, just as in later years an inclination to *verbal* disputes,[2] is a convincing sign that object-choice has fallen on him. One of the roots of the sadistic instinct would seem to lie in the encouragement of sexual excitation by muscular activity. In many people the infantile connection between romping and sexual excitation is among the determinants of the direction subsequently taken by their sexual instinct.[3]

1. [The last two words were added in 1924.]
2. 'Was sich liebt, das neckt sich.' [Lovers' quarrels are proverbial.]
3. [*Footnote added* 1910:] The analysis of cases of neurotic abasia and agoraphobia removes all doubt as to the sexual nature of pleasure in movement. Modern education, as we know, makes great use of games in order to divert young people from sexual activity. It would be more correct to say that in these young people it replaces sexual enjoyment by pleasure in movement – and forces sexual activity back to one of its auto-erotic components.

Affective Processes

The further sources of sexual excitation in children are open to less doubt. It is easy to establish, whether by contemporary observation or by subsequent research, that all comparatively intense affective processes, including even terrifying ones, trench upon sexuality – a fact which may incidentally help to explain the pathogenic effect of emotions of that kind. In schoolchildren dread of going in for an examination or tension over a difficult piece of work can be important not only in affecting the child's relations at school but also in bringing about an irruption of sexual manifestations. For quite often in such circumstances a stimulus may be felt which urges the child to touch his genitals, or something may take place akin to a nocturnal emission with all its bewildering consequences. The behaviour of children at school, which confronts a teacher with plenty of puzzles, deserves in general to be brought into relation with their budding sexuality. The sexually exciting effect of many emotions which are in themselves unpleasurable, such as feelings of apprehension, fright or horror, persists in a great number of people throughout their adult life. There is no doubt that this is the explanation of why so many people seek opportunities for sensations of this kind, subject to the proviso that the seriousness of the unpleasurable feeling is damped down by certain qualifying facts, such as its occurring in an imaginary world, in a book or in a play.

If we assume that a similar erotogenic effect attaches even to intensely painful feelings, especially when the pain is toned down or kept at a distance by some accompanying condition, we should here have one of the main roots of the masochistic-sadistic instinct, into whose numerous complexities we are very gradually gaining some insight.[1]

1. [*Footnote added* 1924:] I am here referring to what is known as 'erotogenic' masochism. [See footnote 2, p. 71f.]

Intellectual Work

Finally, it is an unmistakable fact that concentration of the attention upon an intellectual task and intellectual strain in general produce a concomitant sexual excitation in many young people as well as adults. This is no doubt the only justifiable basis for what is in other respects the questionable practice of ascribing nervous disorders to intellectual 'overwork'.

If we now cast our eyes over the tentative suggestions which I have made as to the sources of infantile sexual excitation, though I have not described them completely nor enumerated them fully, the following conclusions emerge with more or less certainty. It seems that the fullest provisions are made for setting in motion the process of sexual excitation – a process the nature of which has, it must be confessed, become highly obscure to us. The setting in motion of this process is first and foremost provided for in a more or less direct fashion by the excitations of the sensory surfaces – the skin and the sense organs – and, most directly of all, by the operation of stimuli on certain areas known as erotogenic zones. The decisive element in these sources of sexual excitation is no doubt the *quality* of the stimuli, though the factor of intensity, in the case of pain, is not a matter of complete indifference. But apart from these sources there are present in the organism contrivances which bring it about that in the case of a great number of internal processes sexual excitation arises as a concomitant effect, as soon as the intensity of those processes passes beyond certain quantitative limits. What we have called the component instincts of sexuality are either derived directly from these internal sources or are composed of elements both from those sources and from the erotogenic zones. It may well be that nothing of considerable importance can occur in the organism without contributing some component to the excitation of the sexual instinct.

It does not seem to me possible at present to state these

general conclusions with any greater clarity or certainty. For this I think two factors are responsible: first, the novelty of the whole method of approach to the subject, and secondly, the fact that the whole nature of sexual excitation is completely unknown to us. Nevertheless I am tempted to make two observations which promise to open out wide future prospects.

Varieties of Sexual Constitution

(a) Just as we saw previously [p. 86f.] that it was possible to derive a multiplicity of innate sexual constitutions from variety in the development of the erotogenic zones, so we can now make a similar attempt by including the *indirect* sources of sexual excitation. It may be assumed that, although contributions are made from these sources in the case of everyone, they are not in all cases of equal strength, and that further help towards the differentiation of sexual constitutions may be found in the varying development of the individual sources of sexual excitation.[1]

Pathways of Mutual Influence

(b) If we now drop the figurative expression that we have so long adopted in speaking of 'sources' of sexual excitation, we are led to the suspicion that all the connecting pathways that lead from other functions to sexuality must also be traversable in the reverse direction. If, for instance, the common possession of the labial zone by the two functions is the reason why sexual satisfaction arises during the taking of nourishment, then the same factor also enables us to understand why there should be disorders of nutrition if the erotogenic func-

1. [*Footnote added* 1920:] An inevitable consequence of these considerations is that we must regard each individual as possessing an oral erotism, an anal erotism, a urethral erotism, etc., and that the existence of mental complexes corresponding to these implies no judgement of abnormality or neurosis. The differences separating the normal from the abnormal can lie only in the relative strength of the individual components of the sexual instinct and in the use to which they are put in the course of development.

tions of the common zone are disturbed. Or again, if we know that concentration of attention may give rise to sexual excitation, it seems plausible to assume that by making use of the same path, but in a contrary direction, the condition of sexual excitation may influence the possibility of directing the attention. A good portion of the symptomatology of the neuroses, which I have traced to disturbances of the sexual processes, is expressed in disturbances of other, non-sexual, somatic functions; and this circumstance, which has hitherto been unintelligible, becomes less puzzling if it is only the counterpart of the influences which bring about the production of sexual excitation.[1]

The same pathways, however, along which sexual disturbances trench upon the other somatic functions must also perform another important function in normal health. They must serve as paths for the attraction of sexual instinctual forces to aims that are other than sexual, that is to say, for the sublimation of sexuality. But we must end with a confession that very little is as yet known with certainty of these pathways, though they certainly exist and can probably be traversed in both directions.

1. [Freud took up this point, with special reference to disorders of vision, in his paper on 'The Psycho-Analytic View of Psychogenic Disturbance of Vision' (1910*i*) *P.F.L.*, **10**, 111–12.]

THE TRANSFORMATIONS
OF PUBERTY

WITH the arrival of puberty, changes set in which are destined to give infantile sexual life its final, normal shape. The sexual instinct has hitherto been predominantly auto-erotic; it now finds a sexual object. Its activity has hitherto been derived from a number of separate instincts and erotogenic zones, which, independently of one another, have pursued a certain sort of pleasure as their sole sexual aim. Now, however, a new sexual aim appears, and all the component instincts combine to attain it, while the erotogenic zones become subordinated to the primacy of the genital zone.[1] Since the new sexual aim assigns very different functions to the two sexes, their sexual development now diverges greatly. That of males is the more straightforward and the more understandable, while that of females actually enters upon a kind of involution. A normal sexual life is only assured by an exact convergence of the two currents directed towards the sexual object and the sexual aim, the affectionate current and the sensual one.[2] (The former, the affectionate current, comprises what remains over of the infantile efflorescence of sexuality.)[3] It is like the completion of a tunnel which has been driven through a hill from both directions.

The new sexual aim in men consists in the discharge of the sexual products. The earlier one, the attainment of pleasure, is by no means alien to it; on the contrary, the highest degree of

1. [*Footnote added* 1915:] The schematic picture which I have given in the text aims at emphasizing differences. I have already shown on p. 118 the extent to which infantile sexuality approximates to the final sexual organization, owing to its choice of object [*added* 1924:] and to the development of the phallic phase.

2. [The last seven words were added in 1915.]

3. [This sentence was added in 1920.]

pleasure is attached to this final act of the sexual process. The sexual instinct is now subordinated to the reproductive function; it becomes, so to say, altruistic. If this transformation is to succeed, the original dispositions and all the other characteristics of the instincts must be taken into account in the process. Just as on any other occasion on which the organism should by rights make new combinations and adjustments leading to complicated mechanisms, here too there are possibilities of pathological disorders if these new arrangements are not carried out. Every pathological disorder of sexual life is rightly to be regarded as an inhibition in development.

[1] THE PRIMACY OF THE GENITAL ZONES AND FORE-PLEASURE

The starting-point and the final aim of the process which I have described are clearly visible. The intermediate steps are still in many ways obscure to us. We shall have to leave more than one of them as an unsolved riddle.

The most striking of the processes at puberty has been picked upon as constituting its essence: the manifest growth of the external genitalia. (The latency period of childhood is, on the other hand, characterized by a relative cessation of their growth.) In the meantime the development of the internal genitalia has advanced far enough for them to be able to discharge the sexual products or, as the case may be, to bring about the formation of a new living organism. Thus a highly complicated apparatus has been made ready and awaits the moment of being put into operation.

This apparatus is to be set in motion by stimuli, and observation shows us that stimuli can impinge on it from three directions: from the external world by means of the excitation of the erotogenic zones with which we are already familiar, from the organic interior by ways which we have still to explore, and from mental life, which is itself a storehouse for external impressions and a receiving-post for internal excitations. All three kinds of stimuli produce the same effect, namely a condition described as 'sexual excitement', which shows itself by two sorts of indication, mental and somatic. The mental indications consist in a peculiar feeling of tension of an extremely compelling character; and among the numerous somatic ones are first and foremost a number of changes in the genitals, which have the obvious sense of being preparations for the sexual act – the erection of the male organ and the lubrication of the vagina.

Sexual Tension.

The fact that sexual excitement possesses the character of tension raises a problem the solution of which is no less difficult than it would be important in helping us to understand the sexual processes. In spite of all the differences of opinion that reign on the subject among psychologists, I must insist that a feeling of tension necessarily involves unpleasure. What seems to me decisive is the fact that a feeling of this kind is accompanied by an impulsion to make a change in the psychological situation, that it operates in an urgent way which is wholly alien to the nature of the feeling of pleasure. If, however, the tension of sexual excitement is counted as an unpleasurable feeling, we are at once brought up against the fact that it is also undoubtedly felt as pleasurable. In every case in which tension is produced by sexual processes it is accompanied by pleasure; even in the preparatory changes in the genitals a feeling of satisfaction of some kind is plainly to be observed. How, then, are this unpleasurable tension and this feeling of pleasure to be reconciled?

Everything relating to the problem of pleasure and unpleasure touches upon one of the sorest spots of present-day psychology. It will be my aim to learn as much as possible from the circumstances of the instance with which we are at present dealing, but I shall avoid any approach to the problem as a whole.[1]

1. [*Footnote added* 1924:] I have made an attempt at solving this

Let us begin by casting a glance at the way in which the erotogenic zones fit themselves into the new arrangement. They have to play an important part in introducing sexual excitation. The eye is perhaps the zone most remote from the sexual object, but it is the one which, in the situation of wooing an object, is liable to be the most frequently stimulated by the particular quality of excitation whose cause, when it occurs in a sexual object, we describe as beauty. (For the same reason the merits of a sexual object are described as 'attractions'.)[1] This stimulation is on the one hand already accompanied by pleasure, while on the other hand it leads to an increase of sexual excitement or produces it if it is not yet present. If the excitation now spreads to another erotogenic zone – to the hand, for instance, through tactile sensations – the effect is the same: a feeling of pleasure on the one side, which is quickly intensified by pleasure arising from the preparatory changes [in the genitals], and on the other side an increase of sexual tension, which soon passes over into the most obvious unpleasure if it cannot be met by a further accession of pleasure. Another instance will perhaps make this even clearer. If an erotogenic zone in a person who is not sexually excited (e.g. the skin of a woman's breast) is stimulated by touch, the contact produces a pleasurable feeling; but it is at the same time better calculated than anything to arouse a sexual excitation that demands an increase of pleasure. The problem is how it can come about that an experience of pleasure can give rise to a need for greater pleasure.

The Mechanism of Fore-pleasure

The part played in this by the erotogenic zones, however, is clear. What is true of one of them is true of all. They are all used to provide a certain amount of pleasure by being stimulated in the way appropriate to them. This pleasure then

---

problem in the first part of my paper on 'The Economic Problem of Masochism' (1924c).

1. [See footnote 2, p. 69.]

leads to an increase in tension which in its turn is responsible for producing the necessary motor energy for the conclusion of the sexual act. The penultimate stage of that act is once again the appropriate stimulation of an erotogenic zone (the genital zone itself, in the glans penis) by the appropriate object (the mucous membrane of the vagina); and from the pleasure yielded by this excitation the motor energy is obtained, this time by a reflex path, which brings about the discharge of the sexual substances. This last pleasure is the highest in intensity, and its mechanism differs from that of the earlier pleasure. It is brought about entirely by discharge: it is wholly a pleasure of satisfaction and with it the tension of the libido is for the time being extinguished.

This distinction between the one kind of pleasure due to the excitation of erotogenic zones and the other kind due to the discharge of the sexual substances deserves, I think, to be made more concrete by a difference in nomenclature. The former may be suitably described as 'fore-pleasure' in contrast to the 'end-pleasure' or pleasure of satisfaction derived from the sexual act. Fore-pleasure is thus the same pleasure that has already been produced, although on a smaller scale, by the infantile sexual instinct; end-pleasure is something new and is thus probably conditioned by circumstances that do not arise till puberty. The formula for the new function of the erotogenic zones runs therefore: they are used to make possible, through the medium of the fore-pleasure which can be derived from them (as it was during infantile life), the production of the greater pleasure of satisfaction.

I was able recently to throw light upon another instance, in a quite different department of mental life, of a slight feeling of pleasure similarly making possible the attainment of a greater resultant pleasure, and thus operating as an 'incentive bonus'. In the same connection I was also able to go more deeply into the nature of pleasure.[1]

1. See my volume on *Jokes and their Relation to the Unconscious* which appeared in 1905 [*P.F.L.*, 6, 187–9]. The 'fore-pleasure' attained by the

Dangers of Fore-pleasure

The connection between fore-pleasure and infantile sexual life is, however, made clearer by the pathogenic part which it can come to play. The attainment of the normal sexual aim can clearly be endangered by the mechanism in which fore-pleasure is involved. This danger arises if at any point in the preparatory sexual processes the fore-pleasure turns out to be too great and the element of tension too small. The motive for proceeding further with the sexual process then disappears, the whole path is cut short, and the preparatory act in question takes the place of the normal sexual aim. Experience has shown that the precondition for this damaging event is that the erotogenic zone concerned or the corresponding component instinct shall already during childhood have contributed an unusual amount of pleasure. If further factors then come into play, tending to bring about a fixation, a compulsion may easily arise in later life which resists the incorporation of this particular fore-pleasure into a new context. Such is in fact the mechanism of many perversions, which consist in a lingering over the preparatory acts of the sexual process.

This failure of the function of the sexual mechanism owing to fore-pleasure is best avoided if the primacy of the genitals too is adumbrated in childhood; and indeed things seem actually arranged to bring this about in the second half of childhood (from the age of eight to puberty). During these years the genital zones already behave in much the same way as in maturity; they become the seat of sensations of excitation and of preparatory changes whenever any pleasure is felt from the satisfaction of other erotogenic zones, though this result is still without a purpose – that is to say, contributes nothing to a continuation of the sexual process. Already in childhood,

---

technique of joking is used in order to liberate a greater pleasure derived from the removal of internal inhibitions. [In a later paper, on creative writing (1908e), Freud attributed a similar mechanism to aesthetic pleasure. *P.F.L.*, **14**, 141 and *n*.]

therefore, alongside of the pleasure of satisfaction there is a certain amount of sexual tension, although it is less constant and less in quantity. We can now understand why, in discussing the sources of sexuality, we were equally justified in saying of a given process that it was sexually satisfying or sexually exciting. [See p. 120f.] It will be noticed that in the course of our inquiry we began by exaggerating the distinction between infantile and mature sexual life, and that we are now setting this right. Not only the deviations from normal sexual life but its normal form as well are determined by the infantile manifestations of sexuality.

[2] THE PROBLEM OF SEXUAL EXCITATION

We remain in complete ignorance both of the origin and of the nature of the sexual tension which arises simultaneously with the pleasure when erotogenic zones are satisfied.[1] The most obvious explanation, that this tension arises in some way out of the pleasure itself, is not only extremely improbable in itself but becomes untenable when we consider that in connection with the greatest pleasure of all, that which accompanies the discharge of the sexual products, no tension is produced, but on the contrary all tension is removed. Thus pleasure and sexual tension can only be connected in an indirect manner.

Part Played by the Sexual Substances

Apart from the fact that normally it is only the discharge of the sexual substances that brings sexual excitation to an end,

1. It is a highly instructive fact that the German language in its use of the word 'Lust' takes into account the part played by the preparatory sexual excitations which, as has been explained above, simultaneously produce an element of satisfaction and a contribution to sexual tension. 'Lust' has two meanings, and is used to describe the sensation of sexual tension ('Ich habe Lust' = 'I should like to', 'I feel an impulse to') as well as the feeling of satisfaction. [Cf. footnote 2, p. 45.]

there are other points of contact between sexual tension and the sexual products. In the case of a man living a continent life, the sexual apparatus, at varying intervals, which, however, are not ungoverned by rules, discharge the sexual substances during the night, to the accompaniment of a pleasurable feeling and in the course of a dream which hallucinates a sexual act. And in regard to this process (nocturnal emission) it is difficult to avoid the conclusion that the sexual tension, which succeeds in making use of the short cut of hallucination as a substitute for the act itself, is a function of the accumulation of semen in the vesicles containing the sexual products. Our experience in connection with the exhaustibility of the sexual mechanism argues in the same sense. If the store of semen is exhausted, not only is it impossible to carry out the sexual act, but the susceptibility of the erotogenic zones to stimulus ceases, and their appropriate excitation no longer gives rise to any pleasure. We thus learn incidentally that a certain degree of sexual tension is required even for the excitability of the erotogenic zones.

This would seem to lead to what is, if I am not mistaken, the fairly wide-spread hypothesis that the accumulation of the sexual substances creates and maintains sexual tension; the pressure of these products upon the walls of the vesicles containing them might be supposed to act as a stimulus upon a spinal centre, the condition of which would be perceived by higher centres and would then give rise in consciousness to the familiar sensation of tension. If the excitation of the erotogenic zones increases sexual tension, this could only come about on the supposition that the zones in question are in an anatomical connection that has already been laid down with these centres, that they increase the tonus of the excitation in them, and, if the sexual tension is sufficient, set the sexual act in motion or, if it is insufficient, stimulate the production of the sexual substances.[1]

1. [This hypothesis had been discussed by Freud earlier: in Section III of his first paper on anxiety neurosis (1895b), P.F.L., **10**, 55ff.]

The weakness of this theory, which we find accepted, for instance, in Krafft-Ebing's account of the sexual processes, lies in the fact that, having been designed to account for the sexual activity of adult males, it takes too little account of three sets of conditions which it should also be able to explain. These are the conditions in children, in females and in castrated males. In none of these three cases can there be any question of an accumulation of sexual products in the same sense as in males, and this makes a smooth application of the theory difficult. Nevertheless it may at once be admitted that it is possible to find means by which the theory may be made to cover these cases as well. In any case we are warned not to lay more weight on the factor of the accumulation of the sexual products than it is able to bear.

Importance of the Internal Sexual Organs

Observations on castrated males seem to show that sexual excitation can occur to a considerable degree independently of the production of the sexual substances. The operation of castration occasionally fails to bring about a limitation of libido, although such limitation, which provides the motive for the operation, is the usual outcome. Moreover, it has long been known that diseases which abolish the production of the masculine sex-cells leave the patient, though he is now sterile, with his libido and potency undamaged.[1] It is therefore by no means as astonishing as Rieger [1900] represents it to be that the loss of the masculine sex-glands in an adult may have no further effect upon his mental behaviour.[2] It is true that if

1. [This sentence was added in 1920.]
2. [The following sentence occurs at this point in editions before 1920, when it was omitted: 'For the sex-glands do not constitute sexuality, and the observations on castrated males merely confirm what had been shown long before by removal of the ovaries – namely that it is impossible to obliterate the sexual characters by removing the sex-glands.' Before 1920, too, the second half of the next sentence began: 'but it seems that what is in question here is not the actual loss of the sex-glands but an inhibition . . .']

castration is performed at a tender age, before puberty, it approximates in its effect to the aim of obliterating the sexual characters; but here too it is possible that what is in question is, besides the actual loss of the sex-glands, an inhibition (connected with that loss) in the development of other factors.

Chemical Theory

Experiments in the removal of the sex-glands (testes and ovaries) of animals, and in the grafting into vertebrates of sex-glands from other individuals of the opposite sex,[1] have at last thrown a partial light on the origin of sexual excitation, and have at the same time still further reduced the significance of a possible accumulation of cellular sexual products. It has become experimentally possible (E. Steinach) to transform a male into a female, and conversely a female into a male. In this process the psychosexual behaviour of the animal alters in accordance with the somatic sexual characters and simultaneously with them. It seems, however, that this sex-determining influence is not an attribute of that part of the sex-glands which gives rise to the specific sex-cells (spermatozoa and ovum) but of their interstitial tissue, upon which special emphasis is laid by being described in the literature as the 'puberty-gland'. It is quite possible that further investigation will show that this puberty-gland has normally a hermaphrodite disposition. If this were so, the theory of the bisexuality of the higher animals would be given anatomical foundation. It is already probable that the puberty-gland is not the only organ concerned with the production of sexual excitation and sexual characters. In any case, what we already know of the part played by the thyroid gland in sexuality fits in with this new biological discovery. It seems probable, then, that special chemical substances are produced in the interstitial portion of the sex-glands; these are then taken up in the blood stream and cause particular parts of the central nervous system to be

1. Cf. Lipschütz's work [1919], quoted on p. 92f. *n.*

charged with sexual tension. (We are already familiar with the fact that other toxic substances, introduced into the body from outside, can bring about a similar transformation of a toxic condition into a stimulus acting on a particular organ.) The question of how sexual excitation arises from the stimulation of erotogenic zones, when the central apparatus has been previously charged, and the question of what interplay arises in the course of these sexual processes between the effects of purely toxic stimuli and of physiological ones – none of this can be treated, even hypothetically, in the present state of our knowledge. It must suffice us to hold firmly to what is essential in this view of the sexual processes: the assumption that substances of a peculiar kind arise from the sexual metabolism.[1] For this apparently arbitrary supposition is supported by

1. [The whole of this paragraph as far as this point dates in its present form from 1920. In the first edition (1905) and the two subsequent ones the following passage appears in its place: 'The truth is that we can give no information on the nature of sexual excitation, especially since (having found that the importance of the sex-glands in this respect has been over-estimated) we are in the dark as to the organ or organs to which sexuality is attached. After the surprising discoveries of the important part played by the thyroid gland in sexuality, it is reasonable to suspect that we are still ignorant of the essential factors of sexuality. Anyone who feels the need of a provisional hypothesis to fill this wide gap in our knowledge may well take as his starting-point the powerful substances which have been found to be present in the thyroid gland and may proceed along some such lines as the following. It may be supposed that, as a result of an appropriate stimulation of erotogenic zones, or in other circumstances that are accompanied by an onset of sexual excitation, some substance that is disseminated generally throughout the organism becomes decomposed and the products of its decomposition give rise to a specific stimulus which acts on the reproductive organs or upon a spinal centre related to them. (We are already familiar with the fact that other toxic substances, introduced into the body from outside, can bring about a similar transformation of a toxic condition into a stimulus acting on a particular organ.) The question of what interplay arises in the course of the sexual processes between the effects of purely toxic stimuli and of physiological ones cannot be treated, even hypothetically, in the present state of our knowledge. I may add that I attach no importance to this particular hypothesis and should be ready

a fact which has received little attention but deserves the closest consideration. The neuroses, which can be derived only from disturbances of sexual life, show the greatest clinical similarity to the phenomena of intoxication and abstinence that arise from the habitual use of toxic, pleasure-producing substances (alkaloids).

[3] THE LIBIDO THEORY[1]

The conceptual scaffolding which we have set up to help us in dealing with the psychical manifestations of sexual life tallies well with these hypotheses as to the chemical basis of sexual excitation. We have defined the concept of 'libido' as a quantitatively variable force which could serve as a measure of processes and transformations occurring in the field of sexual excitation. We distinguish this libido in respect of its special origin from the energy which must be supposed to underlie mental processes in general, and we thus also attribute a *qualitative* character to it. In thus distinguishing between libidinal and other forms of psychical energy we are giving expression to the presumption that the sexual processes occurring in the organism are distinguished from the nutritive

to abandon it at once in favour of another, provided that its fundamental nature remained unchanged – that is, the emphasis which it lays upon sexual chemistry.' – It is worth remarking how small a modification was made necessary in Freud's hypothesis by the discovery of the sex hormones, which, indeed, he had anticipated not merely in 1905 but at least as early as in 1896, as may be seen from his two letters to Fliess, of March 1 and April 2 of that year (Freud, 1950a, Letters 42 and 44). He further insisted upon the importance of the chemical factor in his second paper on the part played by sexuality in the neuroses, published at about the same time as the first edition of the *Three Essays* (1906a.) See also some remarks in the paper on 'Female Sexuality' (1931b), below, p. 388.]

1. [This whole section, except for its last paragraph, dates from 1915. It is largely based on Freud's paper on narcissism (1914c).]

processes by a special chemistry. The analysis of the perversions and psychoneuroses has shown us that this sexual excitation is derived not from the so-called sexual parts alone, but from all the bodily organs. We thus reach the idea of a quantity of libido, to the mental representation of which we give the name of 'ego-libido', and whose production, increase or diminution, distribution and displacement should afford us possibilities for explaining the psychosexual phenomena observed.

This ego-libido is, however, only conveniently accessible to analytic study when it has been put to the use of cathecting sexual objects, that is, when it has become 'object-libido'. We can then perceive it concentrating upon objects,[1] becoming fixated to them or abandoning them, moving from one object to another and, from these situations, directing the subject's sexual activity, which leads to the satisfaction, that is, to the partial and temporary extinction, of the libido. The psychoanalysis of what are termed transference neuroses (hysteria and obsessional neurosis) affords us a clear insight at this point.

We can follow the object-libido through still further vicissitudes. When it is withdrawn from objects, it is held in suspense in peculiar conditions of tension and is finally drawn back into the ego, so that it becomes ego-libido once again. In contrast to object-libido, we also describe ego-libido as 'narcissistic' libido. From the vantage-point of psychoanalysis we can look across a frontier, which we may not pass, at the activities of narcissistic libido, and may form some idea of the relation between it and object-libido.[2] Narcissistic or ego-libido seems to be the great reservoir from which the object-cathexes are sent out and into which they are withdrawn once

1. [It is scarcely necessary to explain that here as elsewhere, in speaking of the libido concentrating on 'objects', withdrawing from 'objects', etc., Freud has in mind the mental presentations (*Vorstellungen*) of objects and not, of course, objects in the external world.]

2. [*Footnote added* 1924:] Since neuroses other than the 'transference neuroses' have become to a greater extent accessible to psychoanalysis, this limitation has lost its earlier validity.

more; the narcissistic libidinal cathexis of the ego is the original state of things, realized in earliest childhood, and is merely covered by the later extrusions of libido, but in essentials persists behind them.

It should be the task of a libido theory of neurotic and psychotic disorders to express all the observed phenomena and inferred processes in terms of the economics of the libido. It is easy to guess that the vicissitudes of the ego-libido will have the major part to play in this connection, especially when it is a question of explaining the deeper psychotic disturbances. We are then faced by the difficulty that our method of research, psychoanalysis, for the moment affords us assured information only on the transformations that take place in the object-libido,[1] but is unable to make any immediate distinction between the ego-libido and the other forms of energy operating in the ego.[2]

For the present, therefore,[3] no further development of the libido theory is possible, except upon speculative lines. It would, however, be sacrificing all that we have gained hitherto from psychoanalytic observation, if we were to follow the example of C. G. Jung and water down the meaning of the concept of libido itself by equating it with psychical instinctual force in general. The distinguishing of the sexual instinctual impulses from the rest and the consequent restriction of the concept of libido to the former receives strong support from the assumption which I have already discussed that there is a special chemistry of the sexual function.

1. [*Footnote added* 1924:] See the previous footnote.
2. [*Footnote added* 1915:] Cf. my paper on narcissism (1914c). [*Added* 1920:] The term 'narcissism' was not introduced, as I erroneously stated in that paper, by Näcke, but by Havelock Ellis. [Ellis himself subsequently (1927) discussed this point in detail and considered that the honours should be divided.]
3. [This paragraph was added in 1920.]

[4] THE DIFFERENTIATION BETWEEN MEN AND WOMEN

As we all know, it is not until puberty that the sharp distinction is established between the masculine and feminine characters. From that time on, this contrast has a more decisive influence than any other upon the shaping of human life. It is true that the masculine and feminine dispositions are already easily recognizable in childhood. The development of the inhibitions of sexuality (shame, disgust, pity, etc.) takes place in little girls earlier and in the face of less resistance than in boys; the tendency to sexual repression seems in general to be greater; and, where the component instincts of sexuality appear, they prefer the passive form. The auto–erotic activity of the erotogenic zones is, however, the same in both sexes, and owing to this uniformity there is no possibility of a distinction between the two sexes such as arises after puberty. So far as the auto–erotic and masturbatory manifestations of sexuality are concerned, we might lay it down that the sexuality of little girls is of a wholly masculine character. Indeed, if we were able to give a more definite connotation to the concepts of 'masculine' and 'feminine', it would even be possible to maintain that libido is invariably and necessarily of a masculine nature, whether it occurs in men or in women and irrespectively of whether its object is a man or a woman.[1]

1. [Before 1924 the words from 'libido' to the end of the sentence were printed in spaced type. – *Footnote added* 1915:] It is essential to understand clearly that the concepts of 'masculine' and 'feminine', whose meaning seems so unambiguous to ordinary people, are among the most confused that occur in science. It is possible to distinguish at least *three* uses. 'Masculine' and 'feminine' are used sometimes in the sense of *activity* and *passivity*, sometimes in a *biological*, and sometimes, again, in a *sociological* sense. The first of these three meanings is the essential one and the most serviceable in psychoanalysis. When, for instance, libido was described in the text above as being 'masculine', the word was being used in this sense, for an instinct is always active even when it has a passive aim in view. The second, or biological, meaning

Since I have become acquainted[1] with the notion of bi-sexuality I have regarded it as the decisive factor, and without taking bisexuality into account I think it would scarcely be possible to arrive at an understanding of the sexual manifestations that are actually to be observed in men and women.

Leading Zones in Men and Women

Apart from this I have only the following to add. The leading erotogenic zone in female children is located at the clitoris, and is thus homologous to the masculine genital zone of the glans penis. All my experience concerning masturbation in little girls has related to the clitoris and not to the regions of the external genitalia that are important in later sexual function-ing. I am even doubtful whether a female child can be led by the influence of seduction to anything other than clitoridal masturbation. If such a thing occurs, it is quite exceptional. The spontaneous discharges of sexual excitement which occur so often precisely in little girls are expressed in spasms of the

---

of 'masculine' and 'feminine' is the one whose applicability can be determined most easily. Here 'masculine' and 'feminine' are character-ized by the presence of spermatozoa or ova respectively and by the functions proceeding from them. Activity and its concomitant pheno-mena (more powerful muscular development, aggressiveness, greater intensity of libido) are as a rule linked with biological masculinity; but they are not necessarily so, for there are animal species in which these qualities are on the contrary assigned to the female. The third, or sociological, meaning receives its connotation from the observation of actually existing masculine and feminine individuals. Such observation shows that in human beings pure masculinity or femininity is not to be found either in a psychological or a biological sense. Every individual on the contrary displays a mixture of the character-traits belonging to his own and to the opposite sex; and he shows a combination of activity and passivity whether or not these last character-traits tally with his biological ones. [A later discussion of this point will be found in a foot-note at the end of Chapter IV of *Civilization and its Discontents* (1930a).]

1. [In 1905 only: 'through Wilhelm Fliess'. Cf. end of footnote, p. 55.]

clitoris. Frequent erections of that organ make it possible for girls to form a correct judgement, even without any instruction, of the sexual manifestations of the other sex: they merely transfer on to boys the sensations derived from their own sexual processes.

If we are to understand how a little girl turns into a woman, we must follow the further vicissitudes of this excitability of the clitoris. Puberty, which brings about so great an accession of libido in boys, is marked in girls by a fresh wave of *repression*, in which it is precisely clitoridal sexuality that is affected. What is thus overtaken by repression is a piece of masculine sexuality. The intensification of the brake upon sexuality brought about by pubertal repression in women serves as a stimulus to the libido in men and causes an increase of its activity. Along with this heightening of libido there is also an increase of sexual overvaluation which only emerges in full force in relation to a woman who holds herself back and who denies her sexuality. When at last the sexual act is permitted and the clitoris itself becomes excited, it still retains a function: the task, namely, of transmitting the excitation to the adjacent female sexual parts, just as – to use a simile – pine shavings can be kindled in order to set a log of harder wood on fire. Before this transference can be effected, a certain interval of time must often elapse, during which the young woman is anaesthetic. This anaesthesia may become permanent if the clitoridal zone refuses to abandon its excitability, an event for which the way is prepared precisely by an extensive activity of that zone in childhood. Anaesthesia in women, as is well known, is often only apparent and local. They are anaesthetic at the vaginal orifice but are by no means incapable of excitement originating in the clitoris or even in other zones. Alongside these erotogenic determinants of anaesthesia must also be set the psychical determinants, which equally arise from repression.

When erotogenic susceptibility to stimulation has been successfully transferred by a woman from the clitoris to the vaginal orifice, it implies that she had adopted a new leading zone for the purposes of her later sexual activity. A man, on the other hand, retains his leading zone unchanged from childhood. The fact that women change their leading erotogenic zone in this way, together with the wave of repression at puberty, which, as it were, puts aside their childish masculinity, are the chief determinants of the greater proneness of women to neurosis and especially to hysteria. These determinants, therefore, are intimately related to the essence of femininity.[1]

[5] THE FINDING OF AN OBJECT

The processes at puberty thus establish the primacy of the genital zones; and, in a man, the penis, which has now become capable of erection, presses forward insistently towards the new sexual aim – penetration into a cavity in the body which excites his genital zone. Simultaneously on the psychical side the process of finding an object, for which preparations have been made from earliest childhood, is completed. At a time at which the first beginnings of sexual satisfaction are still linked with the taking of nourishment, the sexual instinct has a sexual object outside the infant's own body in the shape of his mother's breast. It is only later that the instinct loses that object, just at the time, perhaps, when the child is able to form a total idea of the person to whom the organ that is giving him satisfaction belongs. As a rule the sexual instinct then becomes auto-erotic, and not until the period of latency has been passed through is the original relation restored. There are thus good

1. [The course of development of sexuality in women was further examined by Freud more particularly on four later occasions: in his case history of a homosexual woman (1920a), in his discussion of the consequences of the anatomical distinction between the sexes (1925j), in his paper on female sexuality (1931b) – both the latter two papers are in the present volume, pp. 323ff. and 367ff. below – and in Lecture 33 of his *New Introductory Lectures* (1933a).]

reasons why a child sucking at his mother's breast has become the prototype of every relation of love. The finding of an object is in fact a refinding of it.[1]

The Sexual Object during Early Infancy

But even after sexual activity has become detached from the taking of nourishment, an important part of this first and most significant of all sexual relations is left over, which helps to prepare for the choice of an object and thus to restore the happiness that has been lost. All through the period of latency children learn to feel for other people who help them in their helplessness and satisfy their needs a love which is on the model of, and a continuation of, their relation as sucklings to their nursing mother. There may perhaps be an inclination to dispute the possibility of identifying a child's affection and esteem for those who look after him with sexual love. I think, however, that a closer psychological examination may make it possible to establish this identity beyond any doubt. A child's intercourse with anyone responsible for his care affords him an unending source of sexual excitation and satisfaction from his erotogenic zones. This is especially so since the person in charge of him, who, after all, is as a rule his mother, herself regards him with feelings that are derived from her own sexual life: she strokes him, kisses him, rocks him and quite clearly treats him as a substitute for a complete sexual object.[2]

1. [*Footnote added* 1915:] Psychoanalysis informs us that there are two methods of finding an object. The first, described in the text, is the 'anaclitic' or 'attachment' one, based on attachment to early infantile prototypes. The second is the narcissistic one, which seeks for the subject's own ego and finds it again in other people. This latter method is of particularly great importance in cases where the outcome is a pathological one, but it is not relevant to the present context. [The point is elaborated in the later part of Section II of Freud's paper on narcissism (1914c). – The paragraph in the text above, written in 1905, does not appear to harmonize with the remarks on the subject on pp. 119 and 158, written in 1915 and 1920 respectively.]

2. Anyone who considers this 'sacrilegious' may be recommended to read Havelock Ellis's views [1903; 2nd ed., 1913, 18] on the

A mother would probably be horrified if she were made aware that all her marks of affection were rousing her child's sexual instinct and preparing for its later intensity. She regards what she does as asexual, 'pure' love, since, after all, she carefully avoids applying more excitations to the child's genitals than are unavoidable in nursery care. As we know, however, the sexual instinct is not aroused only by direct excitation of the genital zone. What we call affection will unfailingly show its effects one day on the genital zones as well. Moreover, if the mother understood more of the high importance of the part played by instincts in mental life as a whole – in all its ethical and psychical achievements – she would spare herself any self-reproaches even after her enlightenment. She is only fufilling her task in teaching the child to love. After all, he is meant to grow up into a strong and capable person with vigorous sexual needs and to accomplish during his life all the things that human beings are urged to do by their instincts. It is true that an excess of parental affection does harm by causing preco-cious sexual maturity and also because, by spoiling the child, it makes him incapable in later life of temporarily doing without love or of being content with a smaller amount of it. One of the clearest indications that a child will later become neurotic is to be seen in an insatiable demand for his parents' affection. And on the other hand neuropathic parents, who are inclined as a rule to display excessive affection, are precisely those who are most likely by their caresses to arouse the child's disposi-tion to neurotic illness. Incidentally, this example shows that there are ways more direct than inheritance by which neurotic parents can hand their disorder on to their children.

Infantile Anxiety

Children themselves behave from an early age as though their dependence on the people looking after them were in the

---

relation between mother and child, which agree almost completely with mine.

nature of sexual love. Anxiety in children is originally nothing other than an expression of the fact that they are feeling the loss of the person they love. It is for this reason that they are frightened of every stranger. They are afraid in the dark because in the dark they cannot see the person they love; and their fear is soothed if they can take hold of that person's hand in the dark. To attribute to bogeys and blood-curdling stories told by nurses the responsibility for making children timid is to overestimate their efficacy. The truth is merely that children who are inclined to be timid are affected by stories which would make no impression whatever upon others, and it is only children with a sexual instinct that is excessive or has developed prematurely or has become vociferous owing to too much petting who are inclined to be timid. In this respect a child, by turning his libido into anxiety when he cannot satisfy it, behaves like an adult. On the other hand an adult who has become neurotic owing to his libido being unsatisfied behaves in his anxiety like a child: he begins to be frightened when he is alone, that is to say when he is away from someone of whose love he had felt secure, and he seeks to assuage this fear by the most childish measures.[1]

1. For this explanation of the origin of infantile anxiety I have to thank a three-year-old boy whom I once heard calling out of a dark room: 'Auntie, speak to me! I'm frightened because it's so dark.' His aunt answered him: 'What good would that do? You can't see me.' 'That doesn't matter,' replied the child, 'if anyone speaks, it gets light.' Thus what he was afraid of was not the dark, but the absence of someone he loved; and he could feel sure of being soothed as soon as he had evidence of that person's presence. [Added 1920:] One of the most important results of psychoanalytic research is this discovery that neurotic anxiety arises out of libido, that it is the product of a transformation of it, and that it is thus related to it in the same kind of way as vinegar is to wine. A further discussion of this problem will be found in my Introductory Lectures on Psycho-Analysis (1916–17), [Lecture 25], though even there, it must be confessed, the question is not finally cleared up. [For Freud's latest views on the subject of anxiety see his Inhibitions, Symptoms and Anxiety (1926d) and his New Introductory Lectures (1933a), Lecture 32.]

The Barrier against Incest [1]

We see, therefore, that the parents' affection for their child may awaken his sexual instinct prematurely (i.e. before the somatic conditions of puberty are present) to such a degree that the mental excitation breaks through in an unmistakable fashion to the genital system. If, on the other hand, they are fortunate enough to avoid this, then their affection can perform its task of directing the child in his choice of a sexual object when he reaches maturity. No doubt the simplest course for the child would be to choose as his sexual objects the same persons whom, since his childhood, he has loved with what may be described as damped-down libido.[2] But, by the postponing of sexual maturation, time has been gained in which the child can erect, among other restraints on sexuality, the barrier against incest, and can thus take up into himself the moral precepts which expressly exclude from his object-choice, as being blood-relations, the persons whom he has loved in his childhood. Respect for this barrier is essentially a cultural demand made by society. Society must defend itself against the danger that the interests which it needs for the establishment of higher social units may be swallowed up by the family; and for this reason, in the case of every individual, but in particular of adolescent boys, it seeks by all possible means to loosen their connection with their family – a connection which, in their childhood, is the only important one.[3]

1. [This side-heading was omitted, probably by an oversight, from 1924 onwards.]

2. [Footnote added 1915:] Cf. what has been said on p. 119 about children's object-choice and the 'affectionate current'.

3. [Footnote added 1915:] The barrier against incest is probably among the historical acquisitions of mankind, and, like other moral taboos, has no doubt already become established in many persons by organic inheritance. (Cf. my Totem and Taboo, 1912–13.) Psychoanalytic investigation shows, however, how intensely the individual struggles with the temptation to incest during his period of growth and how frequently the barrier is transgressed in phantasies and even in reality. – [This is the first published appearance of the 'horror of incest'.]

It is in the world of ideas, however, that the choice of an object is accomplished at first; and the sexual life of maturing youth is almost entirely restricted to indulging in phantasies, that is, in ideas that are not destined to be carried into effect.[1]

1. [*Footnote added* 1920:] The phantasies of the pubertal period have as their starting-point the infantile sexual researches that were abandoned in childhood. No doubt, too, they are also present before the end of the latency period. They may persist wholly, or to a great extent, unconsciously and for that reason it is often impossible to date them accurately. They are of great importance in the origin of many symptoms, since they precisely constitute preliminary stages of these symptoms and thus lay down the forms in which the repressed libidinal components find satisfaction. In the same way, they are the prototypes of the nocturnal phantasies which become conscious as dreams. Dreams are often nothing more than revivals of pubertal phantasies of this kind under the influence of, and in relation to, some stimulus left over from the waking life of the previous day (the 'day's residues'). [See Chapter VI, Section I, of *The Interpretation of Dreams* (1900a); P.F.L., 4, 632–3.] Some among the sexual phantasies of the pubertal period are especially prominent, and are distinguished by their very general occurrence and by being to a great extent independent of individual experience. Such are the adolescent's phantasies of overhearing his parents in sexual intercourse, of having been seduced at an early age by someone he loves and of having been threatened with castration [cf. the discussion of 'primal phantasies' in Lecture 23 of Freud's *Introductory Lectures* (1916–17), P.F.L., 1, 416–18]; such, too, are his phantasies of being in the womb, and even of experiences there, and the so-called 'Family Romance', in which he reacts to the difference between his attitude towards his parents now and in his childhood. The close relations existing between these phantasies and myths has been demonstrated in the case of the last instance by Otto Rank (1909). [Cf. also Freud's own paper on 'Family Romances' (1909c), p. 217ff. below, and his long footnote to Part I (G) of his case of the 'Rat Man' (1909d), P.F.L., 9, 86–8.]

It has justly been said that the Oedipus complex is the nuclear complex of the neuroses, and constitutes the essential part of their content. It represents the peak of infantile sexuality, which, through its after-effects, exercises a decisive influence on the sexuality of adults. Every new arrival on this planet is faced by the task of mastering the Oedipus complex; anyone who fails to do so falls a victim to neurosis. With the progress of psychoanalytic studies the importance of the Oedipus complex has become more and more clearly evident; its recog-

In these phantasies the infantile tendencies invariably emerge once more, but this time with intensified pressure from somatic sources. Among these tendencies the first place is taken with uniform frequency by the child's sexual impulses towards his parents, which are as a rule already differentiated owing to the attraction of the opposite sex – the son being drawn towards his mother and the daughter towards her father.[1] At the same time as these plain incestuous phantasies are overcome and repudiated, one of the most significant, but also one of the most painful, psychical achievements of the pubertal period is completed: detachment from parental authority, a process that alone makes possible the opposition, which is so important for the progress of civilization, between the new generation and the old. At every stage in the course of development through which all human beings ought by rights to pass, a certain number are held back; so there are some who have never got over their parents' authority and have withdrawn their affection from them either very incompletely or not at all. They are mostly girls, who, to the delight of their parents, have persisted in all their childish love far beyond puberty. It is most instructive to find that it is precisely these girls who in their later marriage lack the capacity to give their husbands what is due to them; they make cold wives and remain sexually anaesthetic. We learn from this that sexual love and what

---

nition has become the shibboleth that distinguishes the adherents of psychoanalysis from its opponents. [Cf. pp. 192 and 238 below.]

[*Added* 1924:] In another work (1924), Rank has traced attachment to the mother back to the prehistoric intra-uterine period and has thus indicated the biological foundation of the Oedipus complex. He differs from what has been said above, by deriving the barrier against incest from the traumatic effect of anxiety at birth. [See Chapter X of *Inhibitions, Symptoms and Anxiety* (1926d), P.F.L., **10**, 308–11.]

1. Cf. my remarks in *The Interpretation of Dreams* (1900a), on the inevitability of Fate in the fable of Oedipus [Chapter V, Section D (β); P.F.L., **4**, 362–6].

appears to be non-sexual love for parents are fed from the same sources; the latter, that is to say, merely corresponds to an infantile fixation of the libido.

The closer one comes to the deeper disturbances of psychosexual development, the more unmistakably the importance of incestuous object-choice emerges. In psychoneurotics a large portion or the whole of their psychosexual activity in finding an object remains in the unconscious as a result of their repudiation of sexuality. Girls with an exaggerated need for affection and an equally exaggerted horror of the real demands made by sexual life have an irresistible temptation on the one hand to realize the ideal of asexual love in their lives and on the other hand to conceal their libido behind an affection which they can express without self-reproaches, by holding fast throughout their lives to their infantile fondness, revived at puberty, for their parents or brothers and sisters. Psychoanalysis has no difficulty in showing persons of this kind that they are *in love*, in the everyday sense of the word, with these blood-relations of theirs; for, with the help of their symptoms and other manifestations of their illness, it traces their unconscious thoughts and translates them into conscious ones. In cases in which someone who has previously been healthy falls ill after an unhappy experience in love it is also possible to show with certainty that the mechanism of his illness consists in a turning-back of his libido on to those whom he preferred in his infancy.

After-effects of Infantile Object-choice

Even a person who has been fortunate enough to avoid an incestuous fixation of his libido does not entirely escape its influence. It often happens that a young man falls in love seriously for the first time with a mature woman, or a girl with an elderly man in a position of authority; this is clearly an echo of the phases of development that we have been discussing, since these figures are able to re-animate pictures of their mother or father.[1] There can be no doubt that every object-choice whatever is based, though less closely, on these proto-types. A man, especially, looks for someone who can represent his picture of his mother, as it has dominated his mind from his earliest childhood; and accordingly, if his mother is still alive, she may well resent this new version of herself and meet her with hostility. In view of the importance of a child's relations to his parents in determining his later choice of a sexual object, it can easily be understood that any disturbance of those relations will produce the gravest effects upon his adult sexual life. Jealousy in a lover is never without an infantile root or at least an infantile reinforcement. If there are quarrels between the parents or if their marriage is unhappy, the ground will be prepared in their children for the severest predisposition to a disturbance of sexual development or to a neurotic illness.

A child's affection for his parents is no doubt the most im-portant infantile trace which, after being revived at puberty, points the way to his choice of an object; but it is not the only one. Other starting-points with the same early origin enable a man to develop more than one *sexual line*, based no less upon his childhood, and to lay down very various conditions for his object-choice.[2]

Prevention of Inversion

One of the tasks implicit in object-choice is that it should find its way to the opposite sex. This, as we know, is not accom-plished without a certain amount of fumbling. Often enough the first impulses after puberty go astray, though without any permanent harm resulting. Dessoir [1894] has justly remarked

1. [*Footnote added* 1920:] Cf. my paper 'A Special Type of Choice of Object made by Men' (1910*h*) [in the present volume, p. 227ff. below].

2. [*Footnote added* 1915:] The innumerable peculiarities of the erotic life of human beings as well as the compulsive character of the process of falling in love itself are quite unintelligible except by reference back to childhood and as being residual effects of childhood.

upon the regularity with which adolescent boys and girls form sentimental friendships with others of their own sex. No doubt the strongest force working against a permanent inversion of the sexual object is the attraction which the opposing sexual characters exercise upon one another. Nothing can be said within the framework of the present discussion to throw light upon it.[1] This factor is not in itself, however, sufficient to exclude inversion; there are no doubt a variety of other contributory factors. Chief among these is its authoritative prohibition by society. Where inversion is not regarded as a crime it will be found that it answers fully to the sexual inclinations of no small number of people. It may be presumed, in the next place, that in the case of men a childhood recollection of the affection shown them by their mother and others of the female sex who looked after them when they were children contributes powerfully to directing their choice towards women;[2] on the other hand their early experience of being deterred by their father from sexual activity and their competitive relation with him deflect them from their own sex. Both of these two factors apply equally to girls, whose sexual activity is particularly subject to the watchful guardianship of their mother. They thus acquire a hostile relation to their own sex which influences their object-choice decisively in what is regarded as the normal direction. The education of boys by male persons (by slaves, in antiquity) seems to encourage homosexuality. The frequency of inversion among the present-day aristocracy is made somewhat more intelligible by their employment of

1. [*Footnote added* 1924:] This is the place at which to draw attention to Ferenczi's *Versuch einer Genitaltheorie* (1924), a work which, though somewhat fanciful, is nevertheless of the greatest interest, and in which the sexual life of the higher animals is traced back to their biological evolution.

2. [The rest of this sentence and the two following ones date from 1915. In the editions of 1905 and 1910 the following passage takes their place: 'while in the case of girls, who in any case enter a period of repression at puberty, impulses of rivalry play a part in discouraging them from loving members of their own sex'.]

menservants, as well as by the fact that their mothers give less personal care to their children. In the case of some hysterics it is found that the early loss of one of their parents, whether by death, divorce or separation, with the result that the remaining parent absorbs the whole of the child's love, determines the sex of the person who is later to be chosen as a sexual object, and may thus open the way to permanent inversion.

SUMMARY

THE time has arrived for me to attempt to summarize what I have said. We started out from the aberrations of the sexual instinct in respect of its object and of its aim and we were faced by the question of whether these arise from an innate disposition or are acquired as a result of experiences in life. We arrived at an answer to this question from an understanding, derived from psychoanalytic investigation, of the workings of the sexual instinct in psychoneurotics, a numerous class of people and one not far removed from the healthy. We found that in them tendencies to every kind of perversion can be shown to exist as unconscious forces and betray their presence as factors leading to the formation of symptoms. It was thus possible to say that neurosis is, as it were, the negative of perversion. In view of what was now seen to be the wide dissemination of tendencies to perversion we were driven to the conclusion that a disposition to perversions is an original and universal disposition of the human sexual instinct and that normal sexual behaviour is developed out of it as a result of organic changes and psychical inhibitions occurring in the course of maturation; we hoped to be able to show the presence of this original disposition in childhood. Among the forces restricting the direction taken by the sexual instinct we laid emphasis upon shame, disgust, pity and the structures of morality and authority erected by society. We were thus led to regard any established aberration from normal sexuality as an instance of developmental inhibition and infantilism. Though it was necessary to place in the foreground the importance of the variations in the original disposition, a co-operative and not an opposing relation was to be assumed as existing between them and the influences of actual life. It appeared, on the other hand, that since the original disposition is necessarily a complex one, the sexual instinct itself must be something put together from various factors, and that in the perversions it falls apart, as it were, into its components. The perversions were thus seen to be on the one hand inhibitions, and on the other hand dissociations, of normal development. Both these aspects were brought together in the supposition that the sexual instinct of adults arises from a combination of a number of impulses of childhood into a unity, an impulsion with a single aim.

After having explained the preponderance of perverse tendencies in psychoneurotics by recognizing it as a collateral filling of subsidiary channels when the main current of the instinctual stream has been blocked by 'repression',[1] we proceeded to a consideration of sexual life in childhood. We found it a regrettable thing that the existence of the sexual instinct in childhood has been denied and that the sexual manifestations not infrequently to be observed in children have been described as irregularities. It seemed to us on the contrary that children bring germs of sexual activity with them into the world, that they already enjoy sexual satisfaction when they begin to take nourishment and that they persistently seek to repeat the experience in the familiar activity of 'thumb-sucking'. The sexual activity of children, however, does not, it appeared, develop *pari passu* with their other functions, but, after a short period of efflorescence from the ages of two to five,[2] enters upon the so-called period of latency. During that period the production of sexual excitation is not by any

1. [*Footnote added* 1915:] This does not apply only to the 'negative' tendencies to perversion which appear in neuroses but equally to the 'positive', properly so-called, perversions. Thus these latter are to be derived not merely from a fixation of infantile tendencies but also from a regression to those tendencies as a result of other channels of the sexual current being blocked. It is for this reason that the positive perversions also are accessible to psychoanalytic therapy.

2. [The last seven words were first inserted in 1915. In the edition of that year, however, the ages given were 'three to five'. The 'two' was substituted in 1920.]

means stopped but continues and produces a store of energy which is employed to a great extent for purposes other than sexual – namely, on the one hand in contributing the sexual components to social feelings and on the other hand (through repression and reaction-forming) in building up the subsequently developed barriers against sexuality. On this view, the forces destined to retain the sexual instinct upon certain lines are built up in childhood chiefly at the cost of perverse sexual impulses and with the assistance of education. A certain portion of the infantile sexual impulses would seem to evade these uses and succeed in expressing itself as sexual activity. We next found that sexual excitation in children springs from a multiplicity of forces. Satisfaction arises first and foremost from the appropriate sensory excitation of what we have described as erotogenic zones. It seems probable that any part of the skin and any sense-organ – probably, indeed, *any* organ[1] – can function as an erotogenic zone, though there are some particularly marked erotogenic zones whose excitation would seem to be secured from the very first by certain organic contrivances. It further appears that sexual excitation arises as a byproduct, as it were, of a large number of processes that occur in the organism, as soon as they reach a certain degree of intensity, and most especially of any relatively powerful emotion, even though it is of a distressing nature. The excitations from all these sources are not yet combined; but each follows its own separate aim, which is merely the attainment of a certain sort of pleasure. In childhood, therefore, the sexual instinct is *not unified* and is at first[2] without an object, that is, *auto-erotic*.

The erotogenic zone of the genitals begins to make itself noticeable, it seems, even during the years of childhood. This may happen in two ways. Either, like any other erotogenic zone, it yields satisfaction in response to appropriate sensory stimulation; or, in a manner which is not quite understand-

1. [This parenthesis was added in 1915.]
2. [The words 'not unified and is at first' were added in 1920.]

able, when satisfaction is derived from other sources, a sexual excitation is simultaneously produced which has a special relation to the genital zone. We were reluctantly obliged to admit that we could not satisfactorily explain the relation between sexual satisfaction and sexual excitation, or that between the activity of the genital zone and the activity of the other sources of sexuality.

We found from the study of neurotic disorders[1] that beginnings of an organization of the sexual instinctual components can be detected in the sexual life of children from its very beginning. During a first, very early phase, *oral erotism* occupies most of the picture. A second of these pregenital organizations is characterized by the predominance of *sadism* and *anal erotism*. It is not until a third phase has been reached that the genital zones proper contribute their share in determining sexual life, and in children this last phase is developed only so far as to a primacy of the phallus.[2]

We were then obliged to recognize, as one of our most surprising findings, that this early efflorescence of infantile sexual life (between the ages of two and five) already gives rise to the choice of an object, with all the wealth of mental activities which such a process involves.[3] Thus, in spite of the lack of synthesis between the different instinctual components and the uncertainty of the sexual aim, the phase of development corresponding to that period must be regarded as an important precursor of the subsequent final sexual organization.

The fact that the *onset* of sexual development in human beings occurs in *two phases*, i.e. that the development is interrupted by the period of latency, seemed to call for particular notice. This appears to be one of the necessary conditions of the aptitude of men for developing a higher civilization, but also of their tendency to neurosis. So far as we know, nothing analogous is to be found in man's animal relatives. It would

1. [This and the next two paragraphs were added in 1920.]
2. [The last clause was added in 1924.]
3. [Cf. the end of footnote 1 on p. 145.]

seem that the origin of this peculiarity of man must be looked for in the prehistory of the human species.

It was not possible to say what amount of sexual activity can occur in childhood without being described as abnormal or detrimental to further development. The nature of these sexual manifestations was found to be predominantly masturbatory. Experience further showed that the external influences of seduction are capable of provoking interruptions of the latency period or even its cessation, and that in this connection the sexual instinct of children proves in fact to be polymorphously perverse; it seems, moreover, that any such premature sexual activity diminishes a child's educability.

In spite of the gaps in our knowledge of infantile sexual life, we had to proceed to an attempt at examining the alterations brought about in it by the arrival of puberty. We selected two of these as being the decisive ones: the subordination of all the other sources of sexual excitation under the primacy of the genital zones and the process of finding an object. Both of these are already adumbrated in childhood. The first is accomplished by the mechanism of exploiting fore-pleasure: what were formerly self-contained sexual acts, attended by pleasure and excitation, become acts preparatory to the new sexual aim (the discharge of the sexual products), the attainment of which, enormously pleasurable, brings the sexual excitation to an end. In this connection we had to take into account the differentiation of sexuality into masculine and feminine; and we found that in order to become a woman a further stage of repression is necessary, which discards a portion of infantile masculinity and prepares the woman for changing her leading genital zone. As regards object-choice, we found that it is given its direction by the childhood hints (revived at puberty) of the child's sexual inclination towards his parents and others in charge of him, but that it is diverted away from them, on to other people who resemble them, owing to the barrier against incest which has meanwhile been erected. Finally it must be added that during the transition period of puberty the processes of somatic and of psychical development continue for a time side by side independently, until the irruption of an intense mental erotic impulse, leading to the innervation of the genitals, brings about the unity of the erotic function which is necessary for normality.

Factors Interfering with Development

Every step on this long path of development can become a point of fixation, every juncture in this involved combination can be an occasion for a dissociation of the sexual instinct, as we have already shown from numerous instances.[1] It remains for us to enumerate the various factors, internal and external, that interfere with development, and to indicate the place in the mechanism on which the disturbance arising from each of them impinges. The factors that we shall enumerate can evidently not be of equal importance, and we must be prepared for difficulties in assigning an appropriate value to each.

Constitution and Heredity

First and foremost we must name the innate *variety of sexual constitutions*, upon which it is probable that the principal weight falls, but which can clearly only be inferred from their later manifestations and even then not always with great certainty. We picture this variety as a preponderance of one or another of the many sources of sexual excitation, and it is our view that a difference in disposition of this kind is always bound to find expression in the final result, even though that result may not overstep the limits of what is normal. No doubt it is conceivable that there may also be variations in the original disposition of a kind which must necessarily, and without the concurrence of any other factors, lead to the development of an abnormal sexual life. These might be described as 'degenera-

1. [The further problem of a possible relation between the point of fixation and the type of neurosis developed – the problem of the 'choice of neurosis' – is not dealt with in these essays, though it had long been in Freud's thoughts. The subject was discussed more fully in 'The Disposition to Obsessional Neurosis' (1913*i*), *P.F.L.*, **10**, 135–7.]

tive' and be regarded as an expression of inherited degeneracy. In this connection I have a remarkable fact to record. In more than half of the severe cases of hysteria, obsessional neurosis, etc., which I have treated psychotherapeutically, I have been able to prove with certainty that the patient's father suffered from syphilis before marriage, whether there was evidence of tabes or general paralysis, or whether the anamnesis indicated in some other way the presence of syphilitic disease. I should like to make it perfectly plain that the children who later became neurotic bore no physical signs of hereditary syphilis, so that it was their abnormal sexual constitution that was to be regarded as the last echo of their syphilitic heritage. Though I am far from wishing to assert that descent from syphilitic parents is an invariable or indispensable aetiological condition of a neuropathic constitution, I am nevertheless of opinion that the coincidence which I have observed is neither accidental nor unimportant.

The hereditary conditions in the case of positive perverts are less well known, for they know how to avoid investigation. Yet there are good reasons to suppose that what is true of the neuroses applies also to the perversions. For it is no rare thing to find perversions and psychoneuroses occurring in the same family, and distributed between the two sexes in such a way that the male members of the family, or one of them, are positive perverts, while the females, true to the tendency of their sex to repression, are negative perverts, that is, hysterics. This is good evidence of the essential connections which we have shown to exist between the two disorders.

Further Modification

On the other hand, it is not possible to adopt the view that the form to be taken by sexual life is unambiguously decided, once and for all, with the inception of the different components of the sexual constitution. On the contrary, the determining process continues, and further possibilities arise according to the vicissitudes of the tributary streams of sexuality springing from their separate sources. This *further modification* is clearly what brings the decisive outcome, and constitutions which might be described as the same can lead to three different final results:

[1] If the relation between all the different dispositions – a relation which we will assume to be abnormal – persists and grows stronger at maturity, the result can only be a perverse sexual life. The analysis of abnormal constitutional dispositions of this kind has not yet been properly taken in hand. But we already know cases which can easily be explained on such a basis as this. Writers on the subject, for instance, have asserted [see p. 53] that the necessary precondition of a whole number of perverse fixations lies in an innate weakness of the sexual instinct. In this form the view seems to me untenable. It makes sense, however, if what is meant is a constitutional weakness of one particular factor in the sexual instinct, namely the genital zone – a zone which takes over the function of combining the separate sexual activities for the purposes of reproduction. For if the genital zone is weak, this combination, which is required to take place at puberty, is bound to fail, and the strongest of the other components of sexuality will continue its activity as a perversion.[1]

Repression

[2] A different result is brought about if in the course of development some of the components which are of excessive strength in the disposition are submitted to the process of *repression* (which, it must be insisted, is not equivalent to their being abolished). If this happens, the excitations concerned continue to be generated as before; but they are prevented by psychical obstruction from attaining their aim and are diverted into numerous other channels till they find their way to expression

1. [*Footnote added* 1915:] In such circumstances one often finds that at puberty a normal sexual current begins to operate at first, but that, as a result of its internal weakness, it breaks down in face of the first external obstacles and is then replaced by regression to the perverse fixation.

as symptoms. The outcome may be an approximately normal sexual life – though usually a restricted one – but there is in addition psychoneurotic illness. These particular cases have become familiar to us from the psychoanalytic investigation of neurotics. Their sexual life begins like that of perverts, and a considerable part of their childhood is occupied with perverse sexual activity which occasionally extends far into maturity. A reversal due to repression then occurs, owing to internal causes (usually before puberty, but now and then even long afterwards), and from that time onwards neurosis takes the place of perversion, without the old impulses being extinguished. We are reminded of the proverb 'Junge Hure, alte Betschwester',[1] only that here youth has lasted all too short a time. The fact that perversion can be replaced by neurosis in the life of the same person, like the fact which we have already mentioned that perversion and neurosis can be distributed among different members of the same family, tallies with the view that neurosis is the negative of perversion.

Sublimation

[3] The third alternative result of an abnormal constitutional disposition is made possible by the process of *sublimation*. This enables excessively strong excitations arising from particular sources of sexuality to find an outlet and use in other fields, so that a not inconsiderable increase in psychical efficiency results from a disposition which in itself is perilous. Here we have one of the origins of artistic activity; and, according to the completeness or incompleteness of the sublimation, a characterological analysis of a highly gifted individual, and in particular of one with an artistic disposition, may reveal a mixture, in every proportion, of efficiency, perversion and neurosis. A sub-species of sublimation is to be found in suppression by *reaction-formation*, which, as we have seen, begins during a child's period of latency and continues in favourable cases throughout his whole life. What we describe as a person's

1. ['A young whore makes an old nun.']

'character' is built up to a considerable extent from the material of sexual excitations and is composed of instincts that have been fixed since childhood, of constructions achieved by means of sublimation, and of other constructions, employed for effectively holding in check perverse impulses which have been recognized as being unutilizable.[1] The multifariously perverse sexual disposition of childhood can accordingly be regarded as the source of a number of our virtues, in so far as through reaction-formation it stimulates their development.[2]

Accidental Experiences

No other influences on the course of sexual development can compare in importance with releases of sexuality, waves of repression and sublimations – the two latter being processes of which the inner causes are quite unknown to us. It might be possible to include repressions and sublimations as a part of the constitutional disposition, by regarding them as manifestations of it in life; and anyone who does so is justified in asserting that the final shape taken by sexual life is principally the outcome of the innate constitution. No one with perception will, however, dispute that an interplay of factors such as this also leaves room for the modifying effects of accidental events experienced in childhood and later. It is not easy[3] to estimate

1. [Footnote added 1920:] In the case of some character-traits it has even been possible to trace a connection with particular erotogenic components. Thus, obstinacy, thrift and orderliness arise from an exploitation of anal erotism, while ambition is determined by a strong urethral-erotic disposition. [See the last paragraph of 'Character and Anal Erotism' (1908b), p. 215 below.]

2. Emile Zola, a keen observer of human nature, describes in La joie de vivre how a girl, cheerfully and selflessly and without thought of reward, sacrificed to those she loved everything that she possessed or could lay claim to – her money and her hopes. This girl's childhood was dominated by an insatiable thirst for affection, which was transformed into cruelty on an occasion when she found herself slighted in favour of another girl.

3. [The remainder of this paragraph and the whole of the next one were added in 1915.]

the relative efficacy of the constitutional and accidental factors. In theory one is always inclined to overestimate the former; therapeutic practice emphasizes the importance of the latter. It should, however, on no account be forgotten that the relation between the two is a co-operative and not a mutually exclusive one. The constitutional factor must await experiences before it can make itself felt; the accidental factor must have a constitutional basis in order to come into operation. To cover the majority of cases we can picture what has been described as a 'complemental series',[1] in which the diminishing intensity of one factor is balanced by the increasing intensity of the other; there is, however, no reason to deny the existence of extreme cases at the two ends of the series.

We shall be in even closer harmony with psychoanalytic research if we give a place of preference among the accidental factors to the experiences of early childhood. The single aetiological series then falls into two, which may be called the *dispositional* and the *definitive*. In the first the constitution and the accidental experiences of childhood interact in the same manner as do the disposition and later traumatic experiences in the second. All the factors that impair sexual development show their effects by bringing about a *regression*, a return to an earlier phase of development.

Let us now resume our task of enumerating the factors which we have found to exercise an influence on sexual development, whether they are themselves operative forces or merely manifestations of such forces.

Precocity

One such factor is spontaneous sexual *precocity*, whose presence at least can be demonstrated with certainty in the aetiology of

1. [In 1915 the term used was 'aetiological series', which was altered to 'complemental series' in 1920. The latter term seems to have been first used by Freud in Lecture 22 of his *Introductory Lectures* (1916–17), *P.F.L.*, **1**, 392. The correction of the phrase was not carried out where it occurs again a few lines lower down.]

the neuroses though, like other factors, it is not in itself a sufficient cause. It is manifested in the interruption, abbreviation or bringing to an end of the infantile period of latency; and it is a cause of disturbances by occasioning sexual manifestations which, owing on the one hand to the sexual inhibitions being incomplete and on the other hand to the genital system being undeveloped, are bound to be in the nature of perversions. These tendencies to perversion may thereafter either persist as such or, after repressions have set in, become the motive forces of neurotic symptoms. In any case sexual precocity makes more difficult the later control of the sexual instinct by the higher mental agencies which is so desirable, and it increases the impulsive quality which, quite apart from this, characterizes the psychical representations of the instinct. Sexual precocity often runs parallel with premature intellectual development and, linked in this way, is to be found in the childhood history of persons of the greatest eminence and capacity; under such conditions its effects do not seem to be so pathogenic as when it appears in isolation.[1]

Temporal Factors

Other factors which, along with precocity, may be classed as *temporal* also deserve attention. The order in which the various instinctual impulses come into activity seems to be phylogenetically determined; so, too, does the length of time during which they are able to manifest themselves before they succumb to the effects of some freshly emerging instinctual impulse or to some typical repression. Variations, however, seem to occur both in temporal sequence and in duration, and these variations must exercise a determining influence upon the final result. It cannot be a matter of indifference whether a given current makes its appearance earlier or later than a current flowing in the opposite direction, for the effect

1. [Cf. some remarks on this point in the case history of 'Little Hans' (1909*b*), *P.F.L.*, **8**, 298–9. – The two paragraphs which follow were added in 1915.]

of a repression cannot be undone. Divergences in the temporal sequence in which the components come together invariably produce a difference in the outcome. On the other hand, instinctual impulses which emerge with special intensity often run a surprisingly short course – as, for instance, the heterosexual attachments of persons who later become manifest homosexuals. There is no justification for the fear that trends which set in with the greatest violence in childhood will permanently dominate the adult character; it is just as likely that they will disappear and make way for an opposite tendency. ('Gestrenge Herren regieren nicht lange.')[1]

We are not in a position to give so much as a hint as to the causes of these temporal disturbances of the process of development. A prospect opens before us at this point upon a whole phalanx of biological and perhaps, too, of historical problems of which we have not even come within striking distance.

Pertinacity of Early Impressions

The importance of all early sexual manifestations is increased by a psychical factor of unknown origin, which at the moment, it must be admitted, can only be brought forward as a provisional psychological concept. I have in mind the fact that, in order to account for the situation, it is necessary to assume that these early impressions of sexual life are characterized by an increased *pertinacity* or *susceptibility to fixation* in persons who are later to become neurotics or perverts. For the same premature sexual manifestations, when they occur in other persons, fail to make so deep an impression; they do not tend in a compulsive manner towards repetition nor do they lay down the path to be taken by the sexual instinct for a whole lifetime. Part of the explanation of this pertinacity of early impressions may perhaps lie in another psychical factor which we must not overlook in the causation of the neuroses,

1. ['Harsh rulers have short reigns.']

namely the preponderance attaching in mental life to memory-traces in comparison with recent impressions. This factor is clearly dependent on intellectual education and increases in proportion to the degree of individual culture. The savage has been described in contrast as 'das unglückselige Kind des Augenblickes'.[1] In consequence of the inverse relation holding between civilization and the free development of sexuality, of which the consequences can be followed far into the structure of our existences, the course taken by the sexual life of a child is just as unimportant for later life where the cultural or social level is relatively low as it is important where that level is relatively high.

Fixation

The ground prepared by the psychical factors which have just been enumerated affords a favourable basis for such stimulations of infantile sexuality as are experienced accidentally. The latter (first and foremost, seduction by other children or by adults) provide the material which, with the help of the former, can become fixated as a permanent disorder. A good proportion of the deviations from normal sexual life which are later observed both in neurotics and in perverts are thus established from the very first by the impressions of childhood – a period which is regarded as being devoid of sexuality. The causation is shared between a compliant constitution, precocity, the characteristic of increased pertinacity of early impressions and the chance stimulation of the sexual instinct by extraneous influences.

1. ['The hapless child of the moment.'] Increase in pertinacity may also possibly be the effect of an especially intense somatic manifestation of sexuality in early years. [What Freud here describes as 'pertinacity of early impressions' and 'susceptibility to fixation' was also termed by him elsewhere 'adhesiveness of the libido'. Cf., for example, Lectures 22 and 28 of the *Introductory Lectures* (1916–17), *P.F.L.*, **1**, 392–3 and 508. See also *Civilization and its Discontents* (1930a), Chapter V, where Freud refers to the special case of 'inertia of the libido'.]

The unsatisfactory conclusion, however, that emerges from these investigations of the disturbances of sexual life is that we know far too little of the biological processes constituting the essence of sexuality to be able to construct from our fragmentary information a theory adequate to the understanding alike of normal and of pathological conditions.

THE SEXUAL ENLIGHTENMENT
OF CHILDREN
(AN OPEN LETTER TO DR M. FÜRST)
(1907)

EDITOR'S NOTE

ZUR SEXUELLEN AUFKLÄRUNG DER KINDER

(OFFENER BRIEF AN DR M. FÜRST)

(A) GERMAN EDITIONS:

1907   *Soziale Medizin und Hygiene*, **2** (6) [June], 360–67.
1924   *Gesammelte Schriften*, **5**, 134–42.
1941   *Gesammelte Werke*, **7**, 19–27.

(B) ENGLISH TRANSLATIONS:

'The Sexual Enlightenment of Children. An Open Letter to
Dr M. Fürst'
1924   *Collected Papers*, **2**, 36–44. (Tr. E. B. M. Herford.)
1959   *Standard Edition*, **9**, 129–39.

The present edition is a corrected reprint of the *Standard Edition* version, with some editorial changes.

This was written at the request of a Hamburg doctor, Dr M. Fürst, for publication in a periodical devoted to social medicine and hygiene of which he was the editor. Freud draws here on some of the material derived from the case history of 'Little Hans' (1909*b*), whose analysis was actually in progress at the time of the publication of the present paper. In the early editions of the 'open letter', the boy was given the name of 'Little Herbert'; this was changed to 'Little Hans' in the German editions of 1924 onwards, though not in the English translation of that year. Some topics treated here (the sexual curiosity and sexual theories of children) are considered in more detail in the next paper in this volume, p. 187ff. below.

THE SEXUAL ENLIGHTENMENT OF CHILDREN

(AN OPEN LETTER TO DR M. FÜRST)

Dear Dr Fürst,

When you ask me for an expression of opinion on 'the sexual enlightenment of children', I assume that what you want is not a regular, formal treatise on the subject which shall take into account the excessive mass of literature that has grown up around it, but the independent judgement of an individual doctor whose professional activities have offered him special opportunities for concerning himself with sexual problems. I know that you have followed my scientific efforts with interest and that, unlike many of our colleagues, you do not dismiss my ideas without examining them because I regard the psychosexual constitution and certain noxae of sexual life as the most important causes of the neurotic disorders that are so common. My *Three Essays on the Theory of Sexuality* [1905d, see above, p. 45ff.], too, where I have described the way in which the sexual instinct is compounded and the disturbances which may occur in its development into the function of sexuality, have recently had a friendly reception in your journal.

I am expected, therefore, to answer questions on the following points: whether children ought to be given any enlightenment at all about the facts of sexual life, at what age this ought to happen and in what manner it should be carried out. Let me admit to you at once that I find a discussion of the second and third points perfectly reasonable, but that to my mind it is quite incomprehensible how there could be a difference of opinion on the first point. What can be the purpose of withholding from children – or, let us say, from young people – enlightenment of this kind about the sexual life of human beings? Is it from a fear of arousing their interest in these matters prematurely, before it awakens in them spontaneously? Is it from a hope that a concealment of this kind may retard the sexual instinct altogether until such time as it can find its way into the only channels open to it in our middle-class social order? Is it supposed that children would show no interest or understanding for the facts and riddles of sexual life if they were not promoted to do so by outside influences? Is it thought possible that the knowledge which is withheld from them will not reach them in other ways? Or is it genuinely and seriously intended that later on they should regard everything to do with sex as something degraded and detestable from which their parents and teachers wished to keep them away as long as possible?

I really do not know in which of these purposes to look for the motive for the concealment of what is sexual from children that is in fact carried out. I only know that they are all equally absurd and that I find it difficult to honour them with a serious refutation. I remember, however, that in the family letters of that great thinker and humanitarian Multatuli, I once found a few lines which are a more than adequate answer:

'To my mind, certain things are in general too much wrapped in a veil. It is right to keep a child's imagination pure, but this purity will not be preserved by ignorance. On the contrary, I think that concealment leads a boy or girl to suspect the truth more than ever. Curiosity leads us to pry into things which, if they had been told us without any great to do, would have aroused little or no interest in us. If this ignorance could be maintained even, I might become reconciled to it, but that is impossible. The child comes into contact with other children, books come his way which lead him to reflect, and the mystery-making with which his parents treat what he has nevertheless discovered actually increases his desire to know more. This desire, which is only partly satisfied and only in secret, excites his feeling and corrupts his imagination, so that the child already sins while his parents still believe that he does not know what sin is.'[1]

I do not know how the case could be better stated, but perhaps I may add a few remarks. It is undoubtedly nothing else but the customary prudishness and their own bad conscience over sexual matters that causes adults to adopt this attitude of 'mystery-making' in front of children; but possibly a part is also played by a piece of theoretical ignorance on their part, which we can counteract by giving the adults some enlightenment. It is commonly believed that the sexual instinct is absent in children and only begins to emerge in them at puberty when the sexual organs mature. This is a gross error, equally serious in its effects both on knowledge and on practice; and it is so easily corrected by observation that one wonders how it could ever have been made. As a matter of fact, the new-born baby brings sexuality with it into the world, certain sexual sensations accompany its development as a suckling and during early childhood, and only very few children would seem to escape sexual activities and sensations before puberty. Anyone who would like to find a detailed exposition of these statements can do so in my *Three Essays on the Theory of Sexuality*, to which I have referred above. There he will learn that the organs of reproduction proper are not the only parts of the body which provide sexual sensations of pleasure, and that nature has even so ordered matters that actual stimulations of the genitals are unavoidable during early childhood. This period of life, during which a certain quota of what is undoubtedly sexual pleasure is produced by the excitation of various parts of the skin (erotogenic zones), by the activity of certain biological instincts and as an accompanying excitation in many affective states, is called the period of *auto-erotism*, to use a term introduced by Havelock Ellis [1898]. All that

1. Multatuli, 1906, 1, 26. ['Multatuli' (Latin for 'I have borne much') was the pseudonym of a well-known Dutch writer E. D. Dekker (1820–87).]

puberty does is to give the genitals primacy among all the other zones and sources which produce pleasure, and thus to force erotism into the service of the function of reproduction. This process can naturally undergo certain inhibitions, and in many people (those who later become perverts and neurotics) it is only incompletely accomplished. On the other hand, the child is capable long before puberty of most of the psychical manifestations of love – tenderness, for example, devotion and jealousy. Often enough, too, an irruption of these mental states is associated with the physical sensations of sexual excitation, so that the child cannot remain in doubt as to the connection between the two. In short, except for his reproductive power, a child has a fully developed capacity for love long before puberty; and it may be asserted that the 'mystery-making' merely prevents him from being able to gain an intellectual grasp of activities for which he is psychically prepared and physically adjusted.

A child's intellectual interest in the riddles of sex, his desire for sexual knowledge, shows itself accordingly at an unexpectedly early age. If it has not been possible to make observations such as I am now going to put before you more frequently, that can only be because parents are either afflicted with blindness in regard to this interest on the part of their children, or, because if they cannot overlook it, they at once take steps to stifle it. I know a delightful little boy, now four years old, whose understanding parents abstain from forcibly suppressing one part of the child's development. Little Hans has certainly not been exposed to anything in the nature of seduction by a nurse, yet he has already for some time shown the liveliest interest in the part of the body which he calls his 'widdler'. When he was only three he asked his mother: 'Mummy, have you got a widdler too?' His mother answered 'Of course. What did you think?' He also asked his father the same question repeatedly. At the same age he was taken to a cow-shed for the first time and saw a cow being milked. 'Oh look!' he said, in surprise, 'there's milk coming out of its widdler!' At the age of three and three quarters he was on the way to making an independent discovery of correct categories by means of his observations. He saw some water being let out of an engine and said. 'Oh, look, the engine's widdling. Where's it got its widdler?' He added afterwards in reflective tones: 'A dog and a horse have widdlers; a table and a chair haven't.' Recently he was watching his seven-day-old little sister being given a bath. 'But her widdler's still quite small,' he remarked; 'when she grows up it'll get bigger all right.' (I have been told of this same attitude towards the problem of sex distinction in other boys of similar age.) I should like to say explicitly that little Hans is not a sensual child or at all pathologically disposed. The fact is simply, I think, that, not having been intimidated or oppressed with a sense of guilt, he gives expression quite ingenuously to what he thinks.[1]

The second great problem which exercises a child's mind – only at a somewhat later age, no doubt[2] – is the question of the origin of babies. This is usually started by the unwelcome arrival of a small brother or sister. It is the oldest and most burning question that confronts immature humanity. Those who understand how to interpret myths and legends can detect it in the riddle which the Theban Sphinx set to Oedipus. The customary answers given to the child in the nursery damage his genuine instinct of research and as a rule

1. [Footnote added 1924:] The history of little Hans's later illness and recovery is described in my 'Analysis of a Phobia in a Five-Year-Old Boy', [(1909b), where this material is repeated. See P.F.L., 8, 170ff. See also the Editor's Note, p. 172 above.]

2. [In Freud's earlier writings he asserts as a rule that the problem of the origin of babies is the first one to engage a child's interest. See, for instance, the paper on the sexual theories of children (1908c), written not long after this one (p. 190f. below), the case history of 'Little Hans' (1909b), Section III, and a passage added in 1915 to the Three Essays (1905d), p. 113 above. In the sentence in the text above, however, he appears to put it second to the problem of the distinction between the sexes; and this is the view to which he reverts, at all events as regards girls, in a footnote to his much later paper on this latter topic (1925j), p. 336 n. 2 below.]

deal the first blow, too, at his confidence in his parents. From that time on he usually begins to mistrust grown-up people, and to keep his most intimate interests secret from them. The following little document shows how tormenting this curiosity can become in older children. It is a letter written by a motherless girl of eleven and a half who had been speculating on the problem with her younger sister.

Dear Aunt Mali,

Will you please be so kind as to tell me how you got Christel and Paul. You must know because you are married. We were arguing about it yesterday evening and we want to know the truth. We have nobody else to ask. When are you coming to Salzburg? You know, Aunt Mali, we simply can't understand how the stork brings babies. Trudel thought the stork brings them in a shirt. Then we want to know as well if the stork gets them out of the pond and why one never sees babies in ponds. And will you please tell me, too, how one knows beforehand when one is going to have one. Write and tell me everything about it.

With thousands of greetings and kisses from us all,

Your inquisitive niece,
Lili.

I do not believe that this touching letter brought the two sisters the enlightenment they wanted. Later on the writer of it fell ill of the neurosis that arises from unanswered unconscious questions – of obsessional brooding.[1]

There does not seem to me to be a single good reason for denying children the enlightenment which their thirst for knowledge demands. To be sure, if it is the purpose of educators to stifle the child's power of independent thought as early as possible, in favour of the 'goodness' which they think so much of, they cannot set about this better than by deceiving him in sexual matters and intimidating him in matters of religion. The stronger natures will, it is true, withstand these

1. [*Footnote added* 1924:] After some years, however, her obsessional brooding gave way to a dementia praecox. – [Freud returns to the subject of unanswered questions in the next paper, on p. 196 below.]

influences and become rebels against the authority of their parents and later against every other authority. If children are not given the explanations for which they turn to their elders, they go on tormenting themselves with the problem in secret and produce attempts at solution in which the truth they have guessed is mingled in the most extraordinary way with grotesque untruths; or they whisper information to one another in which, because of the young enquirers' sense of guilt, everything sexual is stamped as being horrible and disgusting. These infantile sexual theories would be well worth collecting and examining.[1] From this time on, children usually lose the only proper attitude to sexual questions, and many of them never regain it.

It seems that the large majority of authors, both men and women, who have written about the sexual enlightenment of youth, have concluded in favour of it. But the clumsiness of most of their proposals as to when and how this enlightenment is to take place tempts one to think that they have not found it easy to arrive at this conclusion. So far as my knowledge of the literature goes, a single outstanding exception is provided by the charming letter of explanation which a certain Frau Emma Eckstein quotes as having been written by her to her son when he was about ten years old.[2] The customary method is obviously not quite the right one: all sexual knowledge is kept from children as long as possible, and then on one single occasion a disclosure is made to them in solemn and turgid language, and even so is only half the truth and generally comes too late. Most of the answers to the question 'How am I to tell my children?' make such a miserable impression, on me at least, that I should prefer parents not to embark on the business of enlightenment at all. What is really important is that children should never get the idea that one wants to make

1. [Freud himself carried out this suggestion soon afterwards. See below, p. 187ff., the paper on these theories, in which much of the present argument is elaborated.]

2. Emma Eckstein (1904).

more of a secret of the facts of sexual life than of any other matter which is not yet accessible to their understanding; and to ensure this it is necessary that from the very first what has to do with sexuality should be treated like anything else that is worth knowing about. Above all, it is the duty of schools not to evade the mention of sexual matters. The main facts of reproduction and their significance should be included in lessons about the animal kingdom, and at the same time stress should be laid on the fact that man shares every essential in his organization with the higher animals. Then, provided that the child's home environment does not aim directly at frightening him off thinking, something that I once overheard in a nursery will probably happen more often. I heard a boy saying to his little sister: 'How can you think babies are brought by the stork! You know man's a mammal; d'you think storks bring other mammals their babies too?'

The child's curiosity will never reach a very high degree of intensity provided it finds appropriate satisfaction at each stage of his learning. Enlightenment about the specific facts of human sexuality and an indication of its social significance should, therefore, be given to the child at the end of his time at his elementary school [*Volksschule*] and before he enters his intermediate school [*Mittelschule*] – that is to say, before he is ten years old. The period of confirmation would be a more suitable time than any other at which to instruct the child, who will by that time have a full knowledge of all the physical facts, in the moral obligations which are attached to the actual satisfaction of the instinct. Enlightenment about sexual life carried out along such lines as this, proceeding step by step and without any real interruption, and in which the school takes the initiative, seems to me to be the only kind which takes into account the child's development and thus successfully avoids the dangers involved.

I consider it the most significant advance in child education that in France the State should have introduced, in place of the catechism, a primer which gives the child his first instruction in his position as a citizen and in the ethical duties which will later devolve on him. But such elementary instruction is seriously deficient, so long as it does not include the field of sexuality. Here is the gap which educators and reformers should set about filling. In countries which have placed the education of children wholly or in part in the hands of the clergy, it will, of course, be impossible to ask for this. A priest will never admit that men and animals have the same nature, since he cannot do without the immortality of the soul, which he requires as the basis for moral precepts. Here, once again, we see the unwisdom of sewing a single silk patch on to a tattered coat – the impossibility of carrying out an isolated reform without altering the foundations of the whole system.[1]

1. [Freud makes the same point, in connection with marriage, in his paper on 'civilized' sexual morality (1908*d*), *P.F.L.*, **12**, 48.]

ON THE SEXUAL THEORIES
OF CHILDREN
(1908)

EDITOR'S NOTE

ÜBER INFANTILE SEXUALTHEORIEN

(A) GERMAN EDITIONS:

1908   *Sexual-Probleme* [*Mutterschutz*, N.F.], **4** (12) [December], 763–79.
1924   *Gesammelte Schriften*, **5**, 168–85.
1941   *Gesammelte Werke*, **7**, 171–88.

(B) ENGLISH TRANSLATIONS:

'On the Sexual Theories of Children'

1924   *Collected Papers*, **2**, 59–75. (Tr. D. Bryan.)
1959   *Standard Edition*, **9**, 205–26.

The present edition is a corrected reprint of the *Standard Edition* version, with some editorial changes.

Though there may be little in the present paper to surprise the modern reader, it in fact launched a quite remarkable quantity of new ideas for the first time on the world. The paradox becomes explicable when we realize that this paper was published some months before the 'Little Hans' case history (1909*b*) (though, as will be seen from footnote 1 on p. 196, that work was probably already in proof) and that the section of the *Three Essays* (1905*d*) on 'The Sexual Researches of Childhood' (pp. 112–15 above) was only added to that work in 1915, eight years after the publication of this paper, of which in fact that section is little more than an abstract.

Here, then, the first readers of the present work were confronted, almost without previous warning, with the notions of fertilization through the mouth and of birth through the anus, of parental intercourse as something sadistic, and of the possession of a penis by members of both sexes. This last notion was the one with the most far-reaching implications, and they in turn find a first mention in these pages: the importance attached to the penis by children of both sexes, the results of the discovery that one sex is without it – the emergence in girls of 'envy for the penis' and in boys of the concept of 'the woman with a penis' and its bearing on one form of homosexuality. Finally, we have here the first explicit mention and discussion of the 'castration complex' itself.

The peculiar wealth of material contained here is no doubt to be attributed largely to the findings in the 'Little Hans' analysis, the report upon which, recently completed, illustrated and expanded much of the content of the present paper.

ON THE SEXUAL THEORIES
OF CHILDREN

THE material on which the following synthesis is based is derived from several sources. Firstly, from the direct observation of what children say and do; secondly, from what adult neurotics consciously remember from their childhood and relate during psychoanalytic treatment; and thirdly, from the inferences and constructions, and from the unconscious memories translated into conscious material, which result from the psychoanalysis of neurotics.

That the first of these three sources has not by itself supplied all that is worth knowing on the subject is due to the attitude which the adult adopts towards the sexual life of children. He does not credit them with having any sexual activity and therefore takes no trouble to observe any such thing while, on the other hand, he suppresses any manifestation of such an activity which might claim his attention. Consequently the opportunity of obtaining information from this, the most unequivocal and fertile source of all, is a very restricted one. Whatever comes from the uninfluenced communications made by adults concerning their own conscious childhood memories is at the best subject to the objection that it may have been falsified in retrospect; but, in addition to this, it has to be viewed in the light of the fact that the informants have subsequently become neurotic. The material that comes from the third source is open to all the criticisms which it is the custom to marshal against the trustworthiness of psychoanalysis and the reliability of the conclusions that are drawn from it. Thus I cannot attempt to justify it here; I can only give an assurance that those who know and practise the psychoanalytic technique acquire an extensive confidence in its findings.

I cannot guarantee the completeness of my results, but I can answer for the care taken in arriving at them.

There remains a difficult question to decide. How far may one assume that what is here reported of children generally is true of all children – that is, of every particular child? Pressure of education and varying intensity of the sexual instinct certainly make great individual variations in the sexual behaviour of children possible, and, above all, influence the date at which a child's sexual interest appears. For this reason, I have not divided my presentation of the material according to the successive epochs of childhood, but have combined into a single account things that come into play in different children sometimes earlier and sometimes later. It is my conviction that no child – none, at least, who is mentally normal and still less one who is intellectually gifted – can avoid being occupied with the problems of sex in the years *before* puberty.

I do not think much of the objection that neurotics are a special class of people, marked by an innate disposition that is 'degenerate', from whose childhood life we must not be allowed to infer anything about the childhood of other people. Neurotics are people much like others. They cannot be sharply differentiated from normal people, and in their childhood they are not always easily distinguishable from those who remain healthy in later life. It is one of the most valuable results of our psychoanalytic investigations to have discovered that the neuroses of such people have no special mental content that is peculiar to them, but that, as Jung has expressed it, they fall ill of the same complexes against which we healthy people struggle as well. The only difference is that healthy people know how to overcome those complexes without any gross damage demonstrable in practical life, whereas in nervous cases the suppression of the complexes succeeds only at the price of costly substitutive formations – that is to say, from a practical point of view it is a failure. In childhood neurotic and normal people naturally approximate to each other much more closely than they do in later life, so that I cannot regard it as a methodological error to make use of the communications of neurotics about their childhood for drawing conclusions by analogy about normal childhood life. But since those who later become neurotics very often have in their inborn constitution an especially strong sexual instinct and a tendency to precocity and to a premature expression of that instinct, they make it possible for us to recognize a great deal of infantile activity more sharply and clearly than our capacity for observation (which is in any case a blunted one) would enable us to do in other children. But we shall of course only be able to assess the true value of these communications made by neurotic adults when, following Havelock Ellis's example, we shall have thought it worth while to collect the childhood memories of *healthy* adults as well.[1]

In consequence of unfavourable circumstances, both of an external and an internal nature, the following observations apply chiefly to the sexual development of one sex only – that is, of males. The value of a compilation such as I am attempting here need not, however, be a purely descriptive one. A knowledge of infantile sexual theories in the shapes they assume in the thoughts of children can be of interest in various ways – even, surprisingly enough, for the elucidation of myths and fairy tales. They are indispensable, moreover, for an understanding of the neuroses themselves; for in them these childish theories are still operative and acquire a determining influence upon the form taken by the symptoms.

If we could divest ourselves of our corporeal existence, and could view the things of this earth with a fresh eye as purely thinking begins, from another planet for instance, nothing perhaps would strike our attention more forcibly than the fact of the existence of two sexes among human beings, who, though so much alike in other respects, yet mark the difference

1. [Cf. Havelock Ellis (1903, Appendix B). See also above, p.108 *n*.]

between them with such obvious external signs. But it does not seem that children choose this fundamental fact in the same way as the starting-point of their researches into sexual problems. Since they have known a father and mother as far back as they can remember in life, they accept their existence as a reality which needs no further inquiry, and a boy has the same attitude towards a little sister from whom he is separated by only a slight difference of age of one or two years. A child's desire for knowledge on this point does not in fact awaken spontaneously, prompted perhaps by some inborn need for established causes; it is aroused under the goad of the self-seeking instincts that dominate him, when – perhaps after the end of his second year – he is confronted with the arrival of a new baby. And a child whose own nursery has received no such addition is able, from observations made in other homes, to put himself in the same situation. The loss of his parents' care, which he actually experiences or justly fears, and the presentiment that from now on he must for evermore share all his possessions with the newcomer, have the effect of awakening his emotions and sharpening his capacities for thought. The elder child expresses unconcealed hostility towards his rival, which finds vent in unfriendly criticisms of it, in wishes that 'the stork should take it away again' and occasionally even in small attacks upon the creature lying helpless in the cradle. A wider difference in age usually softens the expression of this primary hostility. In the same way, at a rather later age, if no small brother or sister has appeared, the child's wish for a playmate, such as he has seen in other families, may gain the upper hand.

At the instigation of these feelings and worries, the child now comes to be occupied with the first, grand problem of life and asks himself the question: '*Where do babies come from?*'[1] – a question which, there can be no doubt, first ran: 'Where did this particular, intruding baby come from?' We seem to hear the echoes of this first riddle in innumerable riddles of

1. [See footnote 2 above, p. 177.]

myth and legend. The question itself is, like all research, the product of a vital exigency,[1] as though thinking were entrusted with the task of preventing the recurrence of such dreaded events. Let us assume, however, that the child's thinking soon becomes independent of this instigation, and henceforward goes on operating as a self-sustained instinct for research. Where a child is not already too much intimidated, he sooner or later adopts the direct method of demanding an answer from his parents or those in charge of him, who are in his eyes the source of all knowledge. This method, however, fails. The child receives either evasive answers or a rebuke for his curiosity, or he is dismissed with the mythologically significant piece of information which, in German countries, runs: 'The stork brings the babies; it fetches them out of the water.' I have reason to believe that far more children than their parents suspect are dissatisfied with this solution and meet it with energetic doubts, which, however, they do not always openly admit. I know of a three-year-old boy who, after receiving this piece of enlightenment, disappeared – to the terror of his nurse. He was found at the edge of the big pond adjoining the country house, to which he had hurried in order to see the babies in the water. I also know of another boy who could only allow his disbelief to find expression in a hesitant remark that he knew better, that it was not a stork that brought babies but a heron. It seems to me to follow from a great deal of information I have received that children refuse to believe the stork theory and that from the time of this first deception and rebuff they nourish a distrust of adults and have a suspicion of there being something forbidden which is being withheld from them by the 'grown-ups', and that they consequently hide their further researches under a cloak of secrecy. With this, however, the child also experiences the first occasion for a

1. [The part played in mental development by the 'exigencies of life' was discussed by Freud in Chapter VII (C) of *The Interpretation of Dreams* (1900a), *P.F.L.*, 4, 719ff.]

'psychical conflict', in that views for which he feels an instinctual kind of preference, but which are not 'right' in the eyes of the grown-ups, come into opposition with other views, which are supported by the authority of the grown-ups without being acceptable to him himself. Such a psychical conflict may soon turn into a 'psychical dissociation'. The set of views which are bound up with being 'good', but also with a cessation of reflection, become the dominant and conscious views; while the other set, for which the child's work of research has meanwhile obtained fresh evidence, but which are not supposed to count, become the suppressed and 'unconscious' ones. The nuclear complex[1] of a neurosis is in this way brought into being.

Recently, the analysis of a five-year-old boy,[2] which his father undertook and which he has handed over to me for publication, has given me irrefutable proof of the correctness of a view towards which the psychoanalysis of adults had long been leading me. I now know that the change which takes place in the mother during pregnancy does not escape the child's sharp eyes and that he is very well able before long to establish the true connection between the increase in his mother's stoutness and the appearance of the baby. In the case just mentioned the boy was three and a half years old when his sister was born and four and three quarters when he showed his better knowledge by the most unmistakable allusions. This precocious discovery, however, is always kept secret, and later, in conformity with the further vicissitudes of the child's sexual researches, it is repressed and forgotten.

The 'stork fable', therefore, is not one of the sexual theories of children. On the contrary, it is the child's observation of

---

1. [Soon after this, e.g. in the 'Rat Man' case history (1909d), Freud was using this term as equivalent to what a little later (1910h, p. 238 below) he called the 'Oedipus complex'. In the present passage, where it first appears, the application is wider. Cf. also p. 149n. above.]

2. [The case history of 'Little Hans' (1909b), which was published shortly after the present paper.]

animals, who hide so little of their sexual life and to whom he feels so closely akin, that strengthens his disbelief in it. With his knowledge, independently obtained, that babies grow inside the mother's body, he would be on the right road to solving the problem on which he first tries out his powers of thinking. But his further progress is inhibited by a piece of ignorance which cannot be made good [see below, p. 196f.] and by false theories which the state of his own sexuality imposes on him.

These false sexual theories, which I shall now discuss, all have one very curious characteristic. Although they go astray in a grotesque fashion, yet each one of them contains a fragment of real truth; and in this they are analogous to the attempts of adults, which are looked at as strokes of genius, at solving the problems of the universe which are too hard for human comprehension. What is correct and hits the mark in such theories is to be explained by their origin from the components of the sexual instinct which are already stirring in the childish organism. For it is not owing to any arbitrary mental act or to chance impressions that those notions arise, but to the necessities of the child's psychosexual constitution; and this is why we can speak of sexual theories in children as being typical, and why we find the same mistaken beliefs in every child whose sexual life is accessible to us.

The first of these theories starts out from the neglect of the differences between the sexes on which I laid stress at the beginning of this paper [p. 189f.] as being characteristic of children. It consists in *attributing to everyone, including females, the possession of a penis*, such as the boy knows from his own body. It is precisely in what we must regard as the 'normal' sexual constitution that already in childhood the penis is the leading erotogenic zone and the chief auto-erotic sexual object; and the boy's estimate of its value is logically reflected in his inability to imagine a person like himself who is without this essential constituent. When a small boy sees his little sister's genitals, what he says shows that his prejudice is already strong enough to falsify his perception.[1] He does not comment on the absence of a penis, but *invariably* says, as though by way of consolation and to put things right: 'Her ——'s still quite small. But when she gets bigger it'll grow all right.'[2] The idea of a woman with a penis returns in later life, in the dreams of adults: the dreamer, in a state of nocturanl sexual excitation, will throw a woman down, strip her and prepare for intercourse – and then, in place of the female genitals, he beholds a well-developed penis and breaks off the dream and the excitation. The numerous hermaphrodites of classical antiquity faithfully reproduce this idea, universally held in childhood; one may observe that to most normal people they cause no offence, while the real hermaphroditic formations of the genitals which are permitted to occur by Nature nearly always excite the greatest abhorrence.

If this idea of a woman with a penis becomes 'fixated' in an individual when he is a child, resisting all the influences of later life and making him as a man unable to do without a penis in his sexual object, then, although in other respects he may lead a normal sexual life, he is bound to become a homo-sexual, and will seek his sexual object among men who, owing to some other physical and mental characteristics, remind him of women.[3] Real women, when he comes to know them later, remain impossible as sexual objects for him, because they lack the essential sexual attraction; indeed, in connection with another impression of his childhood life, they may even become abhorrent to him. The child, having been mainly dominated by excitations in the penis, will usually have

1. [This 'falsified perception', or, as Freud afterwards named it, this 'denial' or 'disavowal', was very much later to become the basis of important theoretical discussions. Cf. in particular the paper on 'Fetishism' (1927e), p. 348ff. below. See also an editorial footnote to 'The Infantile Genital Organization' (1923e), p. 310 *n*. 1. below.]

2. [Cf. an almost identical remark by 'Little Hans' (1909b), *P.F.L.*, 8, 175, also quoted in the last paper, p. 177 above.]

3. [Freud returned to this in Section III of his case history of 'Little Hans', *P.F.L.*, 8, 267-8.]

obtained pleasure by stimulating it with his hand; he will have been detected in this by his parents or nurse and terrorized by the threat of having his penis cut off. The effect of this 'threat of castration' is proportionate to the value set upon that organ and is quite extraordinarily deep and persistent. Legends and myths testify to the upheaval in the child's emotional life and to the horror which is linked with the castration complex[1] – a complex which is subsequently remembered by consciousness with corresponding reluctance. The woman's genitalia, when seen later on, are regarded as a mutilated organ and recall this threat, and they therefore arouse horror instead of pleasure in the homosexual. This reaction cannot be altered in any way when the homosexual comes to learn from science that his childish assumption that women had a penis too was not so far wrong after all. Anatomy has recognized the clitoris within the female pudenda as being an organ that is homologous to the penis; and the physiology of the sexual processes has been able to add that this small penis which does not grow any bigger behaves in fact during childhood like a real and genuine penis – that it becomes the seat of excitations which lead to its being touched, that its excitability gives the little girl's sexual activity a masculine character and that a wave of repression in the years of puberty is needed in order for this masculine sexuality to be discarded and the woman to emerge. Since the sexual function of many women is crippled, whether by their obstinate clinging on to this excitability of the clitoris so that they remain anaesthetic in intercourse, or by such excessive repression occurring that its operation is partly replaced by hysterical compensatory formations – all this seems to show that there is some truth in the infantile sexual theory that women, like men, possess a penis.[2]

It is easy to observe that little girls fully share their brother's

1. [This is the first published appearance of the term. The idea of a threat of castration occurs in a single sentence in *The Interpretation of Dreams* (1900a), *P.F.L.*, 4, 781.]

2. [Cf. *Three Essays* (1905d), pp. 143-4 above.]

opinion of it. They develop a great interest in that part of the boy's body. But this interest promptly falls under the sway of envy. They feel themselves unfairly treated. They make attempts to micturate in the posture that is made possible for boys by their possessing a big penis; and when a girl declares that 'she would rather be a boy', we know what deficiency her wish is intended to put right.

If children could follow the hints given by the excitation of the penis they would get a little nearer to the solution of their problem. That the baby grows inside the mother's body is obviously not a sufficient explanation. How does it get inside? What starts its development? That the father has something to do with it seems likely; he says that the baby is *his* baby as well.[1] Again, the penis certainly has a share, too, in these mysterious happenings; the excitation in it which accompanies all these activities of the child's thoughts bears witness to this. Attached to this excitation are impulsions which the child cannot account for – obscure urges to do something violent, to press in, to knock to pieces, to tear open a hole somewhere. But when the child thus seems to be well on the way to postulating the existence of the vagina and to concluding that an incursion of this kind by his father's penis into his mother is the act by means of which the baby is created in his mother's body – at this juncture his inquiry is broken off in helpless perplexity. For standing in its way is his theory that his mother possesses a penis just as a man does, and the existence of the cavity which receives the penis remains undiscovered by him. It is not hard to guess that the lack of success of his intellectual efforts makes it easier for him to reject and forget them. This brooding and doubting, however, becomes the prototype of all later intellectual work directed towards the solution of problems, and the first failure has a crippling effect on the child's whole future.[2]

1. Cf. the 'Analysis of a Five-Year-Old Boy' [*P.F.L.*, **8**, 290–91].
2. [Freud quoted this last sentence in a footnote near the end of Chapter I of his study of Leonardo (1910*c*), where this same subject is

Their ignorance of the vagina also makes it possible for children to believe in the second of their sexual theories. If the baby grows in the mother's body and is then removed from it, this can only happen along the one possible pathway – the anal aperture. *The baby must be evacuated like a piece of excrement, like a stool.* When, in later childhood, the same question is the subject of solitary reflection or of a discussion between two children, the explanations probably arrived at are that the baby emerges from the navel, which comes open, or that the abdomen is slit up and the baby taken out – which was what happened to the wolf in the story of Little Red Riding-Hood. These theories are expressed aloud and also consciously remembered later on; they no longer contain anything objectionable. These same children have by then completely forgotten that in earlier years they believed in another theory of birth, which is now obstructed by the repression of the anal sexual components that has meanwhile occurred. At that time a motion was something which could be talked about in the nursery without shame. The child was still not so distant from his constitutional coprophilic inclinations. There was nothing degraded about coming into the world like a heap of faeces, which had not yet been condemned by feelings of disgust. The cloacal theory, which, after all, is valid for so many animals, was the most natural theory, and it alone could obtrude upon the child as being a probable one.

This being so, however, it was only logical that the child should refuse to grant women the painful prerogative of giving birth to children. If babies are born through the anus, then a man can give birth just as well as a woman. It is therefore possible for a boy to imagine that he, too, has children of his own, without there being any need to accuse him on that account of having feminine inclinations.[1] He is merely giving

discussed. The question had in fact already been approached by Freud (see above, pp. 177–8).]

1. [Cf. a similar remark in the case history of 'Little Hans', in a

evidence in this of the anal erotism which is still alive in him.

If the cloacal theory of birth is preserved in consciousness during later years of childhood, as occasionally happens, it is accompanied too by a solution – no longer, it is true, a primary one – of the problem of the origin of babies. Here it is like being in a fairy story; one eats some particular thing and gets a child from it. This infantile theory of birth is revived in cases of insanity. A manic woman, for instance, will lead the visiting doctor to a little heap of faeces which she has deposited in a corner of her cell, and say to him with a laugh: 'That's the baby I had today.'

The third of the typical sexual theories arises in children if, through some chance domestic occurrence, they become witnesses of sexual intercourse between their parents. Their perceptions of what is happening are bound, however, to be only very incomplete. Whatever detail it may be that comes under their observation – whether it is the relative positions of the two people, or the noises they make, or some accessory circumstance – children arrive in every case at the same conclusion. They adopt what may be called a *sadistic view of coition*. They see it as something that the stronger participant is forcibly inflicting on the weaker, and they (especially boys) compare it to the romping familiar to them from their childish experience – romping which, incidentally, is not without a dash of sexual excitation. I have not been able to ascertain that children recognize this behaviour which they have witnessed between their parents as the missing link needed for solving the problem of babies; it appears more often that the connection is overlooked by them for the very reason that they have interpreted the act of love as an act of violence. But this view of it itself gives an impression of being a return of

footnote, *P.F.L.*, **8**, 252 *n.*1 It was only later, especially in the analysis of the 'Wolf Man' (1918*b*), that Freud drew attention to the close connection that can exist between anal erotism and a feminine attitude. See, for instance, Section VII of that case history, *P.F.L.*, **9**, 318.]

the obscure impulse towards cruel behaviour which became attached to the excitations of the child's penis when he first began to think about the problem of where babies came from [cf. above, p. 196]. The possibility, too, cannot be excluded that this premature sadistic impulse, which might so nearly have led to the discovery of coition, itself first emerged under the influence of extremely obscure memories of parental intercourse, for which the child had obtained the material – though at the time he made no use of it – while he was still in his first years and was sharing his parents' bedroom.[1]

The sadistic theory of coitus which, taken in isolation, is misleading where it might have provided confirmatory evidence, is, once again, the expression of one of the innate components of the sexual instinct, any of which may be strongly marked to a greater or lesser degree in each particular child. For this reason the theory is correct up to a certain point; it has in part divined the nature of the sexual act and the 'sex-battle' that precedes it. Not infrequently, too, the child is in a position to support this view by accidental observations which he understands in part correctly, but also in part incorrectly and indeed in a reversed sense. In many marriages the wife does in fact recoil from her husband's embraces, which bring her no pleasure, but the risk of a fresh pregnancy. And so the child who is believed to be asleep (or who is pretending to be asleep) may receive an impression from his mother which he can only interpret as meaning that she is defending herself against an act of violence. At other times the whole marriage offers an observant child the spectacle of an unceasing quarrel, expressed in loud words and unfriendly gestures; so that he need not be surprised if the quarrel is

1. Restif de la Bretonne, in his autobiographical work *Monsieur Nicolas* (1794), tells a story of an impression he received at the age of four, which confirms this sadistic misunderstanding of coitus. – [This question came up for lengthy discussion some ten years later, in Freud's 'Wolf Man' case history. (See in particular the opening pages of Section V, *P.F.L.*, **9**, 281ff.)]

carried on at night as well, and finally settled by the same method which he himself is accustomed to use in his relations with his brothers and sisters or playmates.

Moreover, if the child discovers spots of blood in his mother's bed or on her underclothes, he regards it as a confirmation of his view. It proves to him that his father has made another similar assault on his mother during the night (whereas we should rather take the fresh spots of blood to mean that there had been a temporary cessation of sexual intercourse). Much of the otherwise inexplicable 'horror of blood' shown by neurotics finds its explanation from this connection. Once again, however, the child's mistake contains a fragment of truth. For in certain familiar circumstances a trace of blood is in fact judged as a sign that sexual intercourse has been begun.

A question connected somewhat indirectly with the insoluble problem of where babies come from also engages the child – the question as to the nature and content of the state called 'being married'; and he answers the question differently according as his chance perceptions in relation to his parents have coincided with instincts of his own which are still pleasurably coloured. All that these answers seem to have in common is that the child promises himself pleasurable satisfaction from being married and supposes that it involves a disregard of modesty. The notion I have most frequently met with is that *each of the married couple urinates in front of the other*. A variation of this, which sounds as if it was meant to indicate a greater knowledge symbolically, is that *the man urinates into the woman's chamber-pot*. In other instances the meaning of marriage is supposed to be that *the two people show their behinds to each other* (without being ashamed). In one case, in which education had succeeded in postponing sexual knowledge especially late, a fourteen-year-old girl, who had already begun to menstruate, arrived from the books she had read at the idea that being married consisted in a 'mixing of blood'; and since her own sister had not yet started her periods, the lustful girl made an assault on a female visitor who had confessed that she was just then menstruating, so as to force her to take part in this 'blood-mixing'.

Childhood opinions about the nature of marriage, which are not seldom retained by conscious memory, have great significance for the symptomatology of later neurotic illness. At first they find expression in children's games in which each child does with another whatever it is that in his view constitutes being married; and then, later on, the wish to be married may choose the infantile form of expression and so make its appearance in a phobia which is at first sight unrecognizable, or in some corresponding symptom.[1]

These seem to be the most important of the typical sexual theories that children produce spontaneously in early childhood, under the sole influence of the components of the sexual instinct. I know that I have not succeeded in making my material complete or in establishing an unbroken connection between it and the rest of infantile life. But I may add one or two supplementary observations, whose absence would otherwise be noticed by any well-informed person. Thus, for instance, there is the significant theory that a baby is got by a kiss – a theory which obviously betrays the predominance of the erotogenic zone of the mouth. In my experience this theory is exclusively feminine and is sometimes found to be pathogenic in girls whose sexual researches have been subjected to exceedingly strong inhibitions in childhood. Again, through an accidental observation, one of my women patients happened upon the theory of the 'couvade', which, as is well known, is a general custom among some races and is probably intended to contradict the doubts as to paternity which can never be entirely overcome. A rather eccentric uncle of this patient's stayed at home for days after the birth of his child and received visitors in his dressing-gown, from which she concluded that both parents took part in the birth of their children and had to go to bed.

1. The games that are most significant for subsequent neuroses are playing at 'doctor' and at 'father and mother'.

In about their tenth or eleventh year, children get to hear about sexual matters. A child who has grown up in a comparatively uninhibited social atmosphere, or who has found better opportunities for observation, tells other children what he knows, because this makes him feel mature and superior. What children learn in this way is mostly correct – that is, the existence of the vagina and its purpose is revealed to them; but otherwise the explanations they get from one another are not infrequently mixed with false ideas and burdened with remains of the older infantile sexual theories. They are scarcely ever complete or sufficient to solve the primordial problem. Just as formerly it was ignorance of the vagina which prevented the whole process from being understood, so now is it ignorance of the semen. The child cannot guess that another substance besides urine is excreted from the male sexual organ, and occasionally an 'innocent' girl on her wedding night is still indignant at her husband 'urinating into her'. This information acquired in the years of pre-puberty is followed by a new access of sexual researches by the child. But the theories which he now produces no longer have the typical and original stamp which was characteristic of the primary theories of early childhood as long as the infantile sexual components could find expression in theories in an uninhibited and unmodified fashion. The child's later intellectual efforts at solving the puzzles of sex have not seemed to me worth collecting, nor can they have much claim to a pathogenic significance. Their multiplicity is of course mainly dependent on the nature of the enlightenment which a child receives; but their significance consists rather in the fact that they re-awaken the traces, which have since become unconscious, of his first period of sexual interest; so that it is not infrequent for masturbatory sexual activity and some degree of emotional detachment from his parents to be linked up with them. Hence the condemnatory judgement of teachers that enlightenment of such a kind at this age 'corrupts' children.

Let me give a few examples to show what elements often enter into these late speculations by children about sexual life. A girl had heard from her schoolmates that the husband gives his wife an egg, which she hatches out in her body. A boy, who had also heard of the egg, identified it with the testicle, which [in German] is vulgarly called by the same word [*Ei*]; and he racked his brains to make out how the contents of the scrotum could be constantly renewed. The information given seldom goes far enough to prevent important uncertainties about sexual events. Thus a girl may arrive at an expectation that intercourse occurs on one occasion only, but that it lasts a very long time – twenty-four hours – and that all the successive babies come from this single occasion. One would suppose that this child had got her knowledge of the reproductive process from certain insects; but it turned out that this was not so and that the theory emerged as a spontaneous creation. Other girls are ignorant of the period of gestation, the life in the womb, and assume that the baby appears immediately after the first night of intercourse. Marcel Prévost has turned this girlhood mistake into an amusing story in one of his '*Lettres de femmes*'.[1] These later sexual researches of children, or of adolescents who have been retarded at the stage of childhood, offer an almost inexhaustible theme and one which is perhaps not uninteresting in general; but it is more remote from my present interest. I must only lay stress on the fact that in this field children produce many incorrect ideas in order to contradict older and better knowledge which has become unconscious and is repressed.

The way in which children react to the information they are given also has its significance. In some, sexual repression has gone so far that they will not listen to anything; and these succeed in remaining ignorant even in later life – *apparently* ignorant, at least – until, in the psychoanalysis of neurotics, the knowledge that originated in early childhood

1. [Cf. Prévost, 'La nuit de Raymonde', *Nouvelles lettres de femmes*.]

comes to light. I also know of two boys between ten and thirteen years old who, though it is true that they listened to the sexual information, rejected it with the words: '*Your* father and other people may do something like that, but I know for certain *my* father never would.'[1] But however widely children's later reactions to the satisfaction of their sexual curiosity may vary, we may assume that in the first years of childhood their attitude was absolutely uniform, and we may feel certain that at that time all of them tried most eagerly to discover what it was that their parents did with each other so as to produce babies.

1. [This anecdote is repeated, with some further remarks on the present subject, in the paper on a special type of object-choice (1910*h*), p. 237 below.]

CHARACTER AND ANAL EROTISM
(1908)

EDITOR'S NOTE

CHARAKTER UND ANALEROTIK

(A) German Editions:

1908   *Psychiat.-neurol. Wschr.*, **9** (52) [March], 465–7.
1924   *Gesammelte Schriften*, **5**, 261–7.
1941   *Gesammelte Werke*, **7**, 203–9.

(B) English Translations:

'Character and Anal Erotism'

1924   *Collected Papers*, **2**, 45–50. (Tr. R. C. McWatters.)
1959   *Standard Edition*, **9**, 167–75.

The present edition is a corrected reprint of the *Standard Edition* version, with some editorial changes.

The theme of this paper has now become so familiar that it is difficult to realize the astonishment and indignation which it aroused on its first publication. The paper was no doubt partly stimulated by the analysis of the 'Rat Man' (1909*d*), which had been concluded shortly before, though the special connection between anal erotism and obsessional neurosis was only brought out some years later, in 'The Disposition to Obsessional Neurosis' (1913*i*). Another case history, that of the 'Wolf Man' (1918*b* [1914]), led to a further expansion of the topic dealt with here – the paper 'On Transformations of Instinct' (1917*c*), p. 295ff. below.

There are not many accounts by Freud of the nature of 'character' and the mechanism of its formation. Apart from the present paper, the subject is specifically dealt with in two later works included in the present volume: 'On Transformations of Instinct' (1917c) and 'Libidinal Types' (1931a), pp. 295ff. and 361ff. below. It is also treated in 'Some Character-Types Met with in Psychoanalytic Work' (1916d). Among other accounts may be mentioned a passage near the end of the Three Essays (1905d), pp. 163-4 above, some remarks in the paper on 'The Disposition to Obsessional Neurosis' (1913i), and especially a discussion in the first half of Chapter III of The Ego and the Id (1923b), the gist of which is repeated in Lecture 32 of the New Introductory Lectures (1933a).

CHARACTER AND ANAL EROTISM

AMONG those whom we try to help by our psychoanalytic efforts we often come across a type of person who is marked by the possession of a certain set of character-traits, while at the same time our attention is drawn to the behaviour in his childhood of one of his bodily functions and the organ concerned in it. I cannot say at this date what particular occasions began to give me an impression that there was some organic connection between this type of character and this behaviour of an organ, but I can assure the reader that no theoretical expectation played any part in that impression.

Accumulated experience has so much strengthened my belief in the existence of such a connection that I am venturing to make it the subject of a communication.

The people I am about to describe are noteworthy for a regular combination of the three following characteristics. They are especially *orderly*, *parsimonious* and *obstinate*. Each of these words actually covers a small group or series of inter-related character-traits. 'Orderly'[1] covers the notion of bodily cleanliness, as well as of conscientiousness in carrying out small duties and trustworthiness. Its opposite would be 'untidy' and 'neglectful'. Parsimony may appear in the exaggerated form of avarice; and obstinacy can go over into defiance, to which rage and revengefulness are easily joined. The two latter qualities – parsimony and obstinacy – are linked with each other more closely than they are with the first – with orderliness. They are, also, the more constant element

1. ['*Ordentlich*' in German. The original meaning of the word is 'orderly'; but it has become greatly extended in use. It can be the equivalent of such English terms as 'correct', 'tidy', 'cleanly', 'trustworthy', as well as 'regular', 'decent' and 'proper', in the more colloquial senses of those words.]

of the whole complex. Yet it seems to me incontestable that all three in some way belong together.

It is easy to gather from these people's early childhood history that they took a comparatively long time to overcome their infantile *incontinentia alvi* [faecal incontinence], and that even in later childhood they suffered from isolated failures of this function. As infants, they seem to have belonged to the class who refuse to empty their bowels when they are put on the pot because they derive a subsidiary pleasure from defaecating;[1] for they tell us that even in somewhat later years they enjoyed holding back their stool, and they remember – though more readily about their brothers and sisters than about themselves – doing all sorts of unseemly things with the faeces that had been passed. From these indications we infer that such people are born with a sexual constitution in which the erotogenicity of the anal zone is exceptionally strong. But since none of these weaknesses and idiosyncrasies are to be found in them once their childhood has been passed, we must conclude that the anal zone had lost its erotogenic significance in the course of development; and it is to be suspected that the regularity with which this triad of properties is present in their character may be brought into relation with the disappearance of their anal erotism.

I know that no one is prepared to believe in a state of things so long as it appears to be unintelligible and to offer no angle from which an explanation can be attempted. But we can at least bring the underlying factors nearer to our understanding by the help of the postulates I laid down in my *Three Essays on the Theory of Sexuality* in 1905.[2] I there attempted to show that the sexual instinct of man is highly complex and is put together from contributions made by numerous constituents

1. Cf. Freud, *Three Essays on the Theory of Sexuality* (1905*d*), p. 103 above.

2. [The material in the present paragraph is derived mainly from Section 5 of the first essay and Section 1 of the second (pp. 82ff. and 92ff. above).]

and component instincts. Important contributions to 'sexual excitation' are furnished by the peripheral excitations of certain specially designated parts of the body (the genitals, mouth, anus, urethra), which therefore deserve to be described as 'erotogenic zones'. But the amounts of excitation coming in from these parts of the body do not all undergo the same vicissitudes, nor is the fate of all of them the same at every period of life. Generally speaking, only a part of them is made use of in sexual life; another part is deflected from sexual aims and directed towards others – a process which deserves the name of 'sublimation'. During the period of life which may be called the period of 'sexual latency' – i.e. from the completion of the fifth year[1] to the first manifestations of puberty (round about the eleventh year) – reaction-formations, or counter-forces, such as shame, disgust and morality, are created in the mind. They are actually formed at the expense of the excitations proceeding from the erotogenic zones, and they rise like dams to oppose the later activity of the sexual instincts. Now anal erotism is one of the components of the [sexual] instinct which, in the course of development and in accordance with the education demanded by our present civilization, have become unserviceable for sexual aims. It is therefore plausible to suppose that these character-traits of orderliness, parsimony and obstinacy, which are so often prominent in people who were formerly anal erotics, are to be regarded as the first and most constant results of the sublimation of anal erotism.[2]

1. [In the German editions before 1924 this read 'from the completion of the fourth year'.]

2. Since it is precisely the remarks in my *Three Essays on the Theory of Sexuality* about the anal erotism of infants that have particularly scandalized uncomprehending readers, I venture at this point to interpolate an observation for which I have to thank a very intelligent patient. 'A friend of mine', he told me, 'who has read your *Three Essays on the Theory of Sexuality*, was talking about the book. He entirely agreed with it, but there was one passage, which – though of course he accepted and understood its meaning like that of the rest

The intrinsic necessity for this connection is not clear, of course, even to myself. But I can make some suggestions which may help towards an understanding of it. Cleanliness, orderliness and trustworthiness give exactly the impression of a reaction-formation against an interest in what is unclean

---

– struck him as so grotesque and comic that he sat down and laughed over it for a quarter of an hour. This passage ran: "One of the clearest signs of subsequent eccentricity or nervousness is to be seen when a baby obstinately refuses to empty his bowels when he is put on the pot – that is, when his nurse wants him to – and holds back that function till he himself chooses to exercise it. He is naturally not concerned with dirtying the bed, he is only anxious not to miss the subsidiary pleasure attached to defaecating." [Cf. p. 103 above.] The picture of this baby sitting on the pot and deliberating whether he would put up with a restriction of this kind upon his personal freedom of will, and feeling anxious, too, not to miss the pleasure attached to defaecating, – this caused my friend the most intense amusement. About twenty minutes afterwards, as we were having some cocoa, he suddenly remarked without any preliminary: "I say, seeing the cocoa in front of me has suddenly made me think of an idea that I always had when I was a child. I used always to pretend to myself that I was the cocoa-manufacturer Van Houten" (he pronounced the name Van 'Hauten' [i.e. with the first syllable rhyming with the English word 'cow']) "and that I possessed a great secret for the manufacture of this cocoa. Everybody was trying to get hold of this secret that was a boon to humanity but I kept it carefully to myself. I don't know why I should have hit specially upon Van Houten. Probably his advertisements impressed me more than any others." Laughing, and without thinking at the time that my words had any deep meaning, I said: "Wann haut'n die Mutter?" ['When does mother smack?' The first two words in the German phrase are pronounced exactly like 'Van Houten'.] It was only later that I realized that my pun in fact contained the key to the whole of my friend's sudden childhood recollection, and I then recognized it as a brilliant example of a screen-phantasy. My friend's phantasy, while keeping to the situation actually involved (the nutritional process) and making use of phonetic associations ("Kakao" ['cocoa'. –. 'Kaka' is the common German nursery word for 'faeces'] and "Wann haut'n"), pacified his sense of guilt by making a complete reversal in the content of his recollection: there was a displacement from the back of the body to the front, excreting food became taking food in, and something that was shameful and had to be concealed became a secret that was a

and disturbing and should not be part of the body. ('Dirt is matter in the wrong place.')[1] To relate obstinacy to an interest in defaecation would seem no easy task; but it should be remembered that even babies can show self-will about parting with their stool, as we have seen above [p. 210], and that it is a general practice in children's upbringing to administer painful stimuli to the skin of the buttocks – which is linked up with the erotogenic anal zone – in order to break their obstinacy and make them submissive. An invitation to a caress of the anal zone is still used today, as it was in ancient times, to express defiance or defiant scorn, and thus in reality signifies an act of tenderness that has been overtaken by repression. An exposure of the buttocks represents a softening down of this spoken invitation into a gesture; in Goethe's *Götz von Berlichingen* both words and gestures are introduced at the most appropriate point as an expression of defiance.[2]

The connections between the complexes of interest in money and of defaecation, which seem so dissimilar, appear to be the most extensive of all. Every doctor who has practised psychoanalysis knows that the most refractory and long-standing cases of what is described as habitual constipation in neurotics can be cured by that form of treatment. This is less surprising if we remember that that function has shown itself similarly amenable to hypnotic suggestion. But in psycho-analysis one only achieves this result if one deals with the patients' money complex and induces them to bring it into consciousness with all its connections. It might be supposed

---

boon to humanity. I was interested to see how, only a quarter of an hour after my friend had fended the phantasy off (though, it is true, in the comparatively mild form of raising an objection on formal grounds), he was, quite involuntarily, presented with the most con-vincing evidence by his own unconscious.'

1. [This sentence is in English in the original.]
2. [The scene occurs in Act III, when Götz is summoned by a Herald to surrender. In the later, acting versions of the play (which Goethe revised several times) the words and gesture are toned down.]

that the neurosis is here only following an indication of common usage in speech, which calls a person who keeps too careful a hold on his money 'dirty' or 'filthy'. But this explanation would be far too superficial. In reality, wherever archaic modes of thought have predominated or persist – in the ancient civilizations, in myths, fairy tales and superstitions, in unconscious thinking, in dreams and in neuroses – money is brought into the most intimate relationship with dirt. We know that the gold which the devil gives his paramours turns into excrement after his departure, and the devil is certainly nothing else than the personification of the repressed unconscious instinctual life.[1] We also know about the superstition which connects the finding of treasure with defaecation, and everyone is familiar with the figure of the 'shitter of ducats [*Dukatenscheisser*]'.[2] Indeed, even according to ancient Babylonian doctrine gold is 'the faeces of Hell' (Mammon = *ilu manman*[3]). Thus in following the usage of language, neurosis, here as elsewhere, is taking words in their original, significant sense, and where it appears to be using a word figuratively it is usually simply restoring its old meaning.

It is possible that the contrast between the most precious substance known to men and the most worthless, which they reject as waste matter ('refuse'[4]), has led to this specific identification of gold with faeces.

Yet another circumstance facilitates this equation in neurotic thought. The original erotic interest in defaecation is, as we know, destined to be extinguished in later years. In those

1. Compare hysterical possession and demoniac epidemics. [Freud discussed this at considerable length in Part III of his paper 'A Seventeenth-Century Demonological Neurosis' (1923*d*).]

2. [A term vulgarly used for a wealthy spendthrift.]

3. Cf. Jeremias [1904*a*, 115 *n*.], 2nd ed., 1906, 216, and (1905, 96): '"Mamon" ("Mammon" is "Manman" in Babylonian and is another name for Nergal, the God of the Underworld. According to Oriental mythology, which has passed over into popular legends and fairy tales, gold is the excrement of Hell; see Jeremias [1904*b*], p. 16 *n*. 1.'

4. [In English in the original.]

years the interest in money makes its appearance as a new interest which had been absent in childhood. This makes it easier for the earlier impulsion, which is in process of losing its aim, to be carried over to the newly emerging aim.

If there is any basis in fact for the relation posited here between anal erotism and this triad of character-traits, one may expect to find no very marked degree of 'anal character' in people who have retained the anal zone's erotogenic character in adult life, as happens, for instance, with certain homosexuals. Unless I am much mistaken, the evidence of experience tallies quite well on the whole with this inference.

We ought in general to consider whether other character-complexes, too, do not exhibit a connection with the excitations of particular erotogenic zones. At present I only know of the intense 'burning' ambition of people who earlier suffered from enuresis.[1] We can at any rate lay down a formula for the way in which character in its final shape is formed out of the constituent instincts: the permanent character-traits are either unchanged prolongations of the original instincts, or sublimations of those instincts, or reaction-formations against them.[2]

1. [The connection between urethral erotism and ambition seems to find its first mention here. Freud occasionally returned to the point, e.g. in a footnote added in 1920 to the *Three Essays* (1905*d*), above, p. 164. In a long footnote to Chapter III of *Civilization and its Discontents* (1930*a*) he brought the present finding into connection with his two other main lines of thought concerning enuresis – its symbolic association with fire and its importance as an infantile equivalent of masturbation. See also the still later paper on 'The Acquisition and Control of Fire' (1932*a*).]

2. [The present is one of Freud's few contributions to the subject of characterology – see the Editor's Note, p. 208 above, where further references are given.]

FAMILY ROMANCES
(1909 [1908])

EDITOR'S NOTE

DER FAMILIENROMAN DER NEUROTIKER

(A) German Editions:

(1908   Probable date of composition.)

1909   In O. Rank, *Der Mythus von der Geburt des Helden*, 64–8, Leipzig and Vienna: Deuticke. (1922, 2nd ed., 82–6.)

1931   *Neurosenlehre und Technik*, 300–304.

1934   *Gesammelte Schriften*, **12**, 367–71.

1941   *Gesammelte Werke*, **7**, 227–31.

(B) English Translations:

1913   In Rank, *Myth of the Birth of the Hero, J. Nerv. Ment. Dis.*, **40**, 668–71, 718–19 (Tr. S. E. Jelliffe, F. Robbins.)

1914   The same, in volume form, 63–8. New York: Nervous and Mental Diseases Publishing Co.

'Family Romances'

1950   *Collected Papers*, **5**, 74–8. (Tr. James Strachey.)

1959   *Standard Edition*, **9**, 235–41.

The present edition is a reprint of the *Standard Edition* version, with one or two editorial modifications.

When this first appeared, in Rank's book, it bore no heading of any kind and did not form a separate section. It was simply introduced into the course of Rank's argument with a few words of acknowledgement. The work was only given a title in German when it was first reprinted. Since the preface to Rank's book is dated 'Christmas, 1908', Freud's contribution was probably written in that year. But the idea of these 'family romances', and even their name, had long been in his mind – though at first he attributed them specially to paranoics – for he mentioned them in 1897 and 1898 in his letters to Fliess (Freud, 1950a).

FAMILY ROMANCES

THE liberation of an individual, as he grows up, from the authority of his parents is one of the most necessary though one of the most painful results brought about by the course of his development. It is quite essential that that liberation should occur and it may be presumed that it has been to some extent achieved by everyone who has reached a normal state. Indeed, the whole progress of society rests upon the opposition between successive generations. On the other hand, there is a class of neurotics whose condition is recognizably determined by their having failed in this task.

For a small child his parents are at first the only authority and the source of all belief. The child's most intense and most momentous wish during these early years is to be like his parents (that is, the parent of his own sex) and to be big like his father and mother. But as intellectual growth increases, the child cannot help discovering by degrees the category to which his parents belong. He gets to know other parents and compares them with his own, and so acquires the right to doubt the incomparable and unique quality which he had attributed to them. Small events in the child's life which make him feel dissatisfied afford him provocation for beginning to criticize his parents, and for using, in order to support his critical attitude, the knowledge which he has acquired that other parents are in some respects preferable to them. The psychology of the neuroses teaches us that, among other factors, the most intense impulses of sexual rivalry contribute to this result. A feeling of being slighted is obviously what constitutes the subject-matter of such provocations. There are only too many occasions on which a child is slighted, or at least *feels* he has been slighted, on which he feels he is not receiving the whole of his parents' love, and, most of all, on

which he feels regrets at having to share it with brothers and
sisters. His sense that his own affection is not being fully
reciprocated then finds a vent in the idea, often consciously
recollected later from early childhood, of being a step-child
or an adopted child. People who have not developed neuroses
very frequently remember such occasions, on which   usually
as a result of something they have read – they interpreted and
responded to their parent's hostile behaviour in this fashion.
But here the influence of sex is already in evidence, for a boy
is far more inclined to feel hostile impulses towards his father
than towards his mother and has a far more intense desire to
get free from *him* than from *her*. In this respect the imagination
of girls is apt to show itself much weaker. These consciously
remembered mental impulses of childhood embody the factor
which enables us to understand the nature of myths.

The later stage in the development of the neurotic's
estrangement from his parents, begun in this manner, might
be described as 'the neurotic's family romance'. It is seldom
remembered consciously but can almost always be revealed
by psychoanalysis. For a quite peculiarly marked imaginative
activity is one of the essential characteristics of neurotics and
also of all comparatively highly gifted people. This activity
emerges first in children's play, and then, starting roughly
from the period before puberty, takes over the topic of family
relations. A characteristic example of this peculiar imaginative
activity is to be seen in the familiar day-dreaming[1] which
persists far beyond puberty. If these day-dreams are carefully
examined, they are found to serve as the fulfilment of wishes
and as a correction of actual life. They have two principal
aims, an erotic and an ambitious one – though an erotic aim
is usually concealed behind the latter too. At about the period
I have mentioned, then, the child's imagination becomes
engaged in the task of getting free from the parents of whom

1. Cf. 'Hysterical Phantasies and their Relation to Bisexuality'
[1908a], where a reference will be found to the literature of the subject
[*P.F.L.*, 10, 87].

he now has a low opinion and of replacing them by others, who, as a rule, are of higher social standing. He will make use in this connection of any opportune coincidences from his actual experience, such as his becoming acquainted with the Lord of the Manor or some landed proprietor if he lives in the country or with some member of the aristocracy if he lives in town. Chance occurrences of this kind arouse the child's envy, which finds expression in a phantasy in which both his parents are replaced by others of better birth. The technique used in developing phantasies like this (which are, of course, conscious at this period) depends upon the ingenuity and the material which the child has at his disposal. There is also the question of whether the phantasies are worked out with greater or less effort to obtain verisimilitude. This stage is reached at a time at which the child is still in ignorance of the sexual determinants of procreation.

When presently the child comes to know the difference in the parts played by fathers and mothers in their sexual relations, and realizes that '*pater semper incertus est*', while the mother is '*certissima*',[1] the family romance undergoes a curious curtailment: it contents itself with exalting the child's father, but no longer casts any doubts on his maternal origin, which is regarded as something unalterable. This second (sexual) stage of the family romance is actuated by another motive as well, which is absent in the first (asexual) stage. The child, having learnt about sexual processes, tends to picture to himself erotic situations and relations, the motive force behind this being his desire to bring his mother (who is the subject of the most intense sexual curiosity) into situations of secret infidelity and into secret love-affairs.[2] In this way the child's phantasies, which started by being, as it were, asexual, are brought up to the level of his later knowledge.

1. [An old legal tag: 'paternity is always uncertain, maternity is most certain'.]
2. [Freud returned to this in the first of his papers on the psychology of love (1910*h*), pp. 238–9 below.]

Moreover the motive of revenge and retaliation, which was in the foreground at the earlier stage, is also to be found at the later one. It is, as a rule, precisely these neurotic children who were punished by their parents for sexual naughtiness and who now revenge themselves on their parents by means of phantasies of this kind.

A younger child is very specially inclined to use imaginative stories such as these in order to rob those born before him of their prerogatives – in a way which reminds one of historical intrigues; and he often has no hesitation in attributing to his mother as many fictitious love-affairs as he himself has competitors. An interesting variant of the family romance may then appear, in which the hero and author returns to legitimacy himself while his brothers and sisters are eliminated by being bastardized. So too if there are any other particular interests at work they can direct the course to be taken by the family romance; for its many-sidedness and its great range of applicability enable it to meet every sort of requirement. In this way, for instance, the young phantasy-builder can get rid of his forbidden degree of kinship with one of his sisters if he finds himself sexually attracted by her.

If anyone is inclined to turn away in horror from this depravity of the childish heart or feels tempted, indeed, to dispute the possibility of such things, he should observe that these works of fiction, which seem so full of hostility, are none of them really so badly intended, and that they still preserve, under a slight disguise, the child's original affection for his parents. The faithlessness and ingratitude are only apparent. If we examine in detail the commonest of these imaginative romances, the replacement of both parents or of the father alone by grander people, we find that these new and aristocratic parents are equipped with attributes that are derived entirely from real recollections of the actual and humble ones; so that in fact the child is not getting rid of his father but exalting him. Indeed the whole effort at replacing the real father by a superior one is only an expression of the child's longing for the happy, vanished days when his father seemed to him the noblest and strongest of men and his mother the dearest and loveliest of women. He is turning away from the father whom he knows today to the father in whom he believed in the earlier years of his childhood; and his phantasy is no more than the expression of a regret that those happy days have gone. Thus in these phantasies the over-valuation that characterizes a child's earliest years comes into its own again. An interesting contribution to this subject is afforded by the study of dreams. We learn from their inter-pretation that even in later years, if the Emperor and Empress appear in dreams, those exalted personages stand for the dreamer's father and mother.[1] So that the child's over-valuation of his parents survives as well in the dreams of normal adults.

1. Cf. my *Interpretation of Dreams* (1900a), *P.F.L.*, 4, 470.

A SPECIAL TYPE OF CHOICE OF OBJECT MADE BY MEN

(CONTRIBUTIONS TO THE PSYCHOLOGY OF LOVE I)

(1910)

EDITOR'S NOTE

BEITRÄGE ZUR PSYCHOLOGIE DES LIEBESLEBENS I
ÜBER EINEN BESONDEREN TYPUS DER OBJEKTWAHL BEIM MANNE

(A) German Editions:

1910   *Jb. psychoan. psychopath. Forsch.*, **2** (2), 389–97. ('Beiträge zur Psychologie des Liebeslebens' I.)

1918   *S.K.S.N.*, **4**, 200–212. (2nd ed. 1922.)

1924   *Gesammelte Schriften*, **5**, 186–97.

1924   In *Beiträge zur Psychologie des Liebeslebens*, Leipzig, Vienna and Zurich: Internationaler Psychoanalytischer Verlag. (Pp. 3–14.)

1931   *Sexualtheorie und Traumlehre*, 69–80.

1943   *Gesammelte Werke*, **8**, 66–77.

(B) English Translations:

'Contributions to the Psychology of Love:
A Special Type of Choice of Object made by Men'

1925   *Collected Papers*, **4**, 192–202. (Tr. Joan Riviere.)

1957   *Standard Edition*, **11**, 163–75. (Tr. Alan Tyson.)

The present edition is a corrected reprint of the *Standard Edition* version, with a few editorial changes.

This and the two following papers, though they were written and published over a period of some years, were brought together by Freud in the fourth series of his shorter papers

(*Sammlung kleiner Schriften zur Neurosenlehre*, 4, 1918) under the collective title printed above. We learn from Ernest Jones (1955, 333) that Freud had announced his intention of writing some such work at a meeting of the Vienna Psycho-Analytical Society on 28 November 1906. The gist of the present paper was given before the same society on 19 May 1909, and discussed a week later. But it was not actually written until the early summer of the following year.

A SPECIAL TYPE OF CHOICE OF OBJECT MADE BY MEN

(CONTRIBUTIONS TO THE PSYCHOLOGY OF LOVE I)

UP till now we have left it to the creative writer to depict for us the 'necessary conditions for loving' which govern people's choice of an object, and the way in which they bring the demands of their imagination into harmony with reality. The writer can indeed draw on certain qualities which fit him to carry out such a task: above all, on a sensitivity that enables him to perceive the hidden impulses in the minds of other people, and the courage to let his own unconscious speak. But there is one circumstance which lessens the evidential value of what he has to say. Writers are under the necessity to produce intellectual and aesthetic pleasure, as well as certain emotional effects. For this reason they cannot reproduce the stuff of reality unchanged, but must isolate portions of it, remove disturbing associations, tone down the whole and fill in what is missing. These are the privileges of what is known as 'poetic licence'. Moreover they can show only slight interest in the origin and development of the mental states which they portray in their completed form. In consequence it becomes inevitable that science should concern herself with the same materials whose treatment by artists has given enjoyment to mankind for thousands of years, though her touch must be clumsier and the yield of pleasure less. These observations will, it may be hoped, serve to justify us in extending a strictly scientific treatment to the field of human love. Science is, after all, the most complete renunciation of the pleasure principle of which our mental activity is capable.

In the course of psychoanalytic treatment there are ample opportunities for collecting impressions of the way in which neurotics behave in love; while at the same time we can recall having observed or heard of similar behaviour in people of average health or even in those with outstanding qualities. When the material happens to be favourable and thus leads to an accumulation of such impressions, distinct types emerge more clearly. I will begin here with a description of one such type of object-choice – which occurs in men – since it is characterized by a number of 'necessary conditions for loving' whose combination is unintelligible, and indeed bewildering, and since it admits of a simple explanation on psychoanalytic lines.

(1) The first of these preconditions for loving can be described as positively specific: wherever it is found, the presence of the other characteristics of this type may be looked for. It may be termed the precondition that there should be 'an injured third party'; it stipulates that the person in question shall never choose as his love-object a woman who is disengaged – that is, an unmarried girl or an unattached married woman – but only one to whom another man can claim right of possession as her husband, fiancé or friend. In some cases this precondition proves so cogent that a woman can be ignored, or even rejected, so long as she does not belong to any man, but becomes the object of passionate feelings immediately she comes into one of these relationships with another man.

(2) The second precondition is perhaps a less constant one, but it is no less striking. It has to be found in conjunction with the first for the type to be realized, whereas the first precondition seems very often to occur independently as well. This second precondition is to the effect that a woman who is chaste and whose reputation is irreproachable never exercises an attraction that might raise her to the status of a love-object, but only a woman who is in some way or other of bad repute sexually, whose fidelity and reliability are open to some doubt.

This latter characteristic may vary within substantial limits, from the faint breath of scandal attaching to a married woman who is not averse to a flirtation up to the openly promiscuous way of life of a *cocotte* or of an adept in the art of love; but the men who belong to our type will not be satisfied without something of the kind. This second necessary condition may be termed, rather crudely, 'love for a prostitute'.

While the first precondition provides an opportunity for gratifying impulses of rivalry and hostility directed at the man from whom the loved woman is wrested, the second one, that of the woman's being like a prostitute, is connected with the experiencing of *jealousy*, which appears to be a necessity for lovers of this type. It is only when they are able to be jealous that their passion reaches its height and the woman acquires her full value, and they never fail to seize on an occasion that allows them to experience these most powerful emotions. What is strange is that it is not the lawful possessor of the loved one who becomes the target of this jealousy, but strangers, making their appearance for the first time, in relation to whom the loved one can be brought under suspicion. In glaring instances the lover shows no wish for exclusive possession of the woman and seems to be perfectly comfortable in the tri-angular situation. One of my patients, who had been made to suffer terribly by his lady's escapades, had no objection to her getting married, and did all he could to bring it about; in the years that followed he never showed a trace of jealousy towards her husband. Another typical patient had, it is true, been very jealous of the husband in his first love affair, and had forced the lady to stop having marital relations; but in his numerous subsequent affairs he behaved like the other mem-bers of this type and no longer regarded the lawful husband as an interference.

So much for the conditions required in the love-object. The following points describe the lover's behaviour towards the object he has chosen.

(3) In normal love the woman's value is measured by her

sexual integrity, and is reduced by any approach to the characteristic of being like a prostitute.[1] Hence the fact that women with this characteristic are considered by men of our type to be *love-objects of the highest value* seems to be a striking departure from the normal. Their love-relationships with these women are carried on with the highest expenditure of mental energy, to the exclusion of all other interests; they are felt as the only people whom it is possible to love, and the demand for fidelity which the lover makes upon himself is repeated again and again, however often it may be broken in reality. These features of the love-relationships which I am here describing show their *compulsive* nature very clearly, though that is something which is found up to a certain degree whenever anyone falls in love. But the fidelity and intensity that mark the attachment must not lead one to expect that a single love-relationship of this kind will make up the whole erotic life of the person in question or occur only once in it. On the contrary, passionate attachments of this sort are repeated with the same peculiarities – each an exact replica of the others – again and again in the lives of men of this type; in fact, owing to external events such as changes of residence and environment, the love-objects may replace one another so frequently that a *long series of them is formed*.

(4) What is most startling of all to the observer in lovers of this type is the urge they show to '*rescue*' the woman they love. The man is convinced that she is in need of him, that without him she would lose all moral control and rapidly sink to a lamentable level. He rescues her, therefore, by not giving her up. In some individual cases the idea of having to rescue her can be justified by reference to her sexual unreliability and the dangers of her social position: but it is no less

---

1. [The German '*Dirne*', here and in several other passages in this paper, is not well rendered by 'prostitute', which in English lays too much stress on the monetary side of the relation. 'Harlot' would give the sense better, if the word had not today acquired an antiquated and even Biblical colouring.]

conspicuous where there is no such basis in reality. One man of the type I am describing, who knew how to win his ladies by clever methods of seduction and subtle arguments, spared no efforts in the subsequent course of these affairs to keep the woman he was for the time being in love with on the path of 'virtue' by presenting her with tracts of his own composition.

If we survey the different features of the picture presented here – the conditions imposed on the man that his loved one should not be unattached and should be like a prostitute, the high value he sets on her, his need for feeling jealousy, his fidelity, which is nevertheless compatible with being broken down into a long series of instances, and the urge to rescue the woman – it will seem scarcely probable that they should all be derived from a single source. Yet psychoanalytic exploration into the life-histories of men of this type has no difficulty in showing that there is such a single source. The object-choice which is so strangely conditioned, and this very singular way of behaving in love, have the same psychical origin as we find in the loves of normal people. They are derived from the infantile fixation of tender feelings on the mother, and represent one of the consequences of that fixation. In normal love only a few characteristics survive which reveal unmistakably the maternal prototype of the object-choice, as, for instance, the preference shown by young men for maturer women; the detachment of libido from the mother has been effected relatively swiftly. In our type, on the other hand, the libido has remained attached to the mother for so long, even after the onset of puberty, that the maternal characteristics remain stamped on the love-objects that are chosen later, and all these turn into easily recognizable mother-surrogates. The comparison with the way in which the skull of a newly born child is shaped[1] springs to mind at this point: after a protracted labour it always takes the form of a cast of the narrow part of the mother's pelvis.

1. [In the editions before 1924 this read 'deformed'.]

We have now to show the plausibility of our assertion that the characteristic features of our type – its conditions for loving and its behaviour in love – do in fact arise from the psychical constellation connected with the mother. This would seem to be easiest where the first precondition is concerned – the condition that the woman should not be unattached, or that there should be an injured third party. It is at once clear that for the child who is growing up in the family circle the fact of the mother belonging to the father becomes an inseparable part of the mother's essence, and that the injured third party is none other than the father himself. The trait of overvaluing the loved one, and regarding her as unique and irreplaceable, can be seen to fall just as naturally into the context of the child's experience, for no one possesses more than one mother, and the relation to her is based on an event that is not open to any doubt and cannot be repeated.

If we are to understand the love-objects chosen by our type as being above all mother-surrogates, then the formation of a series of them, which seems so flatly to contradict the condition of being faithful to one, can now also be understood. We have learnt from psychoanalysis in other examples that the notion of something irreplaceable, when it is active in the unconscious, frequently appears as broken up into an endless series: endless for the reason that every surrogate nevertheless fails to provide the desired satisfaction. This is the explanation of the insatiable urge to ask questions shown by children at a certain age: they have one single question to ask, but it never crosses their lips.[1] It explains, too, the garrulity of some people affected by neurosis; they are under the pressure of a secret which is burning to be disclosed but which, despite all temptation, they never reveal.

On the other hand the second precondition for loving – the condition that the object chosen should be like a prostitute – seems energetically to oppose a derivation from the mother-

1. [This point is also made by Freud in his essay on Leonardo da Vinci (1910c), near the end of Chapter I.]

complex. The adult's conscious thought likes to regard his mother as a person of unimpeachable moral purity; and there are few ideas which he finds so offensive when they come from others, or feels as so tormenting when they spring from his own mind, as one which calls this aspect of his mother in question. This very relation of the sharpest contrast between 'mother' and 'prostitute' will however encourage us to enquire into the history of the development of these two complexes and the unconscious relation between them, since we long ago discovered that what, in the conscious, is found split into a pair of opposites often occurs in the unconscious as a unity.[1] Investigation then leads us back to the time in a boy's life at which he first gains a more or less complete knowledge of the sexual relations between adults, somewhere about the years of pre-puberty. Brutal pieces of information, which are undisguisedly intended to arouse contempt and rebelliousness, now acquaint him with the secret of sexual life and destroy the authority of adults, which appears incompatible with the revelation of their sexual activities. The aspect of these disclosures which affects the newly initiated child most strongly is the way in which they apply to his own parents. This application is often flatly rejected by him, in some such words as these: ' Your parents and other people may do something like that with one another, but my parents can't possibly do it.'[2]

As an almost invariable corollary to this 'sexual enlightenment', the boy at the same time gains a knowledge of the existence of certain women who practise sexual intercourse as a means of livelihood, and who are for this reason held in general contempt. The boy himself is necessarily far from feeling this contempt: as soon as he learns that he too can be initiated by these unfortunates into sexual life, which till then

1. [This fact had already been hinted at in Freud's Interpretation of Dreams (1900a), P.F.L., 4, 429f., and explicitly mentioned in Chapter VI of his book on jokes (1905c), P.F.L., 6, 231ff.]

2. [Cf. the last paragraph of Freud's paper on the sexual theories of children (1908c), p. 204 above.]

he accepted as being reserved exclusively for 'grown-ups', he regards them only with a mixture of longing and horror. When after this he can no longer maintain the doubt which makes his parents an exception to the universal and odious norms of sexual activity, he tells himself with cynical logic that the difference between his mother and a whore is not after all so very great, since basically they do the same thing. The enlightening information he has received has in fact awakened the memory-traces of the impressions and wishes of his early infancy, and these have led to a reactivation in him of certain mental impulses. He begins to desire his mother herself in the sense with which he has recently become acquainted, and to hate his father anew as a rival who stands in the way of this wish; he comes, as we say, under the dominance of the Oedipus complex.[1] He does not forgive his mother for having granted the favour of sexual intercourse not to himself but to his father, and he regards it as an act of unfaithfulness. If these impulses do not quickly pass, there is no outlet for them other than to run their course in phantasies which have as their subject his mother's sexual activities under the most diverse circumstances; and the consequent tension leads particularly readily to his finding relief in masturbation. As a result of the constant combined operation of the two driving forces, desire and thirst for revenge, phantasies of his mother's unfaithfulness are by far the most preferred; the lover with whom she commits her act of infidelity almost always exhibits the features of the boy's own ego, or more accurately, of his own idealized personality, grown up and so raised to a level with his father. What I have elsewhere[2] described as the 'family romance' comprises the manifold ramifications of

1. [This appears to be Freud's first published use of the actual term. The concept had, of course, long been familiar to him, and he had already spoken of the 'nuclear complex', e.g. in the paper referred to in the last footnote, see above, p. 192 and *n*. 1.]

2. In [a discussion included in] Rank's *The Myth of the Birth of the Hero* (1909) [Freud (1909*c*), p. 221ff. above].

this imaginative activity and the way in which they are inter-woven with various egoistic interests of this period of life.

Now that we have gained an insight into this piece of mental development we can no longer regard it as contradictory and incomprehensible that the precondition of the loved one's being like a prostitute should derive directly from the mother-complex. The type of male love which we have described bears the traces of this evolution and is simple to understand as a fixation on the phantasies formed by the boy in puberty – phantasies which have later after all found a way out into real life. There is no difficulty in assuming that the masturbation assiduously practised in the years of puberty has played its part in the fixation of the phantasies.

To these phantasies which have succeeded in dominating the man's love in real life, the urge to *rescue* the loved one seems to bear merely a loose and superficial relation, and one that is fully accounted for by conscious reasons. By her propensity to be fickle and unfaithful the loved one brings herself into dangerous situations, and thus it is understandable that the lover should be at pains to protect her from these dangers by watching over her virtue and counteracting her bad inclinations. However, the study of people's screen-memories, phantasies and nocturnal dreams shows that we have here a particularly felicitous 'rationalization' of an unconscious motive. a process which may be compared to a successful secondary revision of a dream. In actual fact the 'rescue-*motif*' has a meaning and history of its own, and is an independent derivative of the mother-complex, or more accurately, of the parental complex. When a child hears that he *owes his life* to his parents, or that his mother *gave him life*, his feelings of tenderness unite with impulses which strive at power and independence, and they generate the wish to return this gift to the parents and to repay them with one of equal value. It is as though the boy's defiance were to make him say: 'I want nothing from my father; I will give him back all I have cost him.' He then forms the phantasy of *rescuing his father from danger and saving his life*; in this way he puts his account square with him. This phantasy is commonly enough displaced on to the emperor, king or some other great man; after being thus distorted it becomes admissible to consciousness, and may even be made use of by creative writers. In its application to a boy's father it is the defiant meaning in the idea of rescuing which is by far the most important; where his mother is concerned it is usually its tender meaning. The mother gave the child life, and it is not easy to find a substitute of equal value for this unique gift. With a slight change of meaning, such as is easily effected in the unconscious and is comparable to the way in which in consciousness concepts shade into one another, rescuing his mother takes on the significance of giving her a child or making a child for her – needless to say, one like himself. This is not too remote from the original sense of rescuing, and the change in meaning is not an arbitrary one. His mother gave him a life – his own life – and in exchange he gives her another life, that of a child which has the greatest resemblance to himself. The son shows his gratitude by wishing to have by his mother a son who is like himself: in other words, in the rescue-phantasy he is completely identifying himself with his father. All his instincts, those of tenderness, gratitude, lustfulness, defiance and independence, find satisfaction in the single wish *to be his own father*. Even the element of danger has not been lost in the change of meaning; for the act of birth itself is the danger from which he was saved by his mother's efforts. Birth is both the first of all dangers to life and the prototype of all the later ones that cause us to feel anxiety, and the experience of birth has probably left behind in us the expression of affect which we call anxiety. Macduff of the Scottish legend, who was not born of his mother but ripped from her womb, was for that reason unacquainted with anxiety.[1]

1. [*Macbeth*, V, 7. This is Freud's first extended allusion to the relation between birth and anxiety. He dealt with it again at some length near the beginning of Lecture XXV, of the *Introductory Lectures* (1916–17), *P.F.L.*, **1**, 444–5. But his longest discussion of it will, of

Artemidorus, the dream-interpreter of antiquity, was certainly right in maintaining that the meaning of a dream depends on who the dreamer happens to be.[1] Under the laws governing the expression of unconscious thoughts, the meaning of rescuing may vary, depending on whether the author of the phantasy is a man or a woman. It can equally mean (in a man) making a child, i.e. causing it to be born, or (in a woman) giving birth oneself to a child. These various meanings of rescuing in dreams and phantasies can be recognized particularly clearly when they are found in connection with water. A man rescuing a woman from the water in a dream means that he makes her a mother, which in the light of the preceding discussion amounts to making her his own mother. A woman rescuing someone else (a child) from the water acknowledges herself in this way as the mother who bore him, like Pharaoh's daughter in the legend of Moses (Rank, 1909). At times there is also a tender meaning contained in rescue-phantasies directed towards the father. In such cases they aim at expressing the subject's wish to have his father as a son – that is, to have a son who is like his father.[2]

It is on account of all these connections between the rescue-motif and the parental complex that the urge to rescue the loved one forms an important feature of the type of loving which I have been discussing.

I do not feel that it is necessary for me to justify my method of work on this subject; as in my presentation of anal erotism [Freud (1908b), see above, p. 209ff.], so here too I have in the first place aimed at singling out from the observational

course, be found in *Inhibitions, Symptoms and Anxiety* (1926d), especially in Chapters II, VIII and XI, A (b), where his former opinions are largely revised.]

1. [Cf. a passage in Chapter II of *The Interpretation of Dreams* (1900a), and a footnote to it added in 1914, *P.F.L.*, **4**, 171 and *n*. 2.]

2. [Dreams of rescuing are mentioned in a paragraph added in 1911 to Chapter VI (E) of *The Interpretation of Dreams*, *P.F.L.*, **4**, 529.]

material extreme and sharply defined types. In both cases we find a far greater number of individuals in whom only a few features of the type can be recognized, or only features which are not distinctly marked, and it is obvious that a proper appreciation of these types will not be possible until the whole context to which they belong has been explored.[1]

1. [In a paper (1920a) written many years after the present one, Freud demonstrated the occurrence of precisely the same type of object-choice in a homosexual girl.]

ON THE UNIVERSAL TENDENCY TO DEBASEMENT IN THE SPHERE OF LOVE

(CONTRIBUTIONS TO THE PSYCHOLOGY OF LOVE II)

(1912)

EDITOR'S NOTE

BEITRÄGE ZUR PSYCHOLOGIE DES LIEBESLEBENS II
ÜBER DIE ALLGEMEINSTE ERNIEDRIGUNG DES LIEBESLEBENS

(A) GERMAN EDITIONS:

1912 *Jb. psychoan. psychopath. Forsch.*, **4** (1), 40–50. ('Beiträge zur Psychologie des Liebeslebens' II.)
1918 *S.K.S.N.*, **4**, 213–28. (2nd ed. 1922.)
1924 *Gesammelte Schriften*, **5**, 198–211.
1924 In *Beiträge zur Psychologie des Liebeslebens*, Leipzig, Vienna and Zurich: Internationaler Psychoanalytischer Verlag. (Pp. 15–28.)
1931 *Sexualtheorie und Traumlehre*, 80–95.
1943 *Gesammelte Werke*, **8**, 78–91.

(B) ENGLISH TRANSLATIONS:

'Contributions to the Psychology of Love:
The Most Prevalent Form of Degradation in Erotic Life'

1925 *Collected Papers*, **4**, 203–16. (Tr. Joan Riviere.)
1957 *Standard Edition*, **11**, 177–90. (Tr., with a different title 'On the Universal Tendency to Debasement in the Sphere of Love', Alan Tyson.)

The present edition is a corrected reprint of the *Standard Edition* version, with some editorial changes.

The discussion of the two sexual currents in the earlier part of the present paper is in effect a supplement to the *Three Essays*

(1905*d*), in the 1915 edition of which, indeed, a short summary of it was included (see p. 119 above). The analysis of psychical impotence, which occupies the central section of the paper, is Freud's principal contribution to that topic. The last part of the paper is one of the long series of his elaborations of the theme of the antagonism between civilization and instinctual life. His fullest arguments on the subject will be found in the paper on '"Civilized" Sexual Morality and Modern Nervous Illness' (1908*d*) and in the very much later *Civilization and its Discontents* (1930*a*).

ON THE UNIVERSAL TENDENCY
TO DEBASEMENT IN THE SPHERE
OF LOVE

(CONTRIBUTIONS TO THE PSYCHOLOGY
OF LOVE II)

I

IF the practising psychoanalyst asks himself on account of what disorder people most often come to him for help, he is bound to reply – disregarding the many forms of anxiety – that it is psychical impotence. This singular disturbance affects men of strongly libidinous[1] natures, and manifests itself in a refusal by the executive organs of sexuality to carry out the sexual act, although before and after they may show themselves to be intact and capable of performing the act, and although a strong psychical inclination to carry it out is present. The first clue to understanding his condition is obtained by the sufferer himself on making the discovery that a failure of this kind only arises when the attempt is made with certain individuals; whereas with others there is never any question of such a failure. He now becomes aware that it is some feature of the sexual object which gives rise to the inhibition of his male potency, and sometimes he reports that he has a feeling of an obstacle inside him, the sensation of a counter-will which successfully interferes with his conscious intention. However, he is unable to guess what this internal obstacle is and what feature of the sexual object brings it into operation. If he has had repeated experience of a failure of this kind, he is likely, by the familiar process of 'erroneous connection', to decide that the recollection of the first occasion evoked the disturbing anxiety-idea

1. ['*Libidinös*'. Here 'libidinous', as contrasted with the technical 'libidinal'.]

and so caused the failure to be repeated each time; while he derives the first occasion itself from some 'accidental' impression.

Pyschoanalytic studies of psychical impotence have already been carried out and published by several writers.[1] Every analyst can confirm the explanations provided by them from his own clinical experience. It is in fact a question of the inhibitory influence of certain psychical complexes which are withdrawn from the subject's knowledge. An incestuous fixation on mother or sister, which has never been surmounted, plays a prominent part in this pathogenic material and is its most universal content. In addition there is the influence to be considered of accidental distressing impressions connected with infantile sexual activity, and also those factors which in a general way reduce the libido that is to be directed on to the female sexual object.[2]

When striking cases of psychical impotence are exhaustively investigated by means of psychoanalysis, the following information is obtained about the psychosexual processes at work in them. Here again – as very probably in all neurotic disturbances – the foundation of the disorder is provided by an inhibition in the developmental history of the libido before it assumes the form which we take to be its normal termination. Two currents whose union is necessary to ensure a completely normal attitude in love have, in the cases we are considering, failed to combine. These two may be distinguished as the *affectionate* and the *sensual* current.

The affectionate current is the older of the two. It springs from the earliest years of childhood; it is formed on the basis of the interests of the self-preservative instinct and is directed to the members of the family and those who look after the child. From the very beginning it carries along with it contributions from the sexual instincts – components of erotic interest – which can already be seen more or less clearly even

1. Steiner (1907), Stekel (1908), Ferenczi (1908). [Freud had written a preface to Stekel's book (Freud, 1908*f*).]
2. Stekel (1908, 191ff.).

in childhood and in any event are uncovered in neurotics by psychoanalysis later on. It corresponds to *the child's primary object-choice*. We learn in this way that the sexual instincts find their first objects by attaching themselves to the valuations made by the ego-instincts, precisely in the way in which the first sexual satisfactions are experienced in attachment to the bodily functions necessary for the preservation of life.[1] The 'affection' shown by the child's parents and those who look after him, which seldom fails to betray its erotic nature ('the child is an erotic plaything'), does a very great deal to raise the contributions made by erotism to the cathexes of his ego-instincts, and to increase them to an amount which is bound to play a part in his later development, especially when certain other circumstances lend their support.

These affectionate fixations of the child persist throughout childhood, and continually carry along with them erotism, which is consequently diverted from its sexual aims. Then at the age of puberty they are joined by the powerful 'sensual' current which no longer mistakes its aims. It never fails, apparently, to follow the earlier paths and to cathect the objects of the primary infantile choice with quotas of libido that are now far stronger. Here, however, it runs up against the obstacles that have been erected in the meantime by the barrier against incest; consequently it will make efforts to pass on from these objects which are unsuitable in reality, and find a way as soon as possible to other, extraneous objects with which a real sexual life may be carried on. These new objects will still be chosen on the model (imago[2]) of the infantile ones, but in the course of time they will attract to themselves the affection

1. [The 'attachment' (or 'anaclitic') type of object-choice was discussed more fully in Freud's later paper on narcissism (1914c).]

2. [This term was not often used by Freud, especially in his later writings. He attributed it to Jung (1911, 164), in which passage Jung in turn says he partly chose the word from the title of a novel by the Swiss writer Carl Spitteler. The psychoanalytic journal *Imago* also owed its title to the same source, according to its co-founder, Hanns Sachs (1945, 63).]

that was tied to the earlier ones. A man shall leave his father and his mother – according to the biblical command – and shall cleave unto his wife; affection and sensuality are then united. The greatest intensity of sensual passion will bring with it the highest psychical valuation of the object – this being the normal overvaluation of the sexual object on the part of a man.

Two factors will decide whether this advance in the developmental path of the libido is to fail. First, there is the amount of *frustration in reality* which opposes the new object-choice and reduces its value for the person concerned. There is after all no point in embarking upon an object-choice if no choice is to be allowed at all or if there is no prospect of being able to choose anything suitable. Secondly, there is the amount of *attraction* which the infantile objects that have to be relinquished are able to exercise, and which is in proportion to the erotic cathexis attaching to them in childhood. If these two factors are sufficiently strong, the general mechanism by which the neuroses are formed comes into operation. The libido turns away from reality, is taken over by imaginative activity (the process of introversion), strengthens the images of the first sexual objects and becomes fixated to them. The obstacle raised against incest, however, compels the libido that has turned to these objects to remain in the unconscious. The masturbatory activity carried out by the sensual current, which is now part of the unconscious, makes its own contribution in strengthening this fixation. Nothing is altered in this state of affairs if the advance which has miscarried in reality is now completed in phantasy, and if in the phantasy-situations that lead to masturbatory satisfaction the original sexual objects are replaced by different ones. As a result of this substitution the phantasies become admissible to consciousness, but no progress is made in the allocation of the libido in reality. In this way it can happen that the whole of a young man's sensuality becomes tied to incestuous objects in the unconscious, or to put it another way, becomes fixated to unconscious incestuous phantasies. The result is then total impotence, which is perhaps further ensured by the simultaneous onset of an actual weakening of the organs that perform the sexual act.

Less severe conditions are required to bring about the state known specifically as psychical impotence. Here the fate of the sensual current must not be that its whole charge has to conceal itself behind the affectionate current; it must have remained sufficiently strong or uninhibited to secure a partial outlet into reality. The sexual activity of such people shows the clearest signs, however, that it has not the whole psychical driving force of the instinct behind it. It is capricious, easily disturbed, often not properly carried out, and not accompanied by much pleasure. But above all it is forced to avoid the affectionate current. A restriction has thus been placed on object-choice. The sensual current that has remained active seeks only objects which do not recall the incestuous figures forbidden to it; if someone makes an impression that might lead to a high psychical estimation of her, this impression does not find an issue in any sensual excitation but in affection which has no erotic effect. The whole sphere of love in such people remains divided in the two directions personified in art as sacred and profane (or animal) love. Where they love they do not desire and where they desire they cannot love. They seek objects which they do not need to love, in order to keep their sensuality away from the objects they love; and, in accordance with the laws of 'complexive sensitiveness'[1] and of the return of the repressed, the strange failure shown in psychical impotence makes its appearance whenever an object which has been chosen with the aim of avoiding incest recalls the prohibited object through some feature, often an inconspicuous one.

The main protective measure against such a disturbance which men have recourse to in this split in their love consists in a psychical *debasement* of the sexual object, the overvaluation

1. [This term is borrowed from Jung's word-association experiments (Jung, 1906, 1909).]

that normally attaches to the sexual object being reserved for the incestuous object and its representatives. As soon as the condition of debasement is fulfilled, sensuality can be freely expressed, and important sexual capacities and a high degree of pleasure can develop. There is a further factor which contributes to this result. People in whom there has not been a proper confluence of the affectionate and the sensual currents do not usually show much refinement in their modes of behaviour in love; they have retained perverse sexual aims whose non-fulfilment is felt as a serious loss of pleasure, and whose fulfilment on the other hand seems possible only with a debased and despised sexual object.

We can now understand the motives behind the boy's phantasies mentioned in the first of these 'Contributions' (above, p. 238), which degrade the mother to the level of a prostitute. They are efforts to bridge the gulf between the two currents in love, at any rate in phantasy, and by debasing the mother to acquire her as an object of sensuality.

2

In the preceding section we have approached the study of psychical impotence from a medico-psychological angle of which the title of this paper gives no indication. It will however become clear that this introduction was required by us to provide an approach to our proper subject.

We have reduced psychical impotence to the failure of the affectionate and the sensual currents in love to combine, and this developmental inhibition has in turn been explained as being due to the influences of strong childhood fixations and of later frustration in reality through the intervention of the barrier against incest. There is one principal objection to the theory we advance; it does too much. It explains why certain people suffer from psychical impotence, but it leaves us with the apparent mystery of how others have been able to escape this disorder. Since we must recognize that all the relevant factors known to us – the strong childhood fixation, the incest-barrier and the frustration in the years of development after puberty – are to be found in practically all civilized human beings, we should be justified in expecting psychical impotence to be a universal affliction under civilization and not a disorder confined to some individuals.

It would be easy to escape from this conclusion by pointing to the quantitative factor in the causation of illness – to the greater or lesser extent of the contribution made by the various elements which determine whether a recognizable illness results or not. But although I accept this answer as correct, it is not my intention to make it a reason for rejecting the conclusion itself. On the contrary, I shall put forward the view that psychical impotence is much more widespread than is supposed, and that a certain amount of this behaviour does in fact characterize the love of civilized man.

If the concept of psychical impotence is broadened and is not restricted to failure to perform the act of coitus in circumstances where a desire to obtain pleasure is present and the genital apparatus is intact, we may in the first place add all those men who are described as psychanaesthetic: men who never fail in the act but who carry it out without getting any particular pleasure from it – a state of affairs that is more common than one would think. Psychoanalytic examination of such cases discloses the same aetiological factors as we found in psychical impotence in the narrower sense, without at first arriving at any explanation of the difference between their symptoms. An easily justifiable analogy takes one from these anaesthetic men to the immense number of frigid women; and there is no better way to describe or understand their behaviour in love than by comparing it with the more conspicuous disorder of psychical impotence in men.[1]

1. I am at the same time very willing to admit that frigidity in women is a complex subject which can also be approached from another angle. [The question is examined at length in 'The Taboo of Virginity' (1918a), p. 274ff. below.]

If however we turn our attention not to an extension of the concept of psychical impotence, but to the gradations in its symptomatology, we cannot escape the conclusion that the behaviour in love of men in the civilized world today bears the stamp altogether of psychical impotence. There are only a very few educated people in whom the two currents of affection and sensuality have become properly fused; the man almost always feels his respect for the woman acting as a restriction on his sexual activity, and only develops full potency when he is with a debased sexual object; and this in its turn is partly caused by the entrance of perverse components into his sexual aims, which he does not venture to satisfy with a woman he respects. He is assured of complete sexual pleasure only when he can devote himself unreservedly to obtaining satisfaction, which with his well-brought-up wife, for instance, he does not dare to do. This is the source of his need for a debased sexual object, a woman who is ethically inferior, to whom he need attribute no aesthetic scruples, who does not know him in his other social relations and cannot judge him in them. It is to such a woman that he prefers to devote his sexual potency, even when the whole of his affection belongs to a woman of a higher kind. It is possible, too, that the tendency so often observed in men of the highest classes of society to choose a woman of a lower class as a permanent mistress or even as a wife is nothing but a consequence of their need for a debased sexual object, to whom, psychologically, the possibility of complete satisfaction is linked.

I do not hestitate to make the two factors at work in psychical impotence in the strict sense – the factors of intense incestuous fixation in childhood and the frustration by reality in adolescence – responsible, too, for this extremely common characteristic of the love of civilized men. It sounds not only disagreeable but also paradoxical, yet it must nevertheless be said that anyone who is to be really free and happy in love must have surmounted his respect for women and have come to terms with the idea of incest with his mother or sister. Anyone who subjects himself to a serious self-examination on the subject of this requirement will be sure to find that he regards the sexual act basically as something degrading, which defiles and pollutes not only the body. The origin of this low opinion, which he will certainly not willingly acknowledge, must be looked for in the period of his youth in which the sensual current in him was already strongly developed but its satisfaction with an object outside the family was almost as completely prohibited as it was with an incestuous one.

In our civilized world women are under the influence of a similar after-effect of their upbringing, and, in addition, of their reaction to men's behaviour. It is naturally just as un-favourable for a woman if a man approaches her without his full potency as it is if his initial overvaluation of her when he is in love gives place to undervaluation after he has possessed her. In the case of women there is little sign of a need to debase their sexual object. This is no doubt connected with the absence in them as a rule of anything similar to the sexual overvaluation found in men. But their long holding back from sexuality and the lingering of their sensuality in phantasy has another important consequence for them. They are subse-quently often unable to undo the connection between sensual activity and the prohibition, and prove to be psychically impotent, that is, frigid, when such activity is at last allowed them. This is the origin of the endeavour made by many women to keep even legitimate relations secret for a while; and of the capacity of other women for normal sensation as soon as the condition of prohibition is re-established by a secret love affair: unfaithful to their husband, they are able to keep a second order of faith with their lover [cf. 'The Taboo of Virginity', p. 276 below].

The condition of forbiddenness in the erotic life of women is, I think, comparable to the need on the part of men to debase their sexual object. Both are consequences of the long period of delay, which is demanded by education for cultural reasons, between sexual maturity and sexual activity. Both aim at abolishing the psychical impotence that results from the failure of affectionate and sensual impulses to coalesce. That the effect of the same causes should be so different in men and in women may perhaps be traced to another difference in the behaviour of the two sexes. Civilized women do not usually transgress the prohibition on sexual activity in the period during which they have to wait, and thus they acquire the intimate connection between prohibition and sexuality. Men usually break through this prohibition if they can satisfy the condition of debasing the object, and so they carry on this condition into their love in later life.

In view of the strenuous efforts being made in the civilized world today to reform sexual life, it will not be superfluous to give a reminder that psychoanalytic research is as remote from tendentiousness as any other kind of research. It has no other end in view than to throw light on things by tracing what is manifest back to what is hidden. It is quite satisfied if reforms make use of its findings to replace what is injurious by something more advantageous; but it cannot predict whether other institutions may not result in other, and perhaps graver, sacrifices.

3

The fact that the curb put upon love by civilization involves a universal tendency to debase sexual objects will perhaps lead us to turn our attention from the object to the instincts themselves. The damage caused by the initial frustration of sexual pleasure is seen in the fact that the freedom later given to that pleasure in marriage does not bring full satisfaction. But at the same time, if sexual freedom is unrestricted from the outset the result is no better. It can easily be shown that the psychical value of erotic needs is reduced as soon as their satisfaction becomes easy. An obstacle is required in order to heighten libido; and where natural resistances to satisfaction have not been sufficient men have at all times erected conventional ones so as to be able to enjoy love. This is true both of individuals and of nations. In times in which there were no difficulties standing in the way of sexual satisfaction, such as perhaps during the decline of the ancient civilizations, love became worthless and life empty, and strong reaction-formations were required to restore indispensable affective values. In this connection it may be claimed that the ascetic current in Christianity created psychical values for love which pagan antiquity was never able to confer on it. This current assumed its greatest importance with the ascetic monks, whose lives were almost entirely occupied with the struggle against libidinal temptation.

One's first inclination is no doubt to trace back the difficulties revealed here to universal characteristics of our organic instincts. It is no doubt also true in general that the psychical importance of an instinct rises in proportion to its frustration. Suppose a number of totally different human beings were all equally exposed to hunger. As their imperative need for food mounted, all the individual differences would disappear and in their place one would see the uniform manifestations of the one unappeased instinct. But is it also true that with the satisfaction of an instinct its psychical value always falls just as sharply? Consider, for example, the relation of a drinker to wine. Is it not true that wine always provides the drinker with the same toxic satisfaction, which in poetry has so often been compared to erotic satisfaction – a comparison acceptable from the scientific point of view as well? Has one ever heard of the drinker being obliged constantly to change his drink because he soon grows tired of keeping to the same one? On the contrary, habit constantly tightens the bond between a man and the kind of wine he drinks. Does one ever hear of a drinker who needs to go to a country where wine is dearer or drinking is prohibited, so that by introducing obstacles he can reinforce the dwindling satisfaction that he obtains? Not at all. If we listen to what our great alcoholics, such as

Böcklin,[1] say about their relation to wine, it sounds like the most perfect harmony, a model of a happy marriage. Why is the relation of the lover to his sexual object so very different?

It is my belief that, however strange it may sound, we must reckon with the possibility that something in the nature of the sexual instinct itself is unfavourable to the realization of complete satisfaction. If we consider the long and difficult developmental history of the instinct, two factors immediately spring to mind which might be made responsible for this difficulty. Firstly, as a result of the diphasic onset of object-choice, and the interposition of the barrier against incest, the final object or the sexual instinct is never any longer the original object but only a surrogate for it. Psychoanalysis has shown us that when the original object of a wishful impulse has been lost as a result of repression, it is frequently represented by an endless series of substitute objects none of which, however, brings full satisfaction. This may explain the inconstancy in object-choice, the 'craving for stimulation'[2] which is so often a feature of the love of adults.

Secondly, we know that the sexual instinct is originally divided into a great number of components – or rather, it develops out of them – some of which cannot be taken up into the instinct in its later form, but have at an earlier stage to be suppressed or put to other uses. These above all the coprophilic instinctual components, which have proved incompatible with our aesthetic standards of culture, probably since, as a result of our adopting an erect gait, we raised our organ of smell from the ground.[3] The same is true of a large portion of the sadistic urges which are a part of erotic life. But all such developmental processes affect only the upper layers of the

1. Floerke (1902, 16).
2. ['*Reizhunger*'. This term seems to have been introduced by Hoche and Bloch. See Freud's *Three Essays* (1905d), p. 63 *n.* 2 above.]
3. [Cf. two long footnotes to Chapter IV of *Civilization and its Discontents* (1930a), in which this idea is explored in greater detail.]

complex structure. The fundamental processes which produce erotic excitation remain unaltered. The excremental is all too intimately and inseparably bound up with the sexual; the position of the genitals – *inter urinas et faeces* – remains the decisive and unchangeable factor. One might say here, varying a well-known saying of the great Napoleon: 'Anatomy is destiny.'[1] The genitals themselves have not taken part in the development of the human body in the direction of beauty: they have remained animal, and thus love, too, has remained in essence just as animal as it ever was. The instincts of love are hard to educate; education of them achieves now too much, now too little. What civilization aims at making out of them seems unattainable except at the price of a sensible loss of pleasure; the persistence of the impulses that could not be made use of can be detected in sexual activity in the form of non-satisfaction.

Thus we may perhaps be forced to become reconciled to the idea that it is quite impossible to adjust the claims of the sexual instinct to the demands of civilization; that in consequence of its cultural development renunciation and suffering, as well as the danger of extinction in the remotest future, cannot be avoided by the human race. This gloomy prognosis rests, it is true, on the single conjecture that the non-satisfaction that goes with civilization is the necessary consequence of certain peculiarities which the sexual instinct has assumed under the pressure of culture. The very incapacity of the sexual instinct to yield complete satisfaction as soon as it submits to the first demands of civilization becomes the source, however, of the noblest cultural achievements which are brought into being by ever more extensive sublimation of its instinctual components. For what motive would men have for putting sexual instinctual forces to other uses if, by any distribution of those forces, they could obtain fully satisfying pleasure? They would never abandon that pleasure and they

1. [This paraphrase appears again in 'The Dissolution of the Oedipus Complex' (1924*d*), below, p. 320.]

would never make any further progress. It seems, therefore, that the irreconcilable difference between the demands of the two instincts – the sexual and the egoistic – has made men capable of ever higher achievements, though subject, it is true, to a constant danger, to which, in the form of neurosis, the weaker are succumbing today.

It is not the aim of science either to frighten or to console. But I myself am quite ready to admit that such far-reaching conclusions as those I have drawn should be built on a broader foundation, and that perhaps developments in other directions may enable mankind to correct the results of the developments I have here been considering in isolation.

THE TABOO OF VIRGINITY
(CONTRIBUTIONS TO THE PSYCHOLOGY OF LOVE III)
(1918 [1917])

EDITOR'S NOTE

BEITRÄGE ZUR PSYCHOLOGIE DES LIEBESLEBENS III

DAS TABU DER VIRGINITÄT

(A) German Editions:

(1917 Read as a communication to the Vienna Psycho-
      Analytical Society, December 12, 1917.)

1918 S.K.S.N., 4, 229–51. ('Beiträge zur Psychologie des
      Liebeslebens' III.) (2nd ed. 1922.)

1924 Gesammelte Schriften, 5, 212–31.

1924 In Beiträge zur Psychologie des Liebeslebens, Leipzig,
      Vienna and Zurich: Internationaler Psychoana-
      lytischer Verlag. (Pp. 29–48.)

1931 Sexualtheorie und Traumlehre, 95–115.

1947 Gesammelte Werke, 12, 161–80.

(B) English Translations:

'Contributions to the Psychology of Love:
The Taboo of Virginity'

1925 Collected Papers, 4, 217–35. (Tr. Joan Riviere.)

1957 Standard Edition, 11, 191–208. (Tr. Angela Richards.)

The present edition is a corrected reprint of the Standard
Edition version, with one or two editorial changes.

This paper was written in September 1917, but was not published till the following year. Totem and Taboo (1912–13) had
appeared in the interval since the second paper in the series of

'Contributions', and this third one may from one point of view be regarded as an addition to the second essay in that work. On the other hand, however, it includes a discussion of the clinical problem of frigidity in women and is in that respect the counterpart of the study of impotence in men in the second paper in the series (see p. 252ff. above).

THE TABOO OF VIRGINITY

(CONTRIBUTIONS TO THE PSYCHOLOGY OF LOVE III)

FEW details of the sexual life of primitive peoples are so alien to our own feelings as their estimate of virginity, the state in a woman of being untouched. The high value which her suitor places on a woman's virginity seems to us so firmly rooted, so much a matter of course, that we find ourselves almost at a loss if we have to give reasons for this opinion. The demand that a girl shall not bring to her marriage with a particular man any memory of sexual relations with another is, indeed, nothing other than a logical continuation of the right to exclusive possession of a woman, which forms the essence of monogamy, the extension of this monopoly to cover the past.

From this point we have no trouble in justifying what looked at first like a prejudice, by referring to our views on the erotic life of women. Whoever is the first to satisfy a virgin's desire for love, long and laboriously held in check, and who in doing so overcomes the resistances which have been built up in her through the influences of her milieu and education, that is the man she will take into a lasting relationship, the possibility of which will never again be open to any other man. This experience creates a state of bondage in the woman which guarantees that possession of her shall continue undisturbed and makes her able to resist new impressions and enticements from outside.

The expression 'sexual bondage' was chosen by von Krafft-Ebing (1892) to describe the phenomenon of a person's acquiring an unusually high degree of dependence and lack of self-reliance in relation to another person with whom he has a sexual relationship. This bondage can on occasion extend very far, as far as the loss of all independent will and as far as causing a person to suffer the greatest sacrifices of his own interests; the author, however, does not fail to remark that a certain measure of such dependence 'is absolutely necessary, if the tie is to last for any length of time'. Some such measure of sexual bondage is, indeed, indispensable to the maintenance of civilized marriage and to holding at bay the polygamous tendencies which threaten it, and in our social communities this factor is regularly reckoned upon.

Von Krafft-Ebing derives the formation of sexual bondage from a conjunction of an 'uncommon degree of the state of being in love and of weakness of character' in one person and unbounded egoism in the other. Analytic experience, however, will not let us rest satisfied with this simple attempt at explanation. We can see, rather, that the decisive factor is the amount of sexual resistance that is overcome and in addition the fact that the process of overcoming the resistance is concentrated and happens only once. This state of bondage is, accordingly, far more frequent and more intense in women than in men, though it is true it occurs in the latter more often nowadays than it did in ancient times. Wherever we have been able to study sexual bondage in men it has shown itself as resulting from an overcoming of psychical impotence through one particular woman, to whom the man in question has remained subsequently bound. Many strange marriages and not a few tragic events – even some with far-reaching consequences – seem to owe their explanation to this origin.

Turning to the attitude of primitive peoples, it is incorrect to describe it by declaring that they set no value on virginity and to submit as proof of this the fact that they perform the defloration of girls outside marriage and before the first act of marital intercourse. On the contrary, it appears that for them, too, defloration is a significant act; but it has become the subject of a taboo – of a prohibition which may be described as religious. Instead of reserving it for the girl's bridegroom and future partner in marriage, custom demands that *he shall shun the performance of it.*[1]

It is no part of my purpose to make a full collection of the literary evidence for the existence of this custom of prohibition, to pursue its geographical distribution and to enumerate all the forms in which it is expressed. I shall content myself, therefore, with stating the fact that the practice of rupturing the hymen in this way outside the subsequent marriage is very widespread among primitive races living today. As Crawley says: 'This marriage ceremony consists in perforation of the hymen by some appointed person other than the husband; it is most common in the lowest stages of culture, especially in Australia.' (Crawley, 1902, 347.)

If, however, defloration is not to result from the first act of marital intercourse, then it must have been carried out beforehand – whatever the way and whoever the agent may have been. I shall quote a few passages from Crawley's book, mentioned above, which provide information on these points but also give grounds for some critical observations.

(Ibid., 191.) 'Thus in the Dieri and neighbouring tribes (in Australia) it is the universal custom when a girl reaches puberty to rupture the hymen(*Journal of the Royal Anthropological Institute*, **24**, 169). In the Portland and Glenelg tribes this is done to the bride by an old woman; and sometimes white men are asked for this reason to deflower maidens (Brough Smith, |1878], **2**, 319).'

(Ibid., 307.) 'The artificial rupture of the hymen sometimes takes place in infancy, but generally at puberty. . . . It is often combined, as in Australia, with a ceremonial act of intercourse.'

(Ibid., 348.) (Of Australian tribes among which the well-known exogamous marriage-restrictions are in force, from communications by Spencer and Gillen [1899]:) 'The hymen is artificially perforated, and then the assisting men have access

1. Cf. Crawley (1902), Ploss and Bartels (1891), Frazer (1911) and Havelock Ellis [1910].

(ceremonial, be it observed) to the girl in a stated order. . . . The act is in two parts, perforation and intercourse.'

(Ibid., 349.) 'An important preliminary of marriage amongst the Masai (in Equatorial Africa) is the performance of this operation on the girl (J. Thomson, [1887], 2, 258). This defloration is performed by the father of the bride amongst the Sakais (Malay), Battas (Sumatra), and Alfoers of Celebes (Ploss and Bartels, [1891], 2, 490). In the Philippines there were certain men whose profession it was to deflower brides, in case the hymen had not been ruptured in childhood by an old woman who was sometimes employed for this (Featherman, [1885–91], 2, 474). The defloration of the bride was amongst some Eskimo tribes entrusted to the *angekok*, or priest (ibid., 3, 406).'

The critical remarks I referred to are concerned with two points. Firstly, it is a pity that in these reports a more careful distinction is not made between simple rupture of the hymen without intercourse, and intercourse for the purpose of effecting this rupture. There is only one passage in which we are told expressly that the procedure falls into two actions: defloration (carried out by hand or with some instrument) and the act of intercourse which follows it. The material in Ploss and Bartels [1891], in other respects so rich, is almost useless for our purpose, because in their presentation of it the psychological importance of the act of defloration is completely displaced in favour of its anatomical results. Secondly, we should be glad to be informed how the 'ceremonial' (purely formal, ritual, or official) coitus, which takes place on these occasions, differs from ordinary sexual intercourse. The authors to whom I have had access either have been too embarrassed to discuss the matter or have once again underestimated the psychological importance of such sexual details. It is to be hoped that the first-hand accounts of travellers and missionaries may be more complete and less ambiguous, but since this literature, which is for the most part foreign, is for the time being inaccessible I cannot say anything definite on the subject.[1] Besides, we may get round the problem arising over this second point if we bear in mind the fact that a ceremonial mock-coitus would after all only represent a substitute for, and perhaps replace altogether, an act that in earlier times would have been carried out completely.[2]

There are various factors which can be adduced to explain this taboo of virginity and which I will enumerate and consider briefly. When a virgin is deflowered, her blood is as a rule shed; the first attempt at explanation, then, is based on the horror of blood among primitive races who consider blood as the seat of life. This blood taboo is seen in numerous kinds of observances which have nothing to do with sexuality; it is obviously connected with the prohibition against murder and forms a protective measure against the primal thirst for blood, primeval man's lust for killing. According to this view the taboo of virginity is connected with the taboo of menstruation which is almost universally maintained. Primitive people cannot dissociate the puzzling phenomenon of this monthly flow of blood from sadistic ideas. Menstruation, especially its first appearance, is interpreted as the bite of some spirit-animal, perhaps as a sign of sexual intercourse with this spirit. Occasionally some report gives grounds for recognizing the spirit as that of an ancestor and then, supported by other findings,[3] we understand that the menstruating girl is taboo because she is the property of this ancestral spirit.

Other considerations, however, warn us not to overestimate the influence of a factor such as the horror of blood. It has not, after all, been strong enough to suppress practices like the circumcision of boys and the still more cruel equivalent with girls (excision of the clitoris and labia minora)

1. [This was written during the first World War.]
2. In numerous other examples of marriage ceremonies there can be no doubt that people other than the bridegroom, for example his assistants and companions (our traditional 'groomsmen'), are granted full sexual access to the bride.
3. Cf. *Totem and Taboo* (1912–13) [*P.F.L.*, **13**, 201–5].

which are to some extent the custom in these same races, nor to abolish the prevalence of other ceremonies involving bloodshed. It would not therefore be surprising, either, if this horror were overcome for the benefit of the husband on the occasion of the first cohabitation.

There is a second explanation, also unconcerned with sexuality, which has, however, a much more general scope than the first. It suggests that primitive man is prey to a perpetual lurking apprehensiveness, just as in the psychoanalytic theory of the neuroses we claim to be the case with people suffering from anxiety neurosis. This apprehensiveness will appear most strongly on all occasions which differ in any way from the usual, which involve something new or unexpected, something not understood or uncanny. This is also the origin of the ceremonial practices, widely adopted in later religions, which are connected with the beginning of every new undertaking, the start of every new period of time, the first-fruits of human, animal and plant life. The dangers which the anxious man believes to be threatening him never appear more vivid in his expectation than on the threshold of a dangerous situation, and then, too, is the only time when protecting himself against them is of any use. The first act of intercourse in marriage can certainly claim, on grounds of importance, to be preceded by such precautionary measures. These two attempts at explanation, based on horror of blood and on fear of first occurrences, do not contradict but rather reinforce each other. The first occasion of sexual intercourse is certainly a critical action, all the more so if it is to involve a flow of blood.

A third explanation – the one which Crawley prefers – draws attention to the fact that the taboo of virginity is part of a large totality which embraces the whole of sexual life. It is not only the first coitus with a woman which is taboo but sexual intercourse in general; one might almost say that women are altogether taboo. A woman is not only taboo in particular situations arising from her sexual life such as menstruation, pregnancy, childbirth and lying-in; apart from these situations, intercourse with women is subject to such solemn and numerous restrictions that we have every reason to doubt the reputed sexual freedom of savages. It is true that, on particular occasions, primitive man's sexuality will override all inhibitions; but for the most part it seems to be more strongly held in check by prohibitions than it is at higher levels of civilization. Whenever the man undertakes some special enterprise, like setting out on an expedition, a hunt or a campaign, he is obliged to keep away from his wife and especially from sexual intercourse with her; otherwise she will paralyse his strength and bring him bad luck. In the usages of daily life as well there is an unmistakable tendency to keep the sexes apart. Women live with women, men with men; family life, in our sense, seems scarcely to exist in many primitive tribes. This separation sometimes goes so far that one sex is not allowed to say aloud the personal names of members of the other sex, and that the women develop a language with a special vocabulary. Sexual needs will from time to time break through these barriers of separation afresh, but in some tribes even the encounters of husband and wife have to take place outside the house and in secret.

Wherever primitive man has set up a taboo he fears some danger and it cannot be disputed that a generalized dread of women is expressed in all these rules of avoidance. Perhaps this dread is based on the fact that woman is different from man, for ever incomprehensible and mysterious, strange and therefore apparently hostile. The man is afraid of being weakened by the woman, infected with her femininity and of then showing himself incapable. The effect which coitus has of discharging tensions and causing flaccidity may be the prototype of what the man fears; and realization of the influence which the woman gains over him through sexual intercourse, the consideration she thereby forces from him, may justify the extension of this fear. In all this there is nothing obsolete, nothing which is not still alive among ourselves.

Many observers of primitive races living today have put forward the view that their impulses in love are relatively weak and never reach the degree of intensity which we are accustomed to meet with in civilized men. Other observers have contradicted this opinion, but in any case the practice of the taboos we have described testifies to the existence of a force which opposes love by rejecting women as strange and hostile.

Crawley, in language which differs only slightly from the current terminology of psychoanalysis, declares that each individual is separated from the others by a 'taboo of personal isolation', and that it is precisely the minor differences in people who are otherwise alike that form the basis of feelings of·strangeness and hostility between them. It would be tempting to pursue this idea and to derive from this 'narcissism of minor differences'[1] the hostility which in every human relation we see fighting successfully against feelings of fellowship and overpowering the commandment that all men should love one another. Psychoanalysis believes that it has discovered a large part of what underlies the narcissistic rejection of women by men, which is so much mixed up with despising them, in drawing attention to the castration complex and its influence on the opinion in which women are held.

We can see, however, that these latter considerations have led us to range far beyond our subject. The general taboo of women throws no light on the particular rules concerning the first sexual act with a virgin. As far as they are concerned, we have not got beyond the first two explanations, based on horror of blood and fear of first occurrences, and even these, we must point out, do not touch the core of the taboo in question. It is quite clear that the intention underlying this taboo is that of *denying or sparing precisely the future husband* something which cannot be dissociated from the first sexual act, although according to our introductory observations

1. [Freud returns to this in Chapter VI of *Group Psychology* (1921c), and in Chapter V of *Civilization and its Discontents* (1930a).]

this very relation would lead to the woman becoming specially bound to this one man.

It is not our task on this occasion to discuss the origin and ultimate significance of taboo observances. I have done this in my book *Totem and Taboo* [1912–13], where I have given due consideration to the part played by primal ambivalence in determining the formation of taboo and have traced the genesis of the latter from the prehistoric events which led to the founding of the human family. We can no longer recognize an original meaning of this kind in taboos observed among primitive tribes today. We forget all too easily, in expecting to find any such thing, that even the most primitive peoples exist in a culture far removed from that of primaeval days, which is just as old as our own from the point of view of time and like ours corresponds to a later, if different, stage of development.

Today we find taboos among primitive peoples already elaborated into an intricate system of just the sort that neurotics among ourselves develop in their phobias, and we find old *motifs* replaced by new ones that fit together harmoniously. Leaving aside these genetic problems, then, we will go back to the idea that primitive man institutes a taboo where he fears some danger. Taking it generally this danger is a psychical one, for primitive man is not impelled at this point to make two distinctions, which to us it seems cannot be disregarded. He does not separate material from psychical danger, nor real from imaginary. In his consistently applied animistic view of the universe, every danger springs from the hostile intention of some being with a soul like himself, and this is as much the case with dangers which threaten him from some natural force as it is with those from other human beings or animals. But on the other hand he is accustomed to project his own internal impulses of hostility on to the external world, to ascribe them, that is, to the objects which he feels to be disagreeable or even merely strange. In this way women also are regarded as being a source of such dangers, and the first act of sexual intercourse with a woman stands out as a danger of particular intensity.

Now I believe that we shall receive some indication as to what this heightened danger is and why it threatens precisely the future husband, if we examine more closely the behaviour under the same circumstances of women of our own stage of civilization today. I will submit in advance, as the result of this examination, that such a danger really exists, so that with the taboo of virginity primitive man is defending himself against a correctly sensed, although psychical, danger.

We consider it to be the normal reaction for a woman after intercourse to embrace the man, pressing him to her at the climax of satisfaction, and we see this as an expression of her gratitude and a token of lasting bondage. But we know it is by no means the rule that the first occasion of intercourse should lead to this behaviour; very frequently it means only disappointment for the woman, who remains cold and un-satisfied, and it usually requires quite a long time and frequent repetition of the sexual act before she too begins to find satis-faction in it. There is an unbroken series from these cases of mere initial frigidity which soon vanishes, up to the cheerless phenomenon of permanent and obstinate frigidity which no tender efforts on the part of the husband can overcome. I believe this frigidity in women is not yet sufficiently under-stood and, except for those cases which must be blamed on the man's insufficient potency, calls for elucidation, possibly through allied phenomena.

I do not want to introduce at this point the attempts – which are so frequent – to take flight from the first occasion of sexual intercourse, because they are open to several interpreta-tions and are in the main, although not altogether, to be understood as an expression of the general female tendency to take a defensive line. As against this, I do believe that light is thrown on the riddle of female frigidity by certain pathological cases in which, after the first and indeed after each repeated instance of sexual intercourse, the woman gives unconcealed expression to her hostility towards the man by abusing him, raising her hand against him or actually striking him. In one very clear case of this kind, which I was able to submit to a thorough analysis, this happened although the woman loved the man very much, used to demand intercourse herself and unmistakably found great satisfaction in it. I think that this strange, contradictory reaction is the result of the very same impulses which ordinarily can only find expression as frigidity – which, that is, can hold back the tender reaction without at the same time being able to put themselves into effect. In the pathological case we find separated so to speak into its two components what in the far more common instance of frigidity is united to produce an inhibiting effect, just like the process we have long recognized in the so-called 'diphasic symptoms' of obsessional neurosis.[1] The danger which is thus aroused through the defloration of a woman would consist in drawing her hostility down upon oneself, and the prospective husband is just the person who would have every reason to avoid such enmity.

Now analysis enables us to infer without difficulty which impulses in women take part in bringing about this paradoxical behaviour, in which I expect to find the explanation of frigidity. The first act of intercourse mobilizes a number of impulses which are out of place in the desired feminine attitude, some of which, incidentally, need not recur during subsequent intercourse. In the first place we think of the pain which defloration causes a virgin, and we are perhaps even inclined to consider this factor as decisive and to give up the search for any others. But we cannot well ascribe such importance to this pain; we must rather substitute for it the narcissistic injury which proceeds from the destruction of an organ and which is even represented in a rationalized form in the knowledge that loss of virginity brings a diminution of sexual value. The marriage customs of primitive peoples,

1. [See a passage and an example in a long footnote to Chapter I (E) of the 'Rat Man' case history (1909d), P.F.L., 9, 71–3 and 73 n. 2.]

however, contain a warning against over-estimating this. We have heard that in some cases the rite falls into two phases: after the hymen has been ruptured (by hand or with some instrument) there follows a ceremonial act of coitus or mock-intercourse with the representatives of the husband, and this proves to us that the purpose of the taboo observance is not fulfilled by avoiding anatomical defloration, that the husband is to be spared something else as well as the woman's reaction to the painful injury.

We find a further reason for the disappointment experienced in the first act of intercourse in the fact that, with civilized women at least, fulfilment cannot be in accordance with expectations. Before this, sexual intercourse has been associated in the strongest possible way with prohibitions; lawful and permissible intercourse is not, therefore, felt to be the same thing. Just how close this association can be is demonstrated in an almost comic fashion by the efforts of so many girls about to be married to keep their new love-relationship secret from everyone outside, and indeed even from their parents, where there is no real necessity to do so and no objection can be looked for. Girls often say openly that their love loses value for them if other people know of it. On occasion this feeling can become dominating and can completely prevent the development of any capacity for love in a marriage. The woman only recovers her susceptibility to tender feelings in an illicit relationship which has to be kept secret, and in which alone she knows for certain that her own will is uninfluenced.[1]

However, this motive does not go deep enough either; besides, being bound up with civilized conditions, it fails to provide a satisfactory connection with the state of affairs among primitive people. All the more important, therefore, is the next factor, which is based on the evolution of the libido. We have learnt from analytic researches how universal and how powerful the earliest allocations of libido are. In

1. [Cf. the last paper, p. 255.]

these we are concerned with infantile sexual wishes which are clung to (in women usually a fixation of the libido on the father or a brother who takes his place) – wishes which frequently enough were directed towards other things than intercourse, or included it only as a dimly perceived goal. The husband is almost always so to speak only a substitute, never the right man; it is another man – in typical cases the father – who has first claim to a woman's love, the husband at most takes second place. It depends on how intense this fixation is and on how obstinately it is maintained whether the substitute is rejected as unsatisfying. Frigidity is thus among the genetic determinants of neuroses. The more powerful the psychical element in a woman's sexual life is, the greater will be the capacity for resistance shown by her distribution of libido to the upheaval of the first sexual act, and the less overpowering will be the effect which bodily possession of her can produce. Frigidity may then become established as a neurotic inhibition or provide the foundation for the development of other neuroses and even a moderate diminution of potency in the man will greatly contribute to help this process.

The customs of primitive peoples seem to take account of this *motif* of the early sexual wish by handing over the task of defloration to an elder, priest or holy man, that is, to a substitute for the father (see above [p. 268]). There seems to me to be a direct path leading from this custom to the highly vexed question of the *jus primae noctis* of the mediaeval lord of the manor. A. J. Storfer (1911) has put forward the same view and has in addition, as Jung (1909) had already done before him, interpreted the widespread tradition of the 'Tobias nights' (the custom of continence during the first three nights of marriage) as an acknowledgement of the privilege of the patriarch. It agrees with our expectations, therefore, when we find the images of gods included among the father-surrogates entrusted with defloration. In some districts of India, the newly married woman was obliged to sacrifice her hymen to the wooden lingam, and, according to St Augustine's account, the same custom existed in the Roman marriage ceremony (of his time?), but modified so that the young wife only had to seat herself on the gigantic stone phallus of Priapus.[1]

There is another motive, reaching down into still deeper layers, which can be shown to bear the chief blame for the paradoxical reaction towards the man, and which, in my view, further makes its influence felt in female frigidity. The first act of intercourse activates in a woman other impulses of long standing as well as those already described, and these are in complete opposition to her womanly role and function.

We have learnt from the analysis of many neurotic women that they go through an early age in which they envy their brothers their sign of masculinity and feel at a disadvantage and humiliated because of the lack of it (actually because of its diminished size) in themselves. We include this 'envy for the penis' in the 'castration complex'. If we understand 'masculine' as including the idea of wishing to be masculine, then the designation 'masculine protest' fits this behaviour; the phrase was coined by Adler [1910] with the intention of proclaiming this factor as being responsible for neurosis in general. During this phase, little girls often make no secret of their envy, nor of the hostility towards their favoured brothers which arises from it. They even try to urinate standing upright like their brothers in order to prove the equality which they lay claim to. In the case already described [p. 275] in which the woman used to show uncontrolled aggression after intercourse towards her husband, whom otherwise she loved, I was able to establish that this phase had existed before that of object-choice. Only later was the little girl's libido directed towards her father, and then, instead of wanting to have a penis, she wanted – a child.[2]

1. Ploss and Bartels (1891, 1, xii) and Dulaure (1905, 142).
2. Cf. 'On Transformations of Instinct as Exemplified in Anal Erotism' (1917c) [p. 297 below].

I should not be surprised if in other cases the order in which these impulses occurred were reversed and this part of the castration complex only became effective after a choice of object had been successfully made. But the masculine phase in the girl in which she envies the boy for his penis is in any case developmentally the earlier, and it is closer to the original narcissism than it is to object-love.

Some time ago I chanced to have an opportunity of obtaining insight into a dream of a newly-married woman which was recognizable as a reaction to the loss of her virginity. It betrayed spontaneously the woman's wish to castrate her young husband and to keep his penis for herself. Certainly there was also room for the more innocent interpretation that what she wished for was the prolongation and repetition of the act, but several details of the dream did not fit into this meaning and the character as well as the subsequent behaviour of the woman who had the dream gave evidence in favour of the more serious view. Behind this envy for the penis, there comes to light the woman's hostile bitterness against the man, which never completely disappears in the relations between the sexes, and which is clearly indicated in the strivings and in the literary productions of 'emancipated' women. In a palaeo-biological speculation, Ferenczi has traced back this hostility of women – I do not know if he is the first to do so – to the period in time when the sexes became differentiated.[1] At first, in his opinion, copulation took place between two similar individuals, one of which, however, developed into the stronger and forced the weaker one to submit to sexual union. The feelings of bitterness arising from this subjection still persist in the present-day disposition of women. I do not think there is any harm in employing such speculations, so long as one avoids setting too much value on them.

After this enumeration of the motives for the paradoxical reaction of women to defloration, traces of which persist in

1. [Cf. Ferenczi (1924), where he explains that he expressed these views privately to Freud before publishing them.]

frigidity, we may sum up by saying that a woman's *immature sexuality* is discharged on to the man who first makes her acquainted with the sexual act. This being so, the taboo of virginity is reasonable enough and we can understand the rule which decrees that precisely the man who is to enter upon a life shared with this woman shall avoid these dangers. At higher stages of civilization the importance attributed to this danger diminishes in face of her promise of bondage and no doubt of other motives and inducements; virginity is looked upon as a possession which the husband is not called upon to renounce. But analysis of disturbed marriages teaches us that the motives which seek to drive a woman to take vengeance for her defloration are not completely extinguished even in the mental life of civilized women. I think it must strike the observer in how uncommonly large a number of cases the woman remains frigid and feels unhappy in a first marriage, whereas after it has been dissolved she becomes a tender wife, able to make her second husband happy. The archaic reaction has, so to speak, exhausted itself on the first object.

The taboo of virginity, however, even apart from this has not died out in our civilized existence. It is known to the popular mind and writers have on occasion made use of this material. A comedy by Anzengruber[1] shows how a simple peasant lad is deterred from marrying his intended bride because she is 'a wench who'll cost her first his life'. For this reason he agrees to her marrying another man and is ready to take her when she is a widow and no longer dangerous. The title of the play, *Das Jungferngift* ['Virgin's Venom'], reminds us of the habit of snake-charmers, who make poisonous snakes first bite a piece of cloth in order to handle them afterwards without danger.[2]

1. [Ludwig Anzengruber, Viennese author and dramatist (1839–89).]

2. A masterly short story by Arthur Schnitzler (*Das Schicksal des Freiherrn von Leisenbogh*) ['The Fate of Freiherr von Leisenbogh'] deserves to be included here, in spite of the rather different situation. The

The taboo of virginity and something of its motivation has been depicted most powerfully of all in a well-known dramatic character, that of Judith in Hebbel's tragedy *Judith und Holofernes*. Judith is one of those women whose virginity is protected by a taboo. Her first husband was paralysed on the bridal night by a mysterious anxiety, and never again dared to touch her. 'My beauty is like belladonna,' she says. 'Enjoyment of it brings madness and death.' When the Assyrian general is besieging her city, she conceives the plan of seducing him by her beauty and of destroying him, thus employing a patriotic motive to conceal a sexual one. After she has been deflowered by this powerful man, who boasts of his strength and ruthlessness, she finds the strength in her fury to strike off his head, and thus becomes the liberator of her people. Beheading is well known to us as a symbolic substitute for castrating; Judith is accordingly the woman who castrates the man who has deflowered her, which was just the wish of the newly-married woman expressed in the dream I reported. It is clear that Hebbel has intentionally sexualized the patriotic narrative from the Apocrypha of the Old Testament, for there Judith is able to boast after her return that she has not been defiled, nor is there in the Biblical text any mention of her uncanny wedding night. But probably, with the fine perception of a poet, he sensed the ancient motive, which had been lost in the tendentious narrative, and has merely restored its earlier content to the material.

Sadger (1912) has shown in a penetrating analysis how Hebbel was determined in his choice of material by his own

lover of an actress who is very experienced in love is dying as the result of an accident. He creates a sort of new virginity for her, by putting a curse of death on the man who is the first to possess her after himself. For a time the woman with this taboo upon her does not venture on any love-affair. However, after she has fallen in love with a singer, she hits on the solution of first granting a night to the Freiherr von Leisenbogh, who has been pursuing her for years. And the curse falls on him: he has a stroke as soon as he learns the motive behind his unexpected good fortune in love.

parental complex, and how he came to take the part of the woman so regularly in the struggle between the sexes, and to feel his way into the most hidden impulses of her mind. He also quotes the motives which the poet himself gives for the alteration he has made in the material, and he rightly finds them artificial and as though intended to justify *outwardly* something the poet himself is unconscious of, while at bottom concealing it. I will not dispute Sadger's explanation of why Judith, who according to the Biblical narrative is a widow, has to become a *virgin* widow. He refers to the purpose found in childish phantasies of disavowing the sexual intercourse of the parents and of turning the mother into an untouched virgin. But I will add: after the poet has established his heroine's virginity, his sensitive imagination dwells on the hostile reaction released by the violation of her maidenhood. [Cf. p. 310 and *n.* 1 below.]

We may say, then, in conclusion that defloration has not only the one, civilized consequence of binding the women lastingly to the man; it also unleashes an archaic reaction of hostility towards him, which can assume pathological forms that are frequently enough expressed in the appearance of inhibitions in the erotic side of married life, and to which we may ascribe the fact that second marriages so often turn out better than first. The taboo of virginity, which seems so strange to us, the horror with which, among primitive peoples, the husband avoids the act of defloration, are fully justified by this hostile reaction.

It is interesting that in one's capacity as analyst one can meet with women in whom the opposed reactions of bondage and hostility both find expression and remain intimately associated with each other. There are women of this kind who seem to have fallen out with their husbands completely and who all the same can only make vain efforts to free themselves. As often as they try to direct their love towards some other man, the image of the first, although he is no longer loved, intervenes with inhibiting effect. Analysis then teaches us that these women, it is true, still cling to their first husbands in a state of bondage, but no longer through affection. They cannot get away from them, because they have not completed their revenge upon them, and in pronounced cases they have not even brought the impulses for vengeance to consciousness.

TWO LIES TOLD BY CHILDREN
(1913)

EDITOR'S NOTE

ZWEI KINDERLÜGEN

(A) German Editions:

1913   Int. Z. ärztl Psychoanal., 1 (4), 359–62.
1918   S.K.S.N., 4, 189–94. (1922, 2nd ed.)
1943   Gesammelte Werke, 8, 422–7.

(B) English Translations:

'Infantile Mental Life: Two Lies Told by Children'
1924   Collected Papers, 2, 144–9. (Tr. E. C. Mayne.)
1958   Standard Edition, 12, 303–09 (under a shortened title).

The present edition is a corrected reprint of the *Standard Edition* version, with one or two editorial changes.

On its first appearance in the *Zeitschrift* (in the summer of 1913) this paper was the first of several by various writers included under a general caption 'Aus dem infantilen Seelenleben'. This caption was incorporated in the 1918 reprint of the paper and was also inserted in the title of the first English translation in 1924; thereafter it was dropped. Two small changes in the text were made in the editions from 1918 onwards.

TWO LIES TOLD BY CHILDREN

WE can understand children telling lies, when in doing so, they are imitating the lies told by grown-up people. But a number of lies told by well-brought-up children have a particular significance and should cause those in charge of them to reflect rather than be angry. These lies occur under the influence of excessive feelings of love, and become momentous when they lead to a misunderstanding between the child and the person it loves.

I

A girl of seven (in her second year at school) had asked her father for some money to buy colours for painting Easter eggs. Her father had refused, saying he had no money. Shortly afterwards the girl asked her father for some money for a contribution towards a wreath for the funeral of their reigning princess, who had recently died. Each of the schoolchildren was to bring fifty pfennigs [sixpence]. Her father gave her ten marks [ten shillings]; she paid her contribution, put nine marks on her father's writing-table, and with the remaining fifty pfennigs bought some paints, which she hid in her toy cupboard. At dinner her father asked suspiciously what she had done with the missing fifty pfennigs, and whether she had not bought paints with them after all. She denied it; but her brother, who was two years her elder and with whom she had planned to paint the eggs, betrayed her; the paints were found in the cupboard. The angry father handed the culprit over to her mother for punishment, and it was severely administered. Afterwards her mother was herself much shaken, when she saw how great the child's despair was. She caressed the little girl after the punishment, and took her for a walk to console her. But the effects of the experience, which were described by the patient herself as the 'turning-point in her life', proved to be ineradicable. Up to then she had been a wild, self-confident child, afterwards she became shy and timid. When she was engaged to be married and her mother undertook the purchase of her furniture and her trousseau, she flew into a rage which was incomprehensible even to herself. She had a feeling that after all it was *her* money, and no one else ought to buy anything with it. As a young wife she was shy of asking her husband for any expenditure on her personal needs, and made an uncalled-for distinction between 'her' money and his. During the treatment it happened now and again that her husband's remittances to her were delayed, so that she was left without resources in a foreign city. After she had told me this once, I made her promise that if it happened again she would borrow the small sum necessary from me. She promised to do so; but on the next occasion of financial embarrassment she did not keep her promise, but preferred to pawn her jewellery. She explained that she could not take money from me.

The appropriation of the fifty pfennigs in her childhood had had a significance which her father could not guess. Some time before she began going to school she had played a singular prank with money. A neighbour with whom they were friendly had sent the girl out with a small sum of money, in the company of her own little boy who was even younger, to buy something in a shop. Being the elder of the two, she was bringing the change back home. But, meeting the neighbour's servant in the street, she threw the money down on the pavement. In the analysis of this action, which she herself found inexplicable, the thought of Judas occurred to her, who threw down the thirty pieces of silver which he had been given for betraying his Master. She said she was certainly acquainted with the story of the Passion before she went to school. But in what way could she identify herself with Judas?

When she was three and a half[1] she had a nursemaid of

1. [In 1913 only, 'three and a quarter'.]

whom she was extremely fond. This girl became involved in a love affair with a doctor whose surgery she visited with the child. It appears that at that time the child witnessed various sexual proceedings. It is not certain whether she saw the doctor give the girl money; but there is no doubt that, to make sure of the child's keeping silence, the girl gave her some small coins, with which purchases were made (probably of sweets) on the way home. It is possible too that the doctor himself occasionally gave the child money. Nevertheless the child betrayed the girl to her mother out of jealousy. She played so ostentatiously with the coins she had brought home that her mother could not help asking: 'Where did you get that money?' The girl was dismissed.

To take money from anyone had thus early come to mean to her a physical surrender, an erotic relation. To take money from her father was equivalent to a declaration of love. The phantasy that her father was her lover was so seductive that with its help her childish wish for paints for the Easter eggs easily put itself into effect in spite of the prohibition. She could not admit, however, that she had appropriated the money; she was obliged to deny[1] it, because her motive for the deed, which was unconscious to herself, could not be admitted. Her father's punishment was thus a rejection of the tenderness she was offering him – a humiliation – and so it broke her spirit. During the treatment a period of severe depression occurred (whose explanation led to her remembering the events described here) when on one occasion I was obliged to reproduce this humiliation by asking her not to bring me any more flowers.

For psychoanalysts I need hardly emphasize the fact that in this little experience of the child's we have before us one of those extremely common cases in which early anal erotism persists into later erotic life. Even her desire to paint the eggs with colours derived from the same source.

1. [The German verb used here is 'leugnen'. Cf. p. 310 n. 1 below.]

2

A woman who is now seriously ill in consequence of a frustration in life was in her earlier years a particularly capable, truth-loving, serious and virtuous girl, and became an affectionate[1] wife. But still earlier, in the first years of her life, she had been a wilful and discontented child, and, though she had changed fairly quickly into an excessively good and conscientious one, there were occurrences in her schooldays, which, when she fell ill, caused her deep self-reproaches, and were regarded by her as proofs of fundamental depravity. Her memory told her that in those days she had often bragged and lied. Once on the way to school a school-fellow had said boastfully: 'Yesterday we had ice at dinner.' She replied: 'Oh we have ice every day.' In reality she did not know what ice at dinner could mean; she only knew ice in the long blocks in which it is carted about, but she assumed that there must be something grand in having it for dinner, so she refused to be outdone by her school-fellow.

When she was ten years old, they were set the task in the drawing lesson of making a free-hand drawing of a circle. But she used a pair of compasses, thus easily producing a perfect circle, and showed her achievement in triumph to her neighbour in class. The mistress came up, heard her boasting, discovered the marks of the compasses in the circle, and questioned the girl. But she stubbornly denied what she had done, would not give way to any evidence, and took refuge in sullen silence. The mistress consulted with her father about it. They were both influenced by the girl's usually good behaviour into deciding not to take any further steps about the matter.

Both the child's lies were instigated by the same complex. As the eldest of five children, the little girl early developed an unusually strong attachment to her father, which was destined when she was grown up to wreck her happiness in life. But she could not long escape the discovery that her beloved father

1. [In 1913 only, the words 'and happy' appeared at this point.]

was not so great a personage as she was inclined to think him. He had to struggle against money difficulties; he was not so powerful or so distinguished as she had imagined. But she could not put up with this departure from her ideal. Since, as women do, she based all her ambition on the man she loved, she became too strongly dominated by the motive of supporting her father against the world. So she boasted to her schoolfellows, in order not to have to belittle her father. When, later on, she learned to translate ice for dinner by 'glace', her self-reproaches about this reminiscence led her by an easy path into a pathological dread of pieces or splinters of glass.[1]

Her father was an excellent draughtsman, and had often enough excited the delight and admiration of the children by exhibitions of his skill. It was as an identification of herself with her father that she had drawn the circle at school – which she could only do successfully by deceitful methods. It was as though she wanted to boast: 'Look at what my father can do!' The sense of guilt that was attached to her excessive fondness for her father found its expression in connection with her attempted deception; an admission was impossible for the same reason that was given in the first of these observations [p. 289]: it would inevitably have been an admission of her hidden incestuous love.

We should not think lightly of such episodes in the life of children. It would be a serious mistake to read into childish misdemeanours like these a prognosis of the development of a bad character. Nevertheless, they are intimately connected with the most powerful motive forces in children's minds, and give notice of dispositions that will lead to later eventualities in their lives or to future neuroses.

1. [The German 'Glas', like its English equivalent 'glass', has a sound similar to that of the French 'glace' ('ice').]

ON TRANSFORMATIONS OF
INSTINCT AS EXEMPLIFIED IN
ANAL EROTISM
(1917)

EDITOR'S NOTE

ÜBER TRIEBUMSETZUNGEN, INSBESONDERE DER ANALEROTIK

(A) German Editions:

1917   *Int. Z. ärztl. Psychoanal.,* **4** (3), 125–30.
1918   *S.K.S.N.,* **4,** 139–48 (1922, 2nd. ed.).
1924   *Gesammelte Schriften,* **5,** 268–76.
1926   *Psychoanalyse der Neurosen,* 40–49.
1931   *Sexualtheorie und Traumlehre,* 116–24.
1946   *Gesammelte Werke,* **10,** 402–10.

(B) English Translations:

'On the Transformation of Instincts with Special Reference
to Anal Erotism'

1924   *Collected Papers,* **2,** 164–71. (Tr. E. Glover.)
1955   *Standard Edition,* **17,** 125–33 (with a modified title).

The present edition is a corrected reprint of the *Standard Edition* version, with a few editorial changes.

Though this paper was not published until 1917, it was probably written considerably earlier – perhaps even in 1915. Long delays in publication were inevitable at this period, owing to the difficulties of war conditions. The gist of it had already appeared in a paragraph added to the 1915 edition of Freud's *Three Essays,* p. 103f. above. Moreover, many conclusions reached here seem to be derived from the analysis of the 'Wolf Man' (1918*b*), whose case history was mostly written in the autumn of 1914. The later part of Section VII of that work exemplifies in some detail the thesis of the present paper.

ON TRANSFORMATIONS OF INSTINCT AS EXEMPLIFIED IN ANAL EROTISM

SOME years ago, observations made during psychoanalysis led me to suspect that the constant co-existence in any one of the three character-traits of *orderliness*, *parsimony* and *obstinacy* indicated an intensification of the anal-erotic components in his sexual constitution, and that these modes of reaction, which were favoured by his ego, had been established during the course of his development through the assimilation of his anal erotism.[1]

In that publication my main object was to make known the fact of this established relation; I was little concerned about its theoretical significance. Since then there has been a general consensus of opinion that each one of the three qualities, avarice, pedantry and obstinacy, springs from anal-erotic sources – or, to express it more cautiously and more completely – draws powerful contributions from those sources. The cases in which these defects of character were combined and which in consequence bore a special stamp (the 'anal character') were merely extreme instances, which were bound to betray the particular connection that interests us here even to an unobservant eye.

As a result of numerous impressions, and in particular of one specially cogent analytical observation, I came to the conclusion a few years later that in the development of the libido in man the phase of genital primacy must be preceded by a 'pregenital organization' in which sadism and anal erotism play the leading parts.[2]

1. 'Character and Anal Erotism' (1908*b*) [see above, p. 207ff.].
2. 'The Disposition to Obsessional Neurosis' (1913*i*).

From that moment we had to face the problem of the later history of the anal-erotic instinctual impulses. What becomes of them when, owing to the establishment of a definitive genital organization, they have lost their importance in sexual life? Do they preserve their original nature, but in a state of repression? Are they sublimated or assimilated by transformation into character-traits? Or do they find a place within the new organization of sexuality characterized by genital primacy? Or, since none of these vicissitudes of anal erotism is likely to be the only one, to what extent and in what way does each of them share in deciding its fate? For the organic sources of anal erotism cannot of course be buried as a result of the emergence of the genital organization.

One would think that there could be no lack of material from which to provide an answer, since the processes of development and transformation in question must have taken place in everyone undergoing analysis. Yet the material is so obscure, the abundance of ever-recurring impressions so confusing, that even now I am unable to solve the problem fully and can do no more than make some contributions to its solution. In making them I need not refrain from mentioning, where the context allows it, other instinctual transformations besides anal-erotic ones. Finally, it scarcely requires to be emphasized that the developmental events here described – just as the others found in psychoanalysis – have been inferred from the regressions into which they had been forced by neurotic processes.

As a starting-point for this discussion we may take the fact that it appears as if in the products of the unconscious – spontaneous ideas, phantasies and symptoms – the concepts *faeces* (money, gift),[1] *baby* and *penis* are ill-distinguished from one another and are easily interchangeable. We realize, of course, that to express oneself in this way is incorrectly to apply to the sphere of the unconscious terms which belong properly

1. [The relations between faeces and money, or gold, are discussed at some length in 'Character and Anal Erotism', pp. 213–15 above.]

to other regions of mental life, and that we have been led astray by the advantages offered by an analogy. To put the matter in a form less open to objection, these elements in the unconscious are often treated as if they were equivalent and could replace one another freely.

This is most easily seen in the relation between 'baby' and 'penis'. It cannot be without significance that in the symbolic language of dreams, as well as of everyday life, both may be replaced by the same symbol; both baby and penis are called a 'little one' ['das Kleine']. It is a well-known fact that symbolic speech often ignores difference of sex. The 'little one', which originally meant the male genital organ, may thus have acquired a secondary application to the female genitals.

If we penetrate deeply enough into the neurosis of a woman, we not infrequently meet with the repressed wish to possess a penis like a man. We call this wish 'envy for a penis' and include it in the castration complex. Chance mishaps in the life of such a woman, mishaps which are themselves frequently the result of a very masculine disposition, have re-activated this infantile wish and, through the backward flow of libido, made it the chief vehicle of her neurotic symptoms. In other women we find no evidence of this wish for a penis; it is replaced by the wish for a baby, the frustration of which in real life can lead to the outbreak of a neurosis. It looks as if such women had understood (although this could not possibly have acted as a motive) that nature has given babies to women as a substitute for the penis that has been denied them. With other women, again, we learn that both wishes were present in their childhood and that one replaced the other. At first they had wanted a penis like a man; then at a later, though still childish, stage there appeared instead the wish for a baby. The impression is forced upon us that this variety in our findings is caused by accidental factors during chidhood (e.g. the presence or absence of brothers or the birth of a new baby at some favourable time of life), so that the wish for a penis and the wish for a baby would be fundamentally identical.

We can say what the ultimate outcome of the infantile wish for a penis is in women in whom the determinants of a neurosis in later life are absent: it changes into the wish for a *man*, and thus puts up with the man as an appendage to the penis. This transformation, therefore, turns an impulse which is hostile to the female sexual function into one which is favourable to it. Such women are in this way made capable of an erotic life based on the masculine type of object-love, which can exist alongside the feminine one proper, derived from narcissism. We already know[1] that in other cases it is only a baby that makes the transition from narcissistic self-love to object-love possible. So that in this respect too a baby can be represented by the penis.

I have had occasional opportunities of being told women's dreams that had occurred after their first experience of intercourse. They revealed an unmistakable wish in the woman to keep for herself the penis which she had felt. Apart from their libidinal origin, then, these dreams indicated a temporary regression from man to penis as the object of her wish. One would certainly be inclined to trace back the wish for a man in a purely rationalistic way to the wish for a baby, since a woman is bound to understand sooner or later that there can be no baby without the co-operation of a man. It is, however, more likely that the wish for a man arises independently of the wish for a baby, and that when it arises – from understandable motives belonging entirely to ego-psychology – the original wish for a penis becomes attached to it as an unconscious libidinal reinforcement. The importance of the process described lies in the fact that a part of the young woman's narcissistic masculinity is thus changed into femininity, and so can no longer operate in a way harmful to the female sexual function.

Along another path, a part of the erotism of the pregenital phase, too, becomes available for use in the phase of genital

1. [See the later part of Section II of Freud's paper on narcissism (1914c).]

primacy. The baby is regarded as 'lumf'[1] (cf. the analysis of 'Little Hans'), as something which becomes detached from the body by passing through the bowel. A certain amount of libidinal cathexis which originally attached to the contents of the bowel can thus be extended to the baby born through it. Linguistic evidence of this identity of baby and faeces is contained in the expression 'to *give* someone a baby'. For its faeces are the infant's first *gift*, a part of his body which he will give up only on persuasion by someone he loves, to whom, indeed, he will make a spontaneous gift of it as a token of affection; for, as a rule, infants do not dirty strangers. (There are similar if less intense reactions with urine.) Defaecation affords the first occasion on which the child must decide between a narcissistic and an object-loving attitude. He either parts obediently with his faeces, 'sacrifices' them to his love, or else retains them for purposes of auto-erotic satisfaction and later as a means of asserting his own will. If he makes the latter choice we are in the presence of *defiance* (obstinacy) which, accordingly, springs from a narcissistic clinging to anal erotism.

It is probable that the first meaning which a child's interest in faeces develops is that of 'gift' rather than 'gold' or 'money'. The child knows no money apart from what is given him – no money acquired and none inherited of his own. Since his faeces are his first gift, the child easily transfers his interest from that substance to the new one which he comes across as the most valuable gift in life. Those who question this derivation of gifts should consider their experience of psychoanalytic treatment, study the gifts they receive as doctors from their patients, and watch the storms of transference which a gift from them can rouse in their patients.

Thus the interest in faeces is continued partly as interest in money, partly as a wish for a baby, in which latter an anal-erotic and a genital impulse ('envy for a penis') converge. But the penis has another anal-erotic significance apart from

1. ['Little Hans's' word for faeces. Cf. (1909*b*), *P.F.L.*, **8**, 215, 229 *n*.]

its relation to the interest in a baby. The relationship between the penis and the passage lined with mucous membrane which it fills and excites already has its prototype in the pregenital, anal-sadistic phase. The faecal mass, or as one patient called it, the faecal 'stick', represents as it were the first penis, and the stimulated mucous membrane of the rectum represents that of the vagina. There are people whose anal erotism remains vigorous and unmodified up to the age preceding puberty (ten to twelve years); we learn from them that during the pregenital phase they had already developed in phantasy and in perverse play an organization analogous to the genital one, in which penis and vagina were represented by the faecal stick and the rectum. In other people – obsessional neurotics – we can observe the result of a regressive debasement of the genital organization. This is expressed in the fact that every phantasy originally conceived on the genital level is transposed to the anal level – the penis being replaced by the faecal mass and the vagina by the rectum.

If the interest in faeces recedes in a normal way, the organic analogy we have described here has the effect of transferring the interest on to the penis. If, later, in the course of the child's sexual researches[1] he should learn that babies are born from the bowel, they inherit the greater part of his anal erotism; they have, however, been preceded by the penis in this as well as in another sense.

I feel sure that by this time the manifold interrelations of the series – faeces, penis, baby – have become totally unintelligible; so I will try to remedy the defect by presenting them diagrammatically, and in considering the diagram we can review the same material in a different order. Unfortunately, this technical device is not sufficiently pliable for our purpose, or possibly we have not yet learned to use it with effect. In any case I hope the reader will not expect too much from it.

1. [See Freud's paper 'On the Sexual Theories of Children' (1908c), p. 197f. above.]

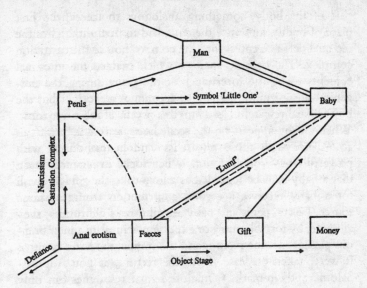

Anal erotism finds a narcissistic application in the production of defiance, which constitutes an important reaction on the part of the ego against demands made by other people. Interest in faeces is carried over first to interest in gifts, and then to interest in money. In girls, the discovery of the penis gives rise to envy for it, which later changes into the wish for a man as the possessor of a penis. Even before this the wish for a penis has changed into the wish for a baby, or the latter wish has taken the place of the former one. An organic analogy between penis and baby (dotted line) is expressed by the existence of a symbol ('little one') common to both. A rational wish (double line) then leads from the wish for a baby to the wish for a man: we have already appreciated the importance of this instinctual transformation.

Another part of the nexus of relations can be observed much more clearly in the male. It arises when the boy's sexual researches lead him to the discovery of the absence of a penis in women. He concludes that the penis must be a detachable part of the body, something analogous to faeces, the first piece of bodily substance the child had to part with. Thus the old anal defiance enters into the composition of the castration complex. The organic analogy which enabled the intestinal contents to be the forerunner of the penis during the pre-genital phase cannot come into account as a motive; but the boy's sexual researches lead him to a psychical substitute for it. When a baby appears on the scene he regards it as 'lumf', in accordance with those researches, and he cathects it with powerful anal-erotic interest. When social experiences teach that a baby is to be regarded as a love-token, a gift, the wish for a baby receives a second contribution from the same source. Faeces, penis and baby are all three solid bodies; they all three, by forcible entry or expulsion, stimulate a membran-ous passage, i.e. the rectum and the vagina, the latter being as it were 'taken on lease' from the rectum, as Lou Andreas-Salomé aptly remarks.[1] Infantile sexual researches can only lead to the conclusion that the baby follows the same route as the faecal mass. The function of the penis is not usually discovered by those researches. But it is interesting to note that after so many détours an organic correspondence reappears in the psychical sphere as an unconscious identity.

1. In her paper '"Anal" und "Sexual"' (1916). [Freud added a foot-note in 1920 to the second of his *Three Essays* (1905*d*, p. 104 *n*. above), in which he summarized the contents of that paper.]

THE INFANTILE GENITAL ORGANIZATION

ORGANIZATION

(AN INTERPOLATION INTO THE THEORY OF SEXUALITY)

(1923)

EDITOR'S NOTE

DIE INFANTILE GENITALORGANISATION
(EINE EINSCHALTUNG IN DIE SEXUALTHEORIE)

(A) GERMAN EDITIONS:

1923 *Int. Z. Psychoanal.*, **9** (2), 168–71.
1930 *Gesammelte Werke*, **13**, 291–8.

(B) ENGLISH TRANSLATIONS:

'The Infantile Genital Organization of the Libido:
A Supplement to the Theory of Sexuality'
1924 *Int. J. Psycho-Anal.*, **5**, 125–9. (Tr. Joan Riviere.)
1961 *Standard Edition*, **19**, 139–45 (with a modified title).

The present edition is a corrected reprint of the *Standard Edition* version, with some editorial changes.

This paper was written in February 1923 (see Jones, 1957, 106). It is essentially, as its sub-title implies, an addition to Freud's *Three Essays on the Theory of Sexuality* (1905*d*); and in fact a new footnote giving the gist of what is put forward here was added to the edition of that work which appeared in the following year (1924), see above, pp. 118–19. The starting-point of this paper is mainly from Sections 5 and 6 of the second *Essay*, pp. 112–19 above, both of which date only from 1915. But it also takes up ideas that will be found in the last pages of the paper on 'The Disposition to Obsessional Neurosis' (1913*i*), where the anal-sadistic pregenital stage of sexual development is discussed (actually for the first time), as well as many that go back earlier still, to 'The Sexual Theories of Children' (1908c), pp. 193–8 above. The phallic stage – the last of the successive immature organizations of the sexual instinct to be described by Freud, and the latest in the developmental series – makes its first appearance in the present paper.

THE INFANTILE GENITAL ORGANIZATION

(AN INTERPOLATION INTO THE THEORY OF SEXUALITY)

THE difficulty of the work of research in psychoanalysis is clearly shown by the fact of its being possible, in spite of whole decades of unremitting observation, to overlook features that are of general occurrence and situations that are characteristic, until at last they confront one in an unmistakable form. The remarks that follow are intended to make good a neglect of this sort in the field of infantile sexual development.

Readers of my *Three Essays on the Theory of Sexuality* (1905*d*) will be aware that I have never undertaken any thorough remodelling of that work in its later editions, but have retained the original arrangement and have kept abreast of the advances made in our knowledge by means of interpolations and alterations in the text.[1] In doing this, it may often have happened that what was old and what was more recent did not admit of being merged into an entirely uncontradictory whole. Originally, as we know, the accent was on a portayal of the fundamental difference between the sexual life of children and of adults; later, the *pregenital organizations* of the libido made their way into the foreground, and also the remarkable and momentous fact of the *diphasic onset* of sexual development. Finally, our interest was engaged by the *sexual researches* of children; and from this we were able to recognize the far-reaching *approximation of the final outcome of sexuality in childhood* (in about the fifth year) to the definitive form taken by it in the adult. This is the point at which I left things in the last (1922) edition of my *Three Essays*.

1. [Cf. the Editor's Note to that work, p. 34 above.]

On p. 63 of that volume[1] I wrote that 'the choice of an object, such as we have shown to be characteristic of the pubertal phase of development, has already frequently or habitually been effected during the years of childhood: that is to say, the whole of the sexual currents have become directed towards a single person in relation to whom they seek to achieve their aims. This then is the closest approximation possible in childhood to the final form taken by sexual life after puberty. The only difference lies in the fact that in childhood the combination of the component instincts and their subordination under the primacy of the genitals have been effected only very incompletely or not at all. Thus the establishment of that primacy in the service of reproduction is the last phase through which the organization of sexuality passes.'

Today I should no longer be satisfied with the statement that in the early period of childhood the primacy of the genitals has been effected only very incompletely or not at all. The approximation of the child's sexual life to that of the adult goes much further and is not limited solely to the coming into being of the choice of an object. Even if a proper combination of the component instincts under the primacy of the genitals is not effected, nevertheless, at the height of the course of development of infantile sexuality, interest in the genitals and in their activity acquires a dominating significance which falls little short of that reached in maturity. At the same time, the main characteristic of this 'infantile genital organization' is its *difference* from the final genital organization of the adult. This consists in the fact that, for both sexes, only one genital, namely the male one, comes into account. What is present, therefore, is not a primacy of the genitals, but a primacy of the *phallus*.

Unfortunately we can describe this state of things only as

1. [This corresponds to p. 118 above (in a Section added in 1915). See also the footnote there, added in 1924, which briefly summarizes the findings in the present paper.]

it affects the male child; the corresponding processes in the little girl are not known to us. The small boy undoubtedly perceives the distinction between men and women, but to begin with he has no occasion to connect it with a difference in their genitals. It is natural for him to assume that all other living beings, humans and animals, possess a genital like his own; indeed, we know that he looks for an organ analogous to his own in inanimate things as well.[1] This part of the body, which is easily excitable, prone to changes and so rich in sensations, occupies the boy's interest to a high degree and is constantly setting new tasks to his instinct for research. He wants to see it in other people as well, so as to compare it with his own; and he behaves as though he had a vague idea that this organ could and should be bigger. The driving force which this male portion of the body will develop later at puberty expresses itself at this period of life mainly as an urge to investigate, as sexual curiosity. Many of the acts of exhibitionism and aggression which children commit, and which in later years would be judged without hesitation to be expressions of lust, prove in analysis to be experiments undertaken in the service of sexual research.

In the course of these researches the child arrives at the discovery that the penis is not a possession which is common to all creatures that are like himself. An accidental sight of the genitals of a little sister of playmate provides the occasion for this discovery. In unusually intelligent children, the observation of girls urinating will even earlier have aroused a suspicion that there is something different here. For they will have seen a different posture and heard a different sound, and will have made attempts to repeat their observations so as to obtain enlightenment. We know how children react to their

---

1. [Cf. the 'Little Hans' analysis (1909b), *P.F.L.*, **8**, 173.] – It is, incidentally, remarkable what a small degree of attention the other part of the male genitals, the little sac with its contents, attracts in children. From all one hears in analyses, one would not guess that the male genitals consisted of anything more than the penis.

first impressions of the absence of a penis. They disavow the fact[1] and believe that they *do* see a penis, all the same. They gloss over the contradiction between observation and pre-conception by telling themselves that the penis is still small and will grow bigger presently;[2] and they then slowly come to the emotionally significant conclusion that after all the penis had at least been there before and been taken away afterwards. The lack of a penis is regarded as a result of castra-tion, and so now the child is faced with the task of coming to terms with castration in relation to himself. The further developments are too well known generally to make it necessary to recapitulate them here. But it seems to me that *the significance of the castration complex can only be rightly appreciated if its origin in the phase of phallic primacy is also taken into account.*[3]

1. [From now on, the concept of 'disavowal' comes to occupy a more and more important place in Freud's writings. In the present passage the German word used is '*leugnen*', but its place is later almost invariably taken by the allied form '*verleugnen*'. Usually, as here, the topic concerned is the castration complex. See, for instance, the papers on masochism (1924c), and on the distinction between the sexes (1925j), p. 336 below. In his later paper on fetishism (1927e) p. 352f. below, Freud differentiates between the correct uses of the words '*Verdrängung* (repression)' and '*Verleugnung* (disavowal)'. The word *Verleugnung* has in the past often been translated 'denial' and the associated verb by 'to deny'. These are, however, ambiguous words and it has been thought better to choose 'to disavow' in order to avoid confusion with the German '*verneinen*', used, for instance, in the paper on 'Negation', 'Die Verneinung', (1925h). This latter German word is, once more in order to avoid ambiguity, there translated by 'to negate'.]

2. [Cf. the 'Little Hans' analysis, *P.F.L.*, 8, 175. See also pp. 177 and 194 above.]

3. It has been quite correctly pointed out that a child gets the idea of a narcissistic injury through a bodily loss from the experience of losing his mother's breast after sucking, from the daily surrender of his faeces and, indeed, even from his separation from the womb at birth. Never-theless, one ought not to speak of a castration complex until this idea of a loss has become connected with the male genitals. [This point is treated at greater length in a footnote added in 1923 to the 'Little Hans'

We know, too, to what a degree depreciation of women, horror of women, and a disposition to homosexuality are derived from the final conviction that women have no penis. Ferenczi (1923) has recently, with complete justice, traced back the mythological symbol of horror – Medusa's head – to the impression of the female genitals devoid of a penis.[1]

It should not be supposed, however, that the child quickly and readily makes a generalization from his observation that some women have no penis. He is in any case debarred from doing so by his assumption that the lack of a penis is the result of having been castrated as a punishment. On the contrary, the child believes that it is only unworthy female persons that have lost their genitals – females who, in all probability, were guilty of inadmissible impulses similar to his own. Women whom he respects, like his mother, retain a penis for a long time. For him, being a woman is not yet synonymous with being without a penis.[2] It is not till later, when the child takes up the problems of the origin and birth of babies, and when he guesses that only women can give birth to them – it is only then that the mother, too, loses her penis. And, along with this, quite complicated theories are built up to explain the exchange of the penis for a baby. In all this, the female genitals never seem to be discovered. The baby, we know, is supposed to live inside the mother's body (in her bowel) and to be born

---

analysis, P.F.L., 8, 172 n. 2. It is also mentioned in 'The Dissolution of the Oedipus Complex' (1924d), p. 317 below.]

1. I should like to add that what is indicated in the myth is the *mother's* genitals. Athene, who carries Medusa's head on her armour, becomes in consequence the unapproachable woman, the sight of whom extinguishes all thought of a sexual approach. – [Freud had himself drafted a short paper on this subject a year earlier, which was published posthumously (1940c [1922]).]

2. I learnt from the analysis of a young married woman who had no father but several aunts that she clung, until quite far on in the latency period, to the belief that her mother and her aunts had a penis. One of her aunts, however, was feeble-minded; and she regarded this aunt as castrated, as she felt herself to be.

through the intestinal outlet. These last theories carry us beyond the stretch of time covered by the infantile sexual period.

It is not unimportant to bear in mind what transformations are undergone, during the sexual development of childhood, by the polarity of sex with which we are familiar. A first antithesis is introduced with the choice of object, which, of course, presupposes a subject and an object. At the stage of the pregenital sadistic-anal organization, there is as yet no question of male and female; the antithesis between *active* and *passive* is the dominant one.[1] At the following stage of infantile genital organization, which we now know about, *maleness* exists, but not femaleness. The antithesis here is between having *a male genital* and being *castrated*. It is not until development has reached its completion at puberty that the sexual polarity coincides with *male* and *female*. Maleness combines [the factors of] subject, activity and possession of the penis; femaleness takes over [those of] object and passivity. The vagina is now valued as a place of shelter for the penis; it enters into the heritage of the womb.

1. Cf. [a passage added in 1915 to] *Three Essays on the Theory of Sexuality*, [p. 117 above. See further a footnote also added to the same work in 1915, pp. 141–2 above].

THE DISSOLUTION OF THE
OEDIPUS COMPLEX
(1924)

EDITOR'S NOTE

DER UNTERGANG DES ÖDIPUSKOMPLEXES

(A) GERMAN EDITIONS:

1924   *Int. Z. Psychoanal.*, **10** (3), 245–52.
1940   *Gesammelte Werke*, **13**, 395–402.

(B) ENGLISH TRANSLATIONS:

'The Passing of the Oedipus Complex'

1924   *Int. J. Psycho-Anal.*, **5** (4), 419–24. (Tr. Joan Riviere.)
1961   *Standard Edition*, **19**, 171–9 (with a changed title.).

The present edition is a corrected reprint of the *Standard Edition* version, with a few editorial changes.

This paper, written in the early months of 1924, was in its essence an elaboration of a passage in Chapter III of *The Ego and the Id* (1923*b*), where the phrase 'the dissolution of the Oedipus complex' was introduced by Freud. It further claims our special interest as laying emphasis for the first time on the different course taken by the development of sexuality in boys and in girls. This fresh line of thought was carried further some eighteen months later in Freud's paper on 'Some Psychical Consequences of the Anatomical Distinction between the Sexes' (1925*j*). The history of Freud's changing views on this subject is outlined in the Editor's Note to the latter paper (p. 325ff. below).

THE DISSOLUTION OF THE
OEDIPUS COMPLEX

To an ever-increasing extent the Oedipus complex reveals its importance as the central phenomenon of the sexual period of early childhood. After that, its dissolution takes place; it succumbs to repression, as we say, and is followed by the latency period. It has not yet become clear, however, what it is that brings about its destruction. Analyses seem to show that it is the experience of painful disappointments. The little girl likes to regard herself as what her father loves above all else; but the time comes when she has to endure a harsh punishment from him and she is cast out of her fool's paradise. The boy regards his mother as his own property; but he finds one day that she has transferred her love and solicitude to a new arrival. Reflection must deepen our sense of the importance of those influences, for it will emphasize the fact that distressing experiences of this sort, which act in opposition to the content of the complex, are inevitable. Even when no special events occur, like those we have mentioned as examples, the absence of the satisfaction hoped for, the continued denial of the desired baby, must in the end lead the small lover to turn away from his hopeless longing. In this way the Oedipus complex would go to its destruction from its lack of success, from the effects of its internal impossibility.

Another view is that the Oedipus complex must collapse because the time has come for its disintegration, just as the milk-teeth fall out when the permanent ones begin to grow. Although the majority of human beings go through the Oedipus complex as an individual experience, it is nevertheless a phenomenon which is determined and laid down by heredity and which is bound to pass away according to programme when the next pre-ordained phase of development sets in.

This being so, it is of no great importance what the occasions are which allow this to happen, or, indeed, whether any such occasions can be discovered at all.

The justice of both these views cannot be disputed. Moreover, they are compatible. There is room for the ontogenetic view side by side with the more far-reaching phylogenetic one. It is also true that even at birth the whole individual is destined to die, and perhaps his organic disposition may already contain the indication of what he is to die from. Nevertheless, it remains of interest to follow out how this innate programme is carried out and in what way accidental noxae exploit his disposition.

We have lately[1] been made more clearly aware than before that a child's sexual development advances to a certain phase at which the genital organ has already taken over the leading role. But this genital is the male one only, or, more correctly, the penis; the female genital has remained undiscovered. This phallic phase, which is contemporaneous with the Oedipus complex, does not develop further to the definitive genital organization, but is submerged, and is succeeded by the latency period. Its termination, however, takes place in a typical manner and in conjunction with events that are of regular recurrence.

When the (male) child's interest turns to his genitals he betrays the fact by manipulating them frequently; and he then finds that the adults do not approve of this behaviour. More or less plainly, more or less brutally, a threat is pronounced that this part of him which he values so highly will be taken away from him. Usually it is from women that the threat emanates; very often they seek to strengthen their authority by a reference to the father or the doctor, who, so they say, will carry out the punishment. In a number of cases the women will themselves mitigate the threat in a symbolic manner by telling the child that what is to be removed is not his genital, which actually plays a passive part, but his hand,

1. [See 'The Infantile Genital Organization' (1923e), p. 308ff. above.]

which is the active culprit. It happens particularly often that the little boy is threatened with castration, not because he plays with his penis with his hand, but because he wets his bed every night and cannot be got to be clean. Those in charge of him behave as if this nocturnal incontinence was the result and the proof of his being unduly concerned with his penis, and they are probably right.[1] In any case, long-continued bed-wetting is to be equated with the emissions of adults. It is an expression of the same excitation of the genitals which has impelled the child to masturbate at this period.

Now it is my view that what brings about the destruction of the child's phallic genital organization is this threat of castration. Not immediately, it is true, and not without other influences being brought to bear as well. For to begin with the boy does not believe in the threat or obey it in the least. Psychoanalysis has recently attached importance to two experiences which all children go through and which, it is suggested, prepare them for the loss of highly valued parts of the body. These experiences are the withdrawal of the mother's breast – at first intermittently and later for good – and the daily demand on them to give up the contents of the bowel. But there is no evidence to show that, when the threat of castration takes place, those experiences have any effect.[2] It is not until a *fresh* experience comes his way that the child begins to reckon with the possibility of being castrated, and then only hesitatingly and unwillingly, and not without making efforts to depreciate the significance of something he has himself observed.

The observation which finally breaks down his unbelief is

1. [Cf. the second of the *Three Essays* (1905*d*), p. 107*f*. above.]

2. [Cf. a footnote added, at about the time this paper was written, to the 'Little Hans' analysis (1909*b*), P.F.L., **8**, 172 *n*. 2. A third experience of separation – that of birth – is also mentioned there, but, as in the present passage, Freud objects to the confusion with the castration complex. Cf. also a footnote to 'The Infantile Genital Organization' (1923*e*), p. 310 *n.* 3 above.]

the sight of the female genitals. Sooner or later the child, who is so proud of his possession of a penis, has a view of the genital region of a little girl, and cannot help being convinced of the absence of a penis in a creature who is so like himself. With this, the loss of his own penis becomes imaginable, and the threat of castration takes its deferred effect.

We should not be as short-sighted as the person in charge of the child who threatens him with castration, and we must not overlook the fact that at this time masturbation by no means represents the whole of his sexual life. As can be clearly shown, he stands in the Oedipus attitude to his parents; his masturbation is only a genital discharge of the sexual excitation belonging to the complex, and throughout his later years will owe its importance to that relationship. The Oedipus complex offered the child two possibilities of satisfaction, an active and a passive one. He could put himself in his father's place in a masculine fashion and have intercourse with his mother as his father did, in which case he would soon have felt the latter as a hindrance; or he might want to take the place of his mother and be loved by his father, in which case his mother would become superfluous. The child may have had only very vague notions as to what constitutes a satisfying erotic intercourse; but certainly the penis must play a part in it, for the sensations in his own organ were evidence of that. So far he had had no occasion to doubt that women possessed a penis. But now his acceptance of the possibility of castration, his recognition that women were castrated, made an end of both possible ways of obtaining satisfaction from the Oedipus complex. For both of them entailed the loss of his penis – the masculine one as a resulting punishment and the feminine one as a precondition. If the satisfaction of love in the field of the Oedipus complex is to cost the child his penis, a conflict is bound to arise between his narcissistic interest in that part of his body and the libidinal cathexis of his parental objects. In this conflict the first of these forces normally triumphs: the child's ego turns away from the Oedipus complex.

I have described elsewhere how this turning away takes place.[1] The object-cathexes are given up and replaced by identifications. The authority of the father or the parents is introjected into the ego, and there it forms the nucleus of the super-ego, which takes over the severity of the father and perpetuates his prohibition against incest, and so secures the ego from the return of the libidinal object-cathexis. The libidinal trends belonging to the Oedipus complex are in part desexualized and sublimated (a thing which probably happens with every transformation into an identification) and in part inhibited in their aim and changed into impulses of affection. The whole process has, on the one hand, preserved the genital organ – has averted the danger of its loss – and, on the other, has paralysed it – has removed its function. This process ushers in the latency period, which now interrupts the child's sexual development.

I see no reason for denying the name of a 'repression' to the ego's turning away from the Oedipus complex, although later repressions come about for the most part with the participation of the super-ego, which in this case is only just being formed. But the process we have described is more than a repression. It is equivalent, if it is ideally carried out, to a destruction and an abolition of the complex. We may plausibly assume that we have here come upon the borderline – never a very sharply drawn one – between the normal and the pathological. If the ego has in fact not achieved much more than a *repression* of the complex, the latter persists in an unconscious state in the id and will later manifest its pathogenic effect.

Analytic observation enables us to recognize or guess these connections between the phallic organization, the Oedipus complex, the threat of castration, the formation of the super-ego and the latency period. These connections justify the statement that the destruction of the Oedipus complex is brought about by the threat of castration. But this does not

1. [See the first part of Chapter III of *The Ego and the Id*.]

dispose of the problem; there is room for a theoretical speculation which may upset the results we have come to or put them
in a new light. Before we start along this new path, however,
we must turn to a question which has arisen in the course of
this discussion and has so far been left on one side. The process
which has been described refers, as has been expressly said, to
male children only. How does the corresponding development
take place in little girls?

At this point our material – for some incomprehensible
reason[1] – becomes far more obscure and full of gaps. The
female sex, too, develops an Oedipus complex, a super-ego
and a latency period. May we also attribute a phallic organization and a castration complex to it? The answer is in the
affirmative; but these things cannot be the same as they are in
boys. Here the feminist demand for equal rights for the sexes
does not take us far, for the morphological distinction is
bound to find expression in differences of psychical development.[2] 'Anatomy is Destiny', to vary a saying of Napoleon's.
The little girl's clitoris behaves just like a penis to begin with;
but, when she makes a comparison with a playfellow of the
other sex, she perceives that she has 'come off badly'[3] and she
feels this as a wrong done to her and as a ground for inferiority.
For a while still she consoles herself with the expectation that
later on, when she grows older, she will acquire just as big an
appendage as the boy's. Here the masculinity complex of
women branches off.[4] But a female child does not understand
her lack of a penis as being a sex character; she explains it by
assuming that at some earlier date she had possessed an equally

1. [Freud suggested some explanation for this in Section I of his
paper on 'Female Sexuality' (1931b), pp. 371–3 below.]

2. [See 'Some Psychical Consequences of the Anatomical Distinction
between the Sexes' (1925j), p. 331ff. below. Much of what follows is
elaborated there. The paraphrase of Napoleon's epigram had appeared
already in the second paper on the psychology of love (1912d), p. 259
above.]

3. [Literally, 'come off too short'.]

4. [Cf. below, p. 336 and n. 3.]

large organ and had then lost it by castration. She seems not to extend this inference from herself to other, adult females, but, entirely on the lines of the phallic phase, to regard them as possession large and complete – that is to say, male – genitals. The essential difference thus comes about that the girl accepts castration as an accomplished fact, whereas the boy fears the possibility of its occurrence.

The fear of castration being thus excluded in the little girl, a powerful motive also drops out for the setting-up of a super-ego and for the breaking-off of the infantile genital organization. In her, far more than in the boy, these changes seem to be the result of upbringing and of intimidation from outside which threatens her with a loss of love. The girl's Oedipus complex is much simpler than that of the small bearer of the penis; in my experience, it seldom goes beyond the taking of her mother's place and the adopting of a feminine attitude towards her father. Renunciation of the penis is not tolerated by the girl without some attempt at compensation. She slips – along the line of a symbolic equation, one might say – from the penis to a baby. Her Oedipus complex culminates in a desire, which is long retained, to receive a baby from her father as a gift – to bear him a child.[1] One has an impression that the Oedipus complex is then gradually given up because this wish is never fulfilled. The two wishes – to possess a penis and a child – remain strongly cathected in the unconscious and help to prepare the female creature for her later sexual role. The comparatively lesser strength of the sadistic contribution to her sexual instinct, which we may no doubt connect with the stunted growth of her penis, makes it easier in her case for the direct sexual trends to be transformed into aim-inhibited trends of an affectionate kind. It must be admitted, however, that in general our insight into these developmental processes in girls is unsatisfactory, incomplete and vague.[2]

1. [Cf. Freud's paper on 'Transformations of Instinct' (1917c), p. 296ff. above; see also below, p. 340.]
2. [Freud discussed this topic much more fully in his papers on the

I have no doubt that the chronological and causal relations described here between the Oedipus complex, sexual intimidation (the threat of castration), the formation of the super-ego and the beginning of the latency period are of a typical kind; but I do not wish to assert that this type is the only possible one. Variations in the chronological order and in the linking-up of these events are bound to have a very important bearing on the development of the individual.

Since the publication of Otto Rank's interesting study, *The Trauma of Birth* [1924], even the conclusion arrived at by this modest investigation, to the effect that the boy's Oedipus complex is destroyed by the fear of castration, cannot be accepted without further discussion. Nevertheless, it seems to me premature to enter into such a discussion at the present time, and perhaps inadvisable to begin a criticism or an appreciation of Rank's view at this juncture.[1]

---

anatomical distinction between the sexes (1925j) and on female sexuality (1931b), pp. 331ff. and 371ff. below, in both of which he gave a very different account of the girl's Oedipus complex from the present one.]

1. [The question was taken up by Freud soon afterwards in *Inhibitions, Symptoms and Anxiety* (1926d). Cf. Section (e) of the Editor's Introduction to that work.]

SOME PSYCHICAL CONSEQUENCES OF THE ANATOMICAL DISTINCTION BETWEEN THE SEXES
(1925)

EDITOR'S NOTE

EINIGE PSYCHISCHE FOLGEN DES ANATOMISCHEN GESCHLECHTSUNTERSCHIEDS

(A) GERMAN EDITIONS:

1925   Int. Z. Psychoanal., II (4), 401–10.
1926   Psychoanalyse der Neurosen, 205–19.
1928   Gesammelte Schriften, II, 8–19.
1931   Sexualtheorie und Traumlehre, 207–20.
1948   Gesammelte Werke, 14, 19–30.

(B) ENGLISH TRANSLATIONS:

'Some Psychological Consequences of the Anatomical Distinction between the Sexes'

1927   Int. J. Psycho-Anal., 8 (2), 133–42. (Tr. James Strachey.)
1950   Collected Papers, 5, 186–97. (Revised reprint of above.)
1961   Standard Edition, 19, 241–58. (A corrected and freshly annotated version, with a slightly modified title, of the one published in 1950.)

The present edition is a corrected reprint of the *Standard Edition* version, with some editorial changes.

This paper was finished by August 1925, when Freud showed it to Ferenczi. It was read on his behalf by Anna Freud the Homburg International Psycho-Analytical Con

September 3, and was published in the *Zeitschrift* later in the autumn (Jones, 1957, 119).

What is in effect a first complete re-assessment of Freud's views on the psychological development of women will be found condensed in this short paper. It contains the germs of all his later work on the subject.

From early days Freud made complaints of the obscurity enveloping the sexual life of females, and of the fact that he had been obliged to base almost all his research into sexual development on material relating to males. See for instance his *Three Essays on the Theory of Sexuality* (1905*d*), p. 63 above, 'On the Sexual Theories of Children' (1908*c*), p. 189 above and again, much later, 'The Infantile Genital Organization' (1923*e*), p. 308f. above. Even after the date of the present paper in his pamphlet on lay analysis (1926*e*), he wrote: 'We know less about the sexual life of little girls than of boys. But we need not feel ashamed of this distinction; after all, the sexual life of adult women is a "dark continent" for psychology.'[1]

One result of this obscurity was to lead Freud to assume very often that the psychology of women could be taken simply as analogous to that of men. In his first full account of the Oedipus situation, for instance, in *The Interpretation of Dreams* (1900*a*), he assumes that there is a complete parallel between the two sexes, that 'a girl's first affection is for her father and a boy's first childish desires are for his mother' (*P.F.L.*, **4,** 358). Similarly, in his long description of the sexual development of children in Lecture 21 of the *Introductory Lectures*

---

1. Ernest Jones writes (1955, 468): 'There is little doubt that Freud found ᵥy of women more enigmatic than that of men. He said once to ... arte: "The great question that has never been answered ... ᵥe not yet been able to answer, despite my thirty years ... the feminine soul, is 'What does a woman want?'" ... ᵤes gives no date for this remark. Freud ... a pa ... ation of his difficulty in the last paragraph ... of his ... on 'Female Sexuality' (1931*b*), where he ... to a ... his transference-relation with women.

(1916–17) he writes: 'As you see, I have only described the relation of a *boy* to his father and mother. Things happen in just the same way with little girls, with the necessary changes: an affectionate attachment to her father, a need to get rid of her mother as superfluous . . .' (*P.F.L.*, **1**, 376.) Even as late as in *The Ego and the Id* (1923*b*) the complicated processes accompanying and following the dissolution of the Oedipus complex are supposed to be 'precisely analogous' in girls and boys (see the middle of Chapter III).

But in fact over a long period from the time of the 'Dora' analysis in 1900 (1905*e*), Freud's interest had not been directed to feminine psychology. It was not for fifteen years that he published any important case material dealing with a woman. Then came the case of female paranoia 'running counter to psychoanalytic theory' (1915*f*), the essence of which lay in the patient's relation to her mother. Not long after came the case of female homosexuality (1920*a*) of which the same might well be said. Between them came the study of beating phantasies (1919*e*), which was almost wholly concerned with the infantile sexual development of girls. And here already there is clear evidence of dissatisfaction with the 'precise analogy' between the two sexes: 'the expectation of there being a complete parallel was mistaken'. Thereafter the problem of the sexual history of women was no doubt constantly in Freud's mind. And although there is little about it in *The Ego and the Id* (1923*b*), it was the theories developed there concerning the end of the Oedipus complex which, linked with fresh clinical observations, gave the key to the new thesis. Freud was already feeling his way towards it in 'The Dissolution of the Oedipus Complex' (1924*d*), p. 315ff. above, but it is fully stated for the first time in the present paper. It was to be further enlarged on in the later paper on 'Female Sexuality' (1931*b*), p. 371ff. below (see the introductory Editor's No to it), in Lecture 33 of the *New Introductory Lectures* (19 and finally in Chapter VII of the posthumous *Ou Psycho-Analysis* (1940*a* [1938]).

Almost every detail is already present in a condensed form in this work. But it is remarkable that many of these details had been ready to hand long before and only required linking up. Thus certain peculiarities in the sexual development of girls had been noted and stressed. Already in the first edition of the *Three Essays* (1905d) Freud had maintained that in little girls the leading sexual organ was the clitoris, that, in conformity with this fact, 'the sexuality of little girls is of a wholly masculine character', and that 'a wave of repression at puberty' is required before the clitoris gives place to the vagina and masculinity to femininity (see above, pp. 141–4). Most of this had, indeed, been indicated many years before in a letter to Fliess of November 14, 1897 (Freud, 1950a, Letter 75). The matter was carried further in the paper on 'The Sexual Theories of Children' (1908c), where it was brought into relation with the girl's envy for the penis and the castration complex (see above, pp. 195–6), and this aspect was discussed afresh in 'The Taboo of Virginity' (1918a), p. 278ff. above. The fact that the injury to her narcissism caused by this leads to resentment against her mother was pointed out at the end of Section I of 'Some Character-Types' (1916d).

Nor had the fundamental basis of the new thesis been unstated – though for long periods it seemed forgotten. In the *Three Essays* we find the plain statement that a child's first sexual object is the mother's breast and that this is the prototype of every later love-relation (see above, p. 144f.). This was clearly meant to be true of girls as well as boys, but it seems to be repeated explicitly for the first time here (p. 334). The twofold change required of the little girl before she could arrive at the normal Oedipus complex thus became evident: a change in her leading sexual organ and a change in her sexual object. The need for an investigation of her 'pre-Oedipus' phase, together with the differences between girls and boys implied by the hypotheses in *The Ego and the Id* – the relation of their castration and Oedipus complexes and the further difference in the construction of their super-egos. It is the synthesis of these various pieces of knowledge, derived from such widely separated historical strata of Freud's work, which gives its importance to the present paper.

SOME PSYCHICAL CONSEQUENCES
OF THE ANATOMICAL DISTINCTION
BETWEEN THE SEXES

IN my own writings and in those of my followers more and more stress is laid on the necessity that the analyses of neurotics shall deal thoroughly with the remotest period of their childhood, the time of the early efflorescence of sexual life. It is only by examining the first manifestations of the patient's innate instinctual constitution and the effects of his earliest experiences that we can accurately gauge the motive forces that have led to his neurosis and can be secure against the errors into which we might be tempted by the degree to which things have become remodelled and overlaid in adult life. This requirement is not only of theoretical but also of practical importance, for it distinguishes our efforts from the work of those physicians whose interests are focused exclusively on therapeutic results and who employ analytic methods, but only up to a certain point. An analysis of early childhood such as we are considering is tedious and laborious and makes demands both upon the physician and upon the patient which cannot always be met. Moreover, it leads us into dark regions where there are as yet no signposts. Indeed, analysts may feel reassured, I think, that there is no risk of their work becoming mechanical, and so of losing its interest, during the next few decades.

In the following pages I bring forward some findings of analytic research which would be of great importance if they could be proved to apply universally. Why do I not postpone publication of them until further experience has given me the necessary proof, if such proof is obtainable? Because the conditions under which I work have undergone a change, with implications which I cannot disguise. Formerly, I was not one of those who are unable to hold back what seems to be a new discovery until it has been either confirmed or corrected. My *Interpretation of Dreams* (1900a) and my 'Fragment of an Analysis of a Case of Hysteria' (1905e) (the case of Dora) were suppressed by me – if not for the nine years enjoined by Horace – at all events for four or five years before I allowed them to be published. But in those days I had unlimited time before me – 'oceans of time'[1] as an amiable author puts it – and material poured in upon me in such quantities that fresh experiences were hardly to be escaped. Moreover, I was the only worker in a new field, so that my reticence involved no danger to myself and no loss to others.

But now everything has changed. The time before me is limited. The whole of it is no longer spent in working, so that my opportunities for making fresh observations are not so numerous. If I think I see something new, I am uncertain whether I can wait for it to be confirmed. And further, everything that is to be seen upon the surface has already been exhausted; what remains has to be slowly and laboriously dragged up from the depths. Finally, I am no longer alone. An eager crowd of fellow-workers is ready to make use of what is unfinished or doubtful, and I can leave to them that part of the work which I should otherwise have done myself. On this occasion, therefore, I feel justified in publishing something which stands in urgent need of confirmation before its value or lack of value can be decided.

In examining the earliest mental shapes assumed by the sexual life of children we have been in the habit of taking as the subject of our investigations the male child, the little boy. With little girls, so we have supposed, things must be similar, though in some way or other they must nevertheless be

1. [In English in the original. It is not clear what author Freud had in mind. – The reference to Horace is to his *Ars Poetica*, line 388.]

different. The point in development at which this difference lay could not be clearly determined.

In boys the situation of the Oedipus complex is the first stage that can be recognized with certainty. It is easy to understand, because at that stage a child retains the same object which he previously cathected with his libido – not as yet a genital one – during the preceding period while he was being suckled and nursed. The fact, too, that in this situation he regards his father as a disturbing rival and would like to get rid of him and take his place is a straightforward consequence of the actual state of affairs. I have shown elsewhere[1] how the Oedipus attitude in little boys belongs to the phallic phase, and how its destruction is brought about by the fear of castration – that is, by narcissistic interest in their genitals. The matter is made more difficult to grasp by the complicating circumstance that even in boys the Oedipus complex has a double orientation, active and passive, in accordance with their bisexual constitution; a boy also wants to take his *mother*'s place as the love-object of his *father* – a fact which we describe as the feminine attitude.[2]

As regards the prehistory of the Oedipus complex in boys we are far from complete clarity. We know that that period includes an identification of an affectionate sort with the boy's father, an identification which is still free from any sense of rivalry in regard to his mother. Another element of that stage is invariably, I believe, a masturbatory activity in connection with the genitals, the masturbation of early childhood, the more or less violent suppression of which by those in charge of the child sets the castration complex in action. It is to be assumed that this masturbation is attached to the Oedipus complex and serves as a discharge for the sexual excitation belonging to it. It is, however, uncertain whether the masturbation has this character from the first, or whether on the

1. 'The Dissolution of the Oedipus Complex' [(1924*d*), this volume p. 315. Much of what follows is an elaboration of that paper.]

2. [Cf. ibid., p. 318.]

contrary it makes its first appearance spontaneously as an activity of a bodily organ and is only brought into relation with the Oedipus complex at some later date; this second possibility is by far the more probable. Another doubtful question is the part played by bed-wetting and by the breaking of that habit through the intervention of training measures. We are inclined to make the simple connection that continued bed-wetting is a result of masturbation and that its suppression is regarded by boys as an inhibition of their genital activity – that is, as having the meaning of a threat of castration;[1] but whether we are always right in supposing this remains to be seen. Finally, analysis shows us in a shadowy way how the fact of a child at a very early age listening to his parents copulating may set up his first sexual excitation, and how that event may, owing to its after-effects, act as a starting-point for the child's whole sexual development. Masturbation, as well as the two attitudes in the Oedipus complex, later on become attached to this early experience, the child having subsequently interpreted its meaning. It is impossible, however, to suppose that these observations of coitus are of universal occurrence, so that at this point we are faced with the problem of 'primal phantasies'.[2] Thus the prehistory of the Oedipus complex, even in boys, raises all of these questions for sifting and explanation; and there is the further problem of whether we are to suppose that the process invariably follows the same course, or whether a great variety of different preliminary stages may not converge upon the same terminal situation.

In little girls the Oedipus complex raises one problem more than in boys. In both cases the mother is the original object; and there is no cause for surprise that boys retain that object in the Oedipus complex. But how does it happen that girls

1. [Cf. ibid., p. 317.]

2. [Cf. the discussion in the 'Wolf Man' analysis (1918b), especially Section V and the passage added later to Section VII (P.F.L., 9, 281–95 and 335–8), and Lecture 23 of the Introductory Lectures (1916–17).]

abandon it and instead take their father as an object? In pursuing this question I have been able to reach some conclusions which may throw light precisely on the prehistory of the Oedipus relation in girls.

Every analyst has come across certain women who cling with especial intensity and tenacity to the attachment to their father and to the wish in which it culminates of having a child by him. We have good reason to suppose that the same wishful phantasy was also the motive force of their infantile masturbation, and it is easy to form an impression that at this point we have been brought up against an elementary and unanalysable fact of infantile sexual life. But a thorough analysis of these very cases brings something different to light – namely, that here the Oedipus complex has a long prehistory and is in some respects a secondary formation.

The old paediatrician Lindner [1879] once remarked that a child discovers the genital zones (the penis or the clitoris) as a source of pleasure while indulging in sensual sucking (thumb-sucking).[1] I shall leave it an open question whether it is really true that the child takes the newly found source of pleasure in exchange for the recent loss of the mother's nipple – a possibility to which later phantasies (fellatio) seem to point. Be that as it may, the genital zone is discovered at some time or other, and there seems no justification for attributing any psychical content to the first activities in connection with it. But the first step in the phallic phase which begins in this way is not the linking-up of the masturbation with the object-cathexes of the Oedipus complex, but a momentous discovery which little girls are destined to make. They notice the penis of a brother or playmate, strikingly visible and of large proportions, at once recognize it as the superior counterpart of their own small and inconspicuous organ, and from that time forward fall a victim to envy for the penis.

There is an interesting contrast between the behaviour of the two sexes. In the analogous situation, when a little boy

1. Cf. *Three Essays on the Theory of Sexuality* [(1905d), p. 95–6 above].

first catches sight of a girl's genital region, he begins by showing irresolution and lack of interest; he sees nothing or disavows[1] what he has seen, he softens it down or looks about for expedients for bringing it into line with his expectations. It is not until later, when some threat of castration has obtained a hold upon him, that the observation becomes important to him: if he then recollects or repeats it, it arouses a terrible storm of emotion in him and forces him to believe in the reality of the threat which he has hitherto laughed at. This combination of circumstances leads to two reactions, which may become fixed and will in that case, whether separately or together or in conjunction with other factors, permanently determine the boy's relations to women: horror of the mutilated creature or triumphant contempt for her. These developments, however, belong to the future, though not to a very remote one.

A little girl behaves differently. She makes her judgement and her decision in a flash. She has seen it and knows that she is without it and wants to have it.[2]

Here what has been named the masculinity complex of women branches off.[3] It may put great difficulties in the way of their regular development towards femininity, if it cannot

1. [See Editor's footnote to 'The Infantile Genital Organization' p. 310 n. 1 above.]

2. This is an opportunity for correcting a statement which I made many years ago. I believed that the sexual interest of children, unlike that of pubescents, was aroused, not by the difference between the sexes, but by the problem of where babies come from. We now see that, at all events with girls, this is certainly not the case. With boys it may no doubt happen sometimes one way and sometimes the other; or with both sexes chance experiences may determine the event. – [The statement mentioned at the beginning of this footnote appears in more than one place; see an editorial footnote to 'The Sexual Enlightenment of Children' (1907c), p. 177 above, where references will be found. In that early paper Freud in fact takes the opposite view – the one advocated here.]

3. [This term seems to have been introduced by Van Ophuijsen (1917). Cf. also p. 320 above, and pp. 376 and 377 n. 1 below.]

be got over soon enough. The hope of some day obtaining a penis in spite of everything and so of becoming like a man may persist to an incredibly late age and may become a motive for strange and otherwise unaccountable actions. Or again, a process may set in which I should like to call a 'dis-avowal',[1] a process which in the mental life of children seems neither uncommon nor very dangerous but which in an adult would mean the beginning of a psychosis. Thus a girl may refuse to accept the fact of being castrated, may harden herself in the conviction that she *does* possess a penis, and may sub-sequently be compelled to behave as though she were a man.

The psychical consequences of envy for the penis, in so far as it does not become absorbed in the reaction-formation of the masculinity complex, are various and far-reaching. After a woman has become aware of the wound to her narcissism, she develops, like a scar, a sense of inferiority. When she has passed beyond her first attempt at explaining her lack of a penis as being a punishment personal to herself and has realized that that sexual character is a universal one, she begins to share the contempt felt by men for a sex which is the lesser in so important a respect, and, at least in holding that opinion, insists on being like a man.[2]

1. [For the parallel process in boys, see 'The Infantile Genital Organ-ization' (1923*e*), pp. 309–10 above.]

2. In my first critical account of the 'History of the Psycho-Analytic Movement' (1914*d*), I recognized that this fact represents the core of truth contained in Adler's theory. That theory has no hesitation in explaining the whole world by this single point ('organ-inferiority', the 'masculine protest', 'breaking away from the feminine line') and prides itself upon having in this way robbed sexuality of its importance and put the desire for power in its place! Thus the only organ which could claim to be called 'inferior' without any ambiguity would be the clitoris. On the other hand, one hears of analysts who boast that, though they have worked for dozens of years, they have never found a sign of the existence of a castration complex. We must bow our heads in recognition of the greatness of this achievement, even though it is only a negative one, a piece of virtuosity in the art of overlooking and mistaking. The two theories form an interesting pair of opposites: in

Even after penis-envy has abandoned its true object, it continues to exist: by an easy displacement it persists in the character-trait of *jealousy*. Of course, jealousy is not limited to one sex and has a wider foundation than this, but I am of opinion that it plays a far larger part in the mental life of women than of men and that that is because it is enormously reinforced from the direction of displaced penis-envy. While I was still unaware of this source of jealousy and was considering the phantasy 'a child is being beaten', which occurs so commonly in girls, I constructed a first phase for it in which its meaning was that another child, a rival of whom the subject was jealous, was to be beaten.[1] This phantasy seems to be a relic of the phallic period in girls. The peculiar rigidity which struck me so much in the monotonous formula 'a child is being beaten' can probably be interpreted in a special way. The child which is being beaten (or caressed) may ultimately be nothing more nor less than the clitoris itself, so that at its very lowest level the statement will contain a confession of masturbation, which has remained attached to the content of the formula from its beginning in the phallic phase till later life.

A third consequence of penis-envy seems to be a loosening of the girl's affectionate relation with her maternal object. The situation as a whole is not very clear, but it can be seen that in the end the girl's mother, who sent her into the world so insufficiently equipped, is almost always held responsible for her lack of a penis. The way in which this comes about historically is often that soon after the girl has discovered that her genitals are unsatisfactory she begins to show jealousy of another child on the ground that her mother is fonder of it than of her, which serves as a reason for her giving up her attachment to her mother. It will fit in with this if the child

---

the latter not a trace of a castration complex, in the former nothing else than its consequences.

1. '"A Child is Being Beaten"' [(1919e), *P.F.L.*, 10, 169–70].

which has been preferred by her mother is made into the first object of the beating-phantasy which ends in masturbation.

There is yet another surprising effect of penis-envy, or of the discovery of the inferiority of the clitoris, which is undoubtedly the most important of all. In the past I had often formed an impression that in general women tolerate masturbation worse than men, that they more frequently fight against it and that they are unable to make use of it in circumstances in which a man would seize upon it as a way of escape without any hesitation. Experience would no doubt elicit innumerable exceptions to this statement, if we attempted to turn it into a rule. The reactions of human individuals of both sexes are of course made up of masculine and feminine traits. But it appeared to me nevertheless as though masturbation were further removed from the nature of women than of men, and the solution of the problem could be assisted by the reflection that masturbation, at all events of the clitoris, is a masculine activity and that the elimination of clitoridal sexuality is a necessary precondition for the development of femininity.[1] Analyses of the remote phallic period have now taught me that in girls, soon after the first signs of penis-envy, an intense current of feeling against masturbation makes its appearance, which cannot be attributed exclusively to the educational influence of those in charge of the child. This impulse is clearly a forerunner of the wave of repression which at puberty will do away with a large amount of the girl's masculine sexuality in order to make room for the development of her femininity. It may happen that this first opposition to auto-erotic activity fails to attain its end. And this was in fact the case in the instances which I analysed. The conflict continued, and both then and later the girl did everything she could to free herself from the compulsion to masturbate. Many of the later

1. [A reference to clitoridal masturbation in girls appeared in the first edition of the *Three Essays* (1905d), p. 142f. above. In the course of his 'Contributions to a Discussion on Masturbation' (1912f), Freud expressed regret at the lack of knowledge about female masturbation.]

manifestations of sexual life in women remain unintelligible unless this powerful motive is recognized.

I cannot explain the opposition which is raised in this way by little girls to phallic masturbation except by supposing that there is some concurrent factor which turns her violently against that pleasurable activity. Such a factor lies close at hand. It cannot be anything else than her narcissistic sense of humiliation which is bound up with penis-envy, the reminder that after all this is a point on which she cannot compete with boys and that it would therefore be best for her to give up the idea of doing so. Thus the little girl's recognition of the anatomical distinction between the sexes forces her away from masculinity and masculine masturbation on to new lines which lead to the development of femininity.

So far there has been no question on the Oedipus complex, nor has it up to this point played any part. But now the girl's libido slips into a new position along the line – there is no other way of putting it – of the equation 'penis-child'. She gives up her wish for a penis and puts in place of it a wish for a child: and *with that purpose in view* she takes her father as a love-object.[1] Her mother becomes the object of her jealousy. The girl has turned into a little woman. If I am to credit a single analytic instance, this new situation can give rise to physical sensations which would have to be regarded as a premature awakening of the female genital apparatus. When the girl's attachment to her father comes to grief later on and has to be abandoned, it may give place to an identification with him and the girl may thus return to her masculinity complex and perhaps remain fixated in it.

I have now said the essence of what I had to say: I will stop, therefore, and cast an eye over our findings. We have gained some insight into the prehistory of the Oedipus complex in girls. The corresponding period in boys is more or less unknown. In girls the Oedipus complex is a secondary for-

1. [Cf. 'The Dissolution of the Oedipus Complex', p. 321 above.]

mation. The operations of the castration complex precede it and prepare for it. As regards the relation between the Oedipus and castration complexes there is a fundamental contrast between the two sexes. *Whereas in boys the Oedipus complex is destroyed by the castration complex,*[1] *in girls it is made possible and led up to by the castration complex.* This contradiction is cleared up if we reflect that the castration complex always operates in the sense implied in its subject-matter: it inhibits and limits masculinity and encourages femininity. The difference between the sexual development of males and females at the stage we have been considering is an intelligible consequence of the anatomical distinction between their genitals and of the psychical situation involved in it; it corresponds to the difference between a castration that has been carried out and one that has merely been threatened. In their essentials, therefore, our findings are self-evident and it should have been possible to foresee them.

The Oedipus complex, however, is such an important thing that the manner in which one enters and leaves it cannot be without its effects. In boys (as I have shown at length in the paper to which I have just referred [1924*d*] and to which all of my present remarks are closely related) the complex is not simply repressed, it is literally smashed to pieces by the shock of threatened castration. Its libidinal cathexes are abandoned, desexualized and in part sublimated; its objects are incorporated into the ego, where they form the nucleus of the super-ego and give that new structure its characteristic qualities. In normal, or, it is better to say, in ideal cases, the Oedipus complex exists no longer, even in the unconscious: the super-ego has become its heir. Since the penis (to follow Ferenczi [1924]) owes its extraordinarily high narcissistic cathexis to its organic significance for the propagation of the species, the catastrophe to the Oedipus complex (the abandonment of incest and the institution of conscience and morality) may be regarded as a victory of the race over the individual. This is

1. [Ibid., p. 319f. above.]

an interesting point of view when one considers that neurosis is based upon a struggle of the ego against the demands of the sexual function. But to leave the standpoint of individual psychology is not of any immediate help in clarifying this complicated situation.

In girls the motive for the demolition of the Oedipus complex is lacking. Castration has already had its effect, which was to force the child into the situation of the Oedipus complex. Thus the Oedipus complex escapes the fate which it meets with in boys: it may be slowly abandoned or dealt with by repression, or its effects may persist far into women's normal mental life. I cannot evade the notion (though I hesitate to give it expression) that for women the level of what is ethically normal is different from what it is in men. Their super-ego is never so inexorable, so impersonal, so independent of its emotional origins as we require it to be in men. Character-traits which critics of every epoch have brought up against women – that they show less sense of justice than men, that they are less ready to submit to the great exigencies of life, that they are more often influenced in their judgements by feelings of affection or hostility – all these would be amply accounted for by the modification in the formation of their super-ego which we have inferred above. We must not allow ourselves to be deflected from such conclusions by the denials of the feminists, who are anxious to force us to regard the two sexes as completely equal in position and worth; but we shall, of course, willingly agree that the majority of men are also far behind the masculine ideal and that all human individuals, as a result of their bisexual disposition and of cross-inheritance, combine in themselves both masculine and feminine characteristics, so that pure masculinity and femininity remain theoretical constructions of uncertain content.

I am inclined to set some value on the considerations I have brought forward upon the psychical consequences of the anatomical distinction between the sexes. I am aware, however, that this opinion can only be maintained if my findings, which are based on a handful of cases, turn out to have general validity and to be typical. If not, they would remain no more than a contribution to our knowledge of the different paths along which sexual life develops.

In the valuable and comprehensive studies on the masculinity and castration complexes in women by Abraham (1921), Horney (1923) and Helene Deutsch (1925) there is much that touches closely on what I have written but nothing that coincides with it completely, so that here again I feel justified in publishing this paper.

FETISHISM
(1927)

EDITOR'S NOTE

FETISCHISMUS

(A) GERMAN EDITIONS:

1927 *Almanach 1928*, 17–24.
1927 *Int. Z. Psychoanal.*, **13** (4), 373–8.
1948 *Gesammelte Werke*, **14**, 311–17.

(B) ENGLISH TRANSLATIONS:

'Fetishism'

1928 *Int. J. Psycho-Anal.*, **9** (2), 161–6. (Tr. Joan Riviere.)
1950 *Collected Papers*, **5**, 198–204. (Revised reprint of above.)
1961 *Standard Edition*, **21**, 147–57.

The present edition is a reprint of the *Standard Edition* version with some editorial changes.

This paper was finished at the end of the first week of August, 1927 (Jones, 1957, 146), and was published the same autumn.

In his earliest discussion of fetishism, in the *Three Essays* (1905*d*), pp. 65–8 above, Freud wrote that 'no other variation of the sexual instinct that borders on the pathological can lay so much claim to our interest as this one', and he in fact returned many times to a consideration of it. In this first account he did not go much further than maintaining that 'the choice of a fetish is an after-effect of some sexual impression, received as a rule in early childhood', and he left it at that in some passing comments on foot-fetishism in Chapter II of his study on *Gradiva* (1907*a*) a year or two later. His next approach to the subject seems to have been in an unpublished paper 'On the Genesis of Fetishism', read to the Vienna Psycho-Analytical Society on February 24, 1909 (Jones, 1955, 332). At that time he was on the point of preparing the 'Rat Man' analysis (1909*d*) for publication, and very near the end of that work he mentioned a fresh point – the connection of fetishism with pleasure in smell – which he enlarged upon in a footnote added to the *Three Essays* in its second edition of 1910 (see p. 68 above). But soon afterwards a new and more important connection must have occurred to him, for this same added footnote contained the first assertion that the fetish stands for the missing penis of the woman, which had figured prominently among the infantile sexual theories to which he had recently devoted a paper (1908*c*), pp. 193–6 above. This new explanation of the fetish was also mentioned (as Freud remarks on p. 352 *n.*1 below) in his study on Leonardo (1910*c*), Chapter III, published very soon after the *Three Essays* footnote.

The special question of the origin of foot-fetishism (referred to in the present paper, p. 354 below) attracted Freud's attention a few years later. On March 11, 1914, he read another paper to the Vienna Psycho-Analytical Society, on 'A Case of Foot-Fetishism'. This too remains unpublished, but this time we fortunately have a summary of it from Ernest Jones (1955, 342–3). The explanation of the choice of the foot as a fetish – approach to the woman's genitals from below –, which was arrived at there, was published in a further addition to the same footnote of the *Three Essays* in its third edition of 1915, p. 68 above. Another similar case history was reported very briefly by Freud in Lecture 22 of his *Introductory Lectures* (1916–17), *P.F.L.*, **1**, 393. But though the present paper is of importance as bringing together and enlarging on Freud's earlier views on fetishism, its major interest lies in a very different direction – namely, in a fresh metapsychological development which it introduces. For several years past Freud had been using the concept of 'disavowal' ('*Verleugnung*') especially in relation to children's reactions to the observation of the anatomical distinction between the sexes.[1] And in the present paper, basing himself on fresh clinical observations, he puts forward reasons for supposing that this 'disavowal' necessarily implies a split in the subject's ego. At the end of his life Freud took up this question again and widened its scope: in an unfinished and posthumously published paper on 'Splitting of the Ego in the Process of Defence' (1940e [1938]) and in the last paragraphs of Chapter VIII of *An Outline of Psycho-Analysis* (1940a [1938]). But though fetishism is specially considered in both these works, Freud there points out that this 'splitting of the ego' is not peculiar to fetishism but is in fact to be found in many other situations in which the ego is faced with the necessity of constructing a defence, and that it occurs not only in disavowal but also in repression.

1. See p. 193f. above and an Editor's footnote, p. 194 *n.* 1, to 'The Infantile Genital Organization' (1923e).

FETISHISM

IN the last few years I have had an opportunity of studying analytically a number of men whose object-choice was dominated by a fetish. There is no need to expect that these people came to analysis on account of their fetish. For though no doubt a fetish is recognized by its adherents as an abnormality, it is seldom felt by them as the symptom of an ailment accompanied by suffering. Usually they are quite satisfied with it, or even praise the way in which it eases their erotic life. As a rule, therefore, the fetish made its appearance in analysis as a subsidiary finding.

For obvious reasons the details of these cases must be withheld from publication; I cannot, therefore, show in what way accidental circumstances have contributed to the choice of a fetish. The most extraordinary case seemed to me to be one in which a young man had exalted a certain sort of 'shine on the nose' into a fetishistic precondition. The surprising explanation of this was that the patient had been brought up in an English nursery but had later come to Germany, where he forgot his mother-tongue almost completely. The fetish, which originated from his earliest childhood, had to be understood in English, not German. The 'shine on the nose' [in German 'Glanz auf der Nase'] – was in reality a 'glance at the nose'. The nose was thus the fetish, which, incidentally, he endowed at will with the luminous shine which was not perceptible to others.

In every instance, the meaning and the purpose of the fetish turned out, in analysis, to be the same. It revealed itself so naturally and seemed to me so compelling that I am prepared to expect the same solution in all cases of fetishism. When now I announce that the fetish is a substitute for the penis, I shall certainly create disappointment; so I hasten to add that it is not a substitute for any chance penis, but for a particular and quite special penis that had been extremely important in early childhood but had later been lost. That is to say, it should normally have been given up, but the fetish is precisely designed to preserve it from extinction. To put it more plainly: the fetish is a substitute for the woman's (the mother's) penis that the little boy once believed in and – for reasons familiar to us – does not want to give up.[1]

What happened, therefore, was that the boy refused to take cognizance of the fact of his having perceived that a woman does not possess a penis. No, that could not be true: for if a woman had been castrated, then his own possession of a penis was in danger; and against that there rose in rebellion the portion of his narcissism which Nature has, as a precaution, attached to that particular organ. In later life a grown man may perhaps experience a similar panic when the cry goes up that Throne and Altar are in danger, and similar illogical con-sequences will ensue. If I am not mistaken, Laforgue would say in this case that the boy 'scotomizes' his perception of the woman's lack of a penis.[2] A new technical term is justified when it describes a new fact or emphasizes it. This is not so here. The oldest word in our psychoanalytic terminology, 'repression', already relates to this pathological process. If we wanted to differentiate more sharply between the vicissitude of the *idea* as distinct from that of the *affect*,[3] and reserve the

1. This interpretation was made as early as 1910, in my study on Leonardo da Vinci, without any reasons being given for it. [See Chapter III of the study. Cf. also the Editor's Note above, p. 348.]

2. I correct myself, however, by adding that I have the best reasons for supposing that Laforgue would not say anything of the sort. It is clear from his own remarks [Laforgue, 1926] that 'scotomization' is a term which derives from descriptions of dementia praecox, which does not arise from a carrying-over of psychoanalytic concepts to the psychoses and which has no application to developmental processes or to the formation of neuroses. In his exposition in the text of his paper, the author has been at pains to make this incompatibility clear.

3. [This is considered in a passage near the middle of the paper on 'Repression' (1915*d*), *P.F.L.*, **11**, 152f.]

word '*Verdrängung*' ['repression'] for the affect, then the correct German word for the vicissitude of the idea would be '*Verleugnung*' ['disavowal'].[1] 'Scotomization' seems to me particularly unsuitable, for it suggests that the perception is entirely wiped out, so that the result is the same as when a visual impression falls on the blind spot in the retina. In the situation we are considering, on the contrary, we see that the perception has persisted, and that a very energetic action has been undertaken to maintain the disavowal. It is not true that, after the child has made his observation of the woman, he has preserved unaltered his belief that women have a phallus. He has retained that belief, but he has also given it up. In the conflict between the weight of the unwelcome perception and the force of his counter-wish, a compromise has been reached, as is only possible under the dominance of the unconscious laws of thought – the primary processes. Yes, in his mind the woman *has* got a penis, in spite of everything; but this penis is no longer the same as it was before. Something else has taken its place, has been appointed its substitute, as it were, and now inherits the interest which was formerly directed to its predecessor. But this interest suffers an extraordinary increase as well, because the horror of castration has set up a memorial to itself in the creation of this substitute. Furthermore, an aversion, which is never absent in any fetishist, to the real female genitals remains a *stigma indelebile* of the repression that has taken place. We can now see what the fetish achieves and what it is that maintains it. It remains a token of triumph over the threat of castration and a protection against it. It also saves the fetishist from becoming a

[1]. [Some discussion of Freud's use of this term and of the English rendering of it appears in an Editor's footnote to the paper on 'The Infantile Genital Organization' (1923e), p. 310, *n.* 1 above. It may be remarked that in Chapter VIII of the *Outline of Psycho-Analysis* (1940a [1938]) Freud makes a different distinction between the uses of the two words: 'repression' applies to defence against internal instinctual demands and 'disavowal' to defence against the claims of external reality.]

homosexual, by endowing women with the characteristic which makes them tolerable as sexual objects. In later life, the fetishist feels that he enjoys yet another advantage from his substitute for a genital. The meaning of the fetish is not known to other people, so the fetish is not withheld from him: it is easily accessible and he can readily obtain the sexual satisfaction attached to it. What other men have to woo and make exertions for can be had by the fetishist with no trouble at all.

Probably no male human being is spared the fright of castration at the sight of a female genital. Why some people become homosexual as a consequence of that impression, while others fend it off by creating a fetish, and the great majority surmount it, we are frankly not able to explain. It is possible that, among all the factors at work, we do not yet know those which are decisive for the rare pathological results. We must be content if we can explain what has happened, and may for the present leave on one side the task of explaining why something has *not* happened.

One would expect that the organs or objects chosen as substitutes for the absent female phallus would be such as appear as symbols of the penis in other connections as well. This may happen often enough, but is certainly not a deciding factor. It seems rather that when the fetish is instituted some process occurs which reminds one of the stopping of memory in traumatic amnesia. As in this latter case, the subject's interest comes to a halt half-way, as it were; it is as though the last impression before the uncanny and traumatic one is retained as a fetish. Thus the foot or shoe owes its preference as a fetish – or a part of it – to the circumstance that the inquisitive boy peered at the woman's genitals from below, from her legs up;[1] fur and velvet – as has long been suspected – are a fixation of the sight of the pubic hair, which should have been followed by the longed-for sight of the female member; pieces of underclothing, which are so often chosen as a fetish, crystallize the moment of undressing, the last

1. [Cf. Editor's Note, p. 348 above.]

moment in which the woman could still be regarded as phallic. But I do not maintain that it is invariably possible to discover with certainty how the fetish was determined.

An investigation of fetishism is strongly recommended to anyone who still doubts the existence of the castration complex or who can still believe that fright at the sight of the female genital has some other ground – for instance, that it is derived from a supposed recollection of the trauma of birth.[1]

For me, the explanation of fetishism had another point of theoretical interest as well. Recently, along quite speculative lines, I arrived at the proposition that the essential difference between neurosis and psychosis was that in the former the ego, in the service of reality, suppresses a piece of the id, whereas in a psychosis it lets itself be induced by the id to detach itself from a piece of reality. I returned to this theme once again later on.[2] But soon after this I had reason to regret that I had ventured so far. In the analysis of two young men I learned that each – one when he was two years old and the other when he was ten – had failed to take cognizance of the death of his beloved father – had 'scotomized' it – and yet neither of them had developed a psychosis. Thus a piece of reality which was undoubtedly important had been disavowed by the ego, just as the unwelcome fact of women's castration is disavowed in fetishists. I also began to suspect that similar occurrences in childhood are by no means rare, and I believed that I had been guilty of an error in my characterization of neurosis and psychosis. It is true that there was one way out of the difficulty. My formula needed only to hold good where there was a higher degree of differentiation in the psychical apparatus; things might be permissible to a child which would entail severe injury to an adult.

But further research led to another solution of the contradiction. It turned out that the two young men had no more

1. [Cf. Rank, 1924, 22–4; English trans., 1929.]
2. 'Neurosis and Psychosis' (1924b) and 'The Loss of Reality in Neurosis and Psychosis' (1924e).

'scotomized' their father's death than a fetishist does the castration of women. It was only one current in their mental life that had not recognized their father's death; there was another current which took full account of that fact. The attitude which fitted in with the wish and the attitude which fitted in with reality existed side by side. In one of my two cases this split had formed the basis of a moderately severe obsessional neurosis. The patient oscillated in every situation in life between two assumptions: the one, that his father was still alive and was hindering his activities; the other, opposite one, that he was entitled to regard himself as his father's successor. I may thus keep to the expectation that in a psychosis the one current – that which fitted in with reality – would have in fact been absent.

Returning to my description of fetishism, I may say that there are many and weighty additional proofs of the divided attitude of fetishists to the question of the castration of women. In very subtle instances both the disavowal and the affirmation of the castration have found their way into the construction of the fetish itself. This was so in the case of a man whose fetish was an athletic support-belt which could also be worn as bathing drawers. This piece of clothing covered up the genitals entirely and concealed the distinction between them. Analysis showed that it signified that women were castrated and that they were not castrated; and it also allowed of the hypothesis that men were castrated, for all these possibilities could equally well be concealed under the belt – the earliest rudiment of which in his childhood had been the fig-leaf on a statue. A fetish of this sort, doubly derived from contrary ideas, is of course especially durable. In other instances the divided attitude shows itself in what the fetishist does with his fetish, whether in reality or in his imagination. To point out that he reveres his fetish is not the whole story; in many cases he treats it in a way which is obviously equivalent to a representation of castration. This happens particularly if he has developed a strong identification with his father and plays the part of the latter; for it is to him that as a child he ascribed the woman's castration. Affection and hostility in the treatment of the fetish – which run parallel with the disavowal and the acknowledgement of castration – are mixed in unequal proportions in different cases, so that the one or the other is more clearly recognizable. We seem here to approach an understanding, even if a distant one, of the behaviour of the '*coupeur de nattes*'.[1] In him the need to carry out the castration which he disavows has come to the front. His action contains in itself the two mutually incompatible assertions: 'the woman has still got a penis' and 'my father has castrated the woman'. Another variant, which is also a parallel to fetishism in social psychology, might be seen in the Chinese custom of mutilating the female foot and then revering it like a fetish after it has been mutilated. It seems as though the Chinese male wants to thank the woman for having submitted to being castrated.

In conclusion we may say that the normal prototype of fetishes is a man's penis, just as the normal prototype of inferior organs is a woman's real small penis, the clitoris.[2]

1. [A pervert who enjoys cutting off the hair of females. Part of the present explanation was given by Freud in his study of Leonardo (1910c), Chapter III.]

2. [This is an allusion to Adler's insistence on 'organ-inferiority' as the basis of all neuroses. Cf. a footnote to the paper on 'Some Psychical Consequences of the Anatomical Distinction between the Sexes' (1925j), p. 337–8 above, and a longer discussion in Lecture 31 of the *New Introductory Lectures* (1933a), *P.F.L.*, 2, 97–8.]

LIBIDINAL TYPES
(1931)

EDITOR'S NOTE

ÜBER LIBIDINÖSE TYPEN

(A) GERMAN EDITIONS:

1931   *Int. Z. Psychoanal.*, **17** (3), 313–16.
1948   *Gesammelte Werke*, **14**, 509–13.

(B) ENGLISH TRANSLATIONS:

'Libidinal Types'

1932   *Psychoan. Quart.*, **1** (1), 3–6. (Tr. E. B. Jackson.)
1932   *Int. J. Psycho-Anal.*, **13** (3), 277–80. (Tr. Joan Riviere.)
1950   *Collected Papers*, **5**, 247–51. (Revised reprint of above.)
1961   *Standard Edition*, **21**, 215–20.

The present edition is a reprint of the *Standard Edition* version, with one or two editorial changes.

Like the next paper ('Female Sexuality'), this was begun early in 1931 and finished during the summer. It is a late addition to the very small number of Freud's papers dealing with characterology. A list of the works and passages in which the topic crops up will be found in the Editor's introductory note to 'Character and Anal Erotism' (1908*b*), pp. 207–8 above. In the present work the subject is considered in the light of Freud's later, structural, view of the mind.

LIBIDINAL TYPES

OBSERVATION teaches us that individual human beings realize the general picture of humanity in an almost infinite variety of ways. If we yield to the legitimate need to distinguish particular types in this multiplicity, we shall at the start have the choice as to what characteristics and what points of view we shall take as the basis of our differentiation. For that purpose physical qualities will doubtless serve no less well than mental ones; the most valuable distinctions will be those which promise to present a regular combination of physical and mental characteristics.

It is doubtful whether we are as yet in a position to discover types to fulfil this requirement – as we shall no doubt be able to do later, on some basis of which we are still ignorant. If we confine our effort to setting up purely psychological types, the libidinal situation will have a first claim to serve as a basis for our classification. It may fairly be demanded that this classification should not merely be deduced from our knowledge or our hypothesis about the libido, but that it should be easily confirmed in actual experience and that it should contribute to the clarification of the mass of our observations and help us to grasp them. It may at once be admitted that these libidinal types need not be the only possible ones even in the psychical field, and that, if we proceeded from other qualities, we might perhaps establish a whole set of other psychological types. But it must be required of all such types that they shall not coincide with clinical pictures. On the contrary, they must comprehend all the variations which according to our practical judgement fall within the limits of the normal. In their extreme developments, however, they may well approximate to clinical pictures and in that way help to bridge the gulf that is supposed to lie between the normal and the pathological.

According, then, as the libido is predominantly allocated to the provinces of the mental apparatus, we can distinguish three main libidinal types. To give names to these types is not particularly easy; following the lines of our depth-psychology, I should like to call them the *erotic*, the *narcissistic* and the *obsessional* types.[1]

The *erotic* type is easily characterized. Erotics are those whose main interest – the relatively largest part of whose libido – is turned towards love. Loving, but above all being loved, is the most important thing for them. They are dominated by the fear of loss of love and are therefore especially dependent on others who may withold their love from them. Even in its pure form this type is a very common one. Variants of it occur according as it is blended with another type and in proportion to the amount of aggressiveness present in it. From the social and cultural standpoint this type represents the elementary instinctual demands of the id, to which the other psychical agencies have become compliant.

The second type is what I have termed the *obsessional* type – a name which may at first seem strange. It is distinguished by the predominance of the super-ego, which is separated from the ego under great tension. People of this type are dominated by fear of their conscience instead of fear of losing love. They exhibit, as it were, an internal instead of an external dependence. They develop a high degree of self-reliance; and, from the social standpoint, they are the true, pre-eminently conservative vehicles of civilization.

The third type, justly called the *narcissistic* type, is mainly to be described in negative terms. There is no tension between ego and super-ego (indeed, on the strength of this type one would scarcely have arrived at the hypothesis of a super-ego),

1. [Freud had approached this classification of types near the end of Chapter II of *Civilization and its Discontents* (1930a).]

and there is no preponderance of erotic needs. The subject's main interest is directed to self-preservation; he is independent and not open to intimidation. His ego has a large amount of aggressiveness at its disposal, which also manifests itself in readiness for activity. In his erotic life loving is preferred above being loved. People belonging to this type impress others as being 'personalities'; they are especially suited to act as a support for others, to take on the role of leaders and to give a fresh stimulus to cultural development or to damage the established state of affairs.

These pure types will hardly escape the suspicion of having been deduced from the theory of the libido. But we feel our-selves on the firm ground of experience when we turn to the mixed types, which are to be observed so much more fre-quently than the unmixed ones. These new types – the *erotic-obsessional*, the *erotic-narcissistic* and the *narcissistic-obsessional* – seem in fact to afford a good classification of the individual psychical structures which we have come to know through analysis. If we study these mixed types we find in them pictures of characters with which we have long been familiar. In the *erotic-obsessional* type it appears that the preponderance of instinctual life is restricted by the influence of the super-ego. In this type, dependence at once on contemporary human objects and on the residues of parents, educators and exemp-lars, is carried to its highest pitch. The *erotic-narcissistic* type is perhaps the one we must regard as the commonest of all. It unites opposites, which are able to moderate one another in it. One may learn from this type, as compared with the two other erotic ones, that aggressiveness and activity go along with a predominance of narcissism. Finally, the *narcissistic-obsessional* type produces the variation which is most valuable from a cultural standpoint; for it adds to independence of the external world and a regard for the demands of conscience a capacity for vigorous action, and it strengthens the ego against the super-ego.

One might think one was making a jest if one asked why no

mention has been made here of another mixed type which is theoretically possible – namely, the *erotic-obsessional-narcissistic* type. But the answer to this jest is serious. Such a type would no longer be a type at all: it would be the absolute norm, the ideal harmony. We thus realize that the phenomenon of types arises precisely from the fact that, of the three main ways of employing the libido in the economy of the mind, one or two have been favoured at the expense of the others.

The question may also be raised of what the relation is of these libidinal types to pathology – whether some of them have a special disposition to pass over into neurosis, and if so, which types lead to which forms of neurosis. The answer is that the setting-up of these libidinal types throws no new light on the genesis of the neuroses. Experience shows that all these types can exist without any neurosis. The pure types, marked by the undisputed preponderance of a single mental agency, seem to have a better chance of manifesting themselves as pure characterological pictures, while we might expect that mixed types would provide a more favourable soil for conditions leading to a neurosis. But I think we should not make up our minds on these matters till they have been submitted to a careful and specially directed examination.

It seems easy to infer that when people of the erotic type fall ill they will develop hysteria, just as those of the obsessional type will develop obsessional neurosis; but these inferences, too, share the uncertainty which I have just stressed. People of the narcissistic type who are exposed to a frustration from the external world, though otherwise independent, are peculiarly disposed to psychosis; and they also present essential preconditions for criminality.

It is a familiar fact that the aetiological preconditions of neurosis are not yet known with certainty. The precipitating causes of it are frustrations and internal conflicts: conflicts between the three major psychical agencies, conflicts arising within the libidinal economy in consequence of our bisexual disposition and conflicts between the erotic and the aggressive instinctual components. It is the endeavour of the psychology of the neuroses to discover what makes these processes, which belong to the normal course of mental life, become pathogenic.

FEMALE SEXUALITY
(1931)

EDITOR'S NOTE

ÜBER DIE WEIBLICHE SEXUALITÄT

(A) GERMAN EDITIONS:

1931 *Int. Z. Psychoanal.*, **17** (3), 317–32.
1934 *Gesammelte Schriften*, **12**, 120–40.
1948 *Gesammelte Werke*, **14**, 517–37.

(B) ENGLISH TRANSLATIONS:

'Concerning the Sexuality of Women'

1932 *Psychoan. Quart.*, **1** (1), 191–209. (Tr. E. B. Jackson.)

'Female Sexuality'

1932 *Int. J. Psycho-Anal.*, **13** (3), 281–97. (Tr. Joan Riviere.)
1950 *Collected Papers*, **5**, 252–72. (Revised reprint of above.)
1961 *Standard Edition*, **21**, 221–43.

The present edition is a corrected reprint of the *Standard Edition* version, with some editorial changes.

The first draft of this paper seems to have been written by the end of February, 1931, but it was only completed in the summer of that year (cf. Jones, 1957, 176).

The present study is in essence a restatement of the findings first announced by Freud six years earlier in his paper on 'Some Psychical Consequences of the Anatomical Distinction between the Sexes' (1925*j*), some discussion of which will be found in the Editor's Note to that work, p. 326 ff. above. The publication of this earlier work had provoked considerable repercussions among psychoanalysts, especially, perhaps, in England, and these may have stimulated Freud to return to the subject. The last section of the present paper contains – and this was a very unusual thing in Freud's writings – some criticisms of a number of other authors' papers. And it is a curious thing that he seems to treat them as though they had arisen spontaneously and not, as was clearly the case, as a reaction to his own somewhat revolutionary paper of 1925 – to which, indeed, he here makes no reference whatever.

There are, however, one or two respects in which this work enlarges upon its predecessor. It lays further emphasis (evidently on the basis of fresh clinical material) on the intensity and long duration of the little girl's pre-Oedipus attachment to her mother. But of most interest, perhaps, it the long discussion of the *active* element in the little girl's attitude towards her mother and in femininity in general.

A year or so after the appearance of this paper Freud returned to the question of female sexuality in Lecture 33 of the *New Introductory Lectures* (1933a). This deals with the subject on very similar lines to the present ones, though in a rather less technical manner; it ends, moreover, with some discussion of the characteristics of women in dault life.

FEMALE SEXUALITY

I

DURING the phase of the normal Oedipus complex we find the child tenderly attached to the parent of the opposite sex, while its relation to the parent of its own sex is predominantly hostile. In the case of a boy there is no difficulty in explaining this. His first love-object was his mother. She remains so; and, with the strengthening of his erotic desires and his deeper insight into the relations between his father and mother, the former is bound to become his rival. With the small girl it is different. Her first object, too, was her mother. How does she find her way to her father? How, when and why does she detach herself from her mother? We have long understood that the development of female sexuality is complicated by the fact that the girl has the task of giving up what was originally her leading genital zone – the clitoris – in favour of a new zone – the vagina.[1] But it now seems to us that there is a second change of the same sort which is no less characteristic and important for the development of the female: the exchange of her original object – her mother – for her father. The way in which the two tasks are connected with each other is not yet clear to us.

It is well known that there are many women who have a strong attachment to their father; nor need they be in any way neurotic. It is upon such women that I have made the observations which I propose to report here and which have led me to adopt a particular view of female sexuality. I was struck, above all, by two facts. The first was that where the woman's attachment to her father was particularly intense, analysis showed that it had been preceded by a phase of exclusive attachment to her mother which had been equally

1. [*Three Essays on the Theory of Sexuality* (1905d), pp. 142–4 above.]

intense and passionate. Except for the change of her love-object, the second phase had scarcely added any new feature to her erotic life. Her primary relation to her mother had been built up in a very rich and many-sided manner. The second fact taught me that the *duration* of this attachment had also been greatly underestimated. In several cases it lasted until well into the fourth year – in one case into the fifth year – so that it covered by far the longer part of the period of early sexual efflorescence. Indeed, we had to reckon with the possibility that a number of women remain arrested in their original attachment to their mother and never achieve a true change-over towards men. This being so, the pre-Oedipus phase in women gains an importance which we have not attributed to it hitherto.

Since this phase allows room for all the fixations and repressions from which we trace the origin of the neuroses, it would seem as though we must retract the universality of the thesis that the Oedipus complex is the nucleus of the neuroses. But if anyone feels reluctant about making this correction, there is no need for him to do so. On the one hand, we can extend the content of the Oedipus complex to include all the child's relations to both parents; or, on the other, we can take due account of our new findings by saying that the female only reaches the normal positive Oedipus situation after she has surmounted a period before it that is governed by the negative complex.[1] And indeed during that phase a little girl's father is not much else for her than a troublesome rival, although her hostility towards him never reaches the pitch which is characteristic of boys. We have, after all, long given up any expectation of a neat parallelism between male and female sexual development.

Our insight into this early, pre-Oedipus, phase in girls comes to us as a surprise, like the discovery, in another field, of the Minoan-Mycenaean civilization behind the civilization of Greece.

1. [The positive and negative Oedipus complexes were discussed by Freud in Chapter III of *The Ego and the Id* (1923b).]

Everything in the sphere of this first attachment to the mother seemed to me so difficult to grasp in analysis – so grey with age and shadowy and almost impossible to revivify – that it was as if it had succumbed to an especially inexorable repression. But perhaps I gained this impression because the women who were in analysis with me were able to cling to the very attachment to the father in which they had taken refuge from the early phase that was in question. It does indeed appear that women analysts – as, for instance, Jeanne Lampl-de Groot and Helene Deutsch – have been able to perceive these facts more easily and clearly because they were helped in dealing with those under their treatment by the transference to a suitable mother-substitute. Nor have I succeeded in seeing my way through any case completely, and I shall therefore confine myself to reporting the most general findings and shall give only a few examples of the new ideas which I have arrived at. Among these is a suspicion that this phase of attachment to the mother is especially intimately related to the aetiology of hysteria, which is not surprising when we reflect that both the phase and the neurosis are characteristically feminine, and further, that in this dependence on the mother we have the germ of later paranoia in women.[1] For this germ appears to be the surprising, yet regular, fear of being killed (? devoured) by the mother. It is plausible to assume that this fear corresponds to a hostility which develops in the child towards her mother in consequence of the manifold restrictions imposed by the latter in the course of training and bodily care and that the mechanism of projection is favoured by the early age of the child's psychical organization.[2]

1. In the well-known case of delusional jealousy reported by Ruth Mack Brunswick (1928), the direct source of the disorder was the patient's pre-Oedipus fixation (to her sister). [Cf. also Freud's own 'Case of Paranoia Running Contrary to the Psycho-Analytic Theory of the Disease' (1915f).]

2. [The girl's fear of being killed by her mother is considered further, on p. 385 below.]

2

I began by stating the two facts which have struck me as new: that a woman's strong dependence on her father merely takes over the heritage of an equally strong attachment to her mother, and that this earlier phase has lasted for an unexpectedly long period of time. I shall now go back a little in order to insert these new findings into the picture of female sexual development with which we are familiar. In doing this, a certain amount of repetition will be inevitable. It will help our exposition if, as we go along, we compare the state of things in women with that in men.

First of all, there can be no doubt that the bisexuality, which is present, as we believe, in the innate disposition of human beings, comes to the fore much more clearly in women than in men. A man, after all, has only one leading sexual zone, one sexual organ, whereas a woman has two: the vagina – the female organ proper – and the clitoris, which is analogous to the male organ. We believe we are justified in assuming that for many years the vagina is virtually non-existent and possibly does not produce sensations until puberty. It is true that recently an increasing number of observers report that vaginal impulses are present even in these early years. In women, therefore, the main genital occurrences of childhood must take place in relation to the clitoris. Their sexual life is regularly divided into two phases, of which the first has a masculine character, while only the second is specifically feminine. Thus in female development there is a process of transition from the one phase to the other, to which there is nothing analogous in the male. A further complication arises from the fact that the clitoris, with its virile character, continues to function in later female sexual life in a manner which is very variable and which is certainly not yet satisfactorily understood. We do not, of course, know the biological basis of these peculiarities in women; and still less are we able to assign them any teleological purpose.

Parallel with this first great difference there is the other, concerned with the finding of the object. In the case of a male, his mother becomes his first love-object as a result of her feeding him and looking after him, and she remains so until she is replaced by someone who resembles her or is derived from her. A female's first object, too, must be her mother: the primary conditions for a choice of object are, of course, the same for all children. But at the end of her development, her father – a man – should have become her new love-object. In other words, to the change in her own sex there must correspond a change in the sex of her object. The new problems that now require investigating are in what way this change takes place, how radically or how incompletely it is carried out, and what the different possibilities are which present themselves in the course of this development.

We have already learned, too, that there is yet another difference between the sexes, which relates to the Oedipus complex. We have an impression here that what we have said about the Oedipus complex applies with complete strictness to the male child only and that we are right in rejecting the term 'Electra complex'[1] which seeks to emphasize the analogy between the attitude of the two sexes. It is only in the male child that we find the fateful combination of love for the one parent and simultaneous hatred for the other as a rival. In his case it is the discovery of the possibility of castration, as proved by the sight of the female genitals, which forces on him the transformation of his Oedipus complex, and which leads to the creation of his super-ego and thus initiates all the processes that are designed to make the individual find a place in the cultural community. After the paternal agency has been internalized and become a super-ego, the next task is to detach the latter from the figures of whom it was originally the psychical representative. In this remarkable course of development it is precisely the boy's narcissistic interest in his

1. [The term had been used by Jung (1913, 370).]

genitals – his interest in preserving his penis – which is turned round into a curtailing of his infantile sexuality.[1]

One thing that is left over in men from the influence of the Oedipus complex is a certain amount of disparagement in their attitude towards women, whom they regard as being castrated. In extreme cases this gives rise to an inhibition in their choice of object, and, if it is supported by organic factors, to exclusive homosexuality.

Quite different are the effects of the castration complex in the female. She acknowledges the fact of her castration, and with it, too, the superiority of the male and her own inferiority; but she rebels against this unwelcome state of affairs. From this divided attitude three lines of development open up. The first leads to a general revulsion from sexuality. The little girl, frightened by the comparison with boys, grows dissatisfied with her clitoris, and gives up her phallic activity and with it her sexuality in general as well as a good part of her masculinity in other fields. The second line leads her to cling with defiant self-assertiveness to her threatened masculinity. To an incredibly late age she clings to the hope of getting a penis some time. That hope becomes her life's aim; and the phantasy of being a man in spite of everything often persists as a formative factor over long periods. This 'masculinity complex' in women can also result in a manifest homosexual choice of object. Only if her development follows the third, very circuitous, path does she reach the final normal female attitude, in which she takes her father as her object and so finds her way to the feminine form of the Oedipus complex. Thus in women the Oedipus complex is the end-result of a fairly lengthy development. It is not destroyed, but created, by the influence of castration; it escapes the strongly hostile influences which, in the male, have a destructive effect on it, and indeed it is all too often not surmounted by the female at all. For this reason, too, the cultural consequences

1. [For all of this see 'The Dissolution of the Oedipus Complex' (1924d), p. 315 ff. above.]

of its break-up are smaller and of less importance in her. We should probably not be wrong in saying that it is this difference in the reciprocal relation between the Oedipus and the castration complex which gives its special stamp to the character of females as social beings.[1]

We see, then, that the phase of exclusive attachment to the mother, which may be called the *pre-Oedipus* phase, possesses a far greater importance in women than it can have in men. Many phenomena of female sexual life which were not properly understood before can be fully explained by reference to this phase. Long ago, for instance, we noticed that many women who have chosen their husband on the model of their father, or have put him in their father's place, nevertheless repeat towards him, in their married life, their bad relations with their mother.[2] The husband of such a woman was meant to be the inheritor of her relation to her father, but in reality he became the inheritor of her relation to her mother. This is easily explained as an obvious case of regression. Her relation to her mother was the original one, and her attachment to her father was built up on it, and now, in marriage,

1. It is to be anticipated that men analysts with feminist views, as well as our women analysts, will disagree with what I have said here. They will hardly fail to object that such notions spring from the 'masculinity complex' of the male and are designed to justify on theoretical grounds his innate inclination to disparage and suppress women. But this sort of psychoanalytic argumentation reminds us here, as it so often does, of Dostoevsky's famous 'knife that cuts both ways'. The opponents of those who argue in this way will on their side think it quite natural that the female sex should refuse to accept a view which appears to contradict their eagerly coveted equality with men. The use of analysis as a weapon of controversy can clearly lead to no decision. [The Dostoevsky phrase (a simile applied to psychology) occurs in the speech for the defence in the account of Mitya's trial in Chapter X of Book XII of *The Brothers Karamazov*. Freud had quoted it already in his paper on 'Dostoevsky and Parricide' (1928b), *P.F.L.*, Volume 14. The actual simile used by Freud and in the Russian original is 'a stick with two ends'. – On the term 'masculinity complex', see p. 336 and *n.* 3 above.]

2. [See 'The Taboo of Virginity' (1918a), p. 278 ff. above.]

the original relation emerges from repression. For the main content of her development to womanhood lay in the carrying over of her affective object attachments from her mother to her father.

With many women we have the impression that their years of maturity are occupied by a struggle with their husband, just as their youth was spent in a struggle with their mother. In the light of the previous discussions we shall conclude that their hostile attitude to their mother is not a consequence of the rivalry implicit in the Oedipus complex, but originates from the preceding phase and has merely been reinforced and exploited in the Oedipus situation. And actual analytic examination confirms this view. Our interest must be directed to the mechanisms that are at work in her turning away from the mother who was an object so intensely and exclusively loved. We are prepared to find, not a single factor, but a whole number of them operating together towards the same end.

Among these factors are some which are determined by the circumstances of infantile sexuality in general, and so hold good equally for the erotic life of boys. First and foremost we may mention jealousy of other people – of brothers and sisters, rivals, among whom the father too has a place. Childhood love is boundless; it demands exclusive possession, it is not content with less than all. But it has a second characteristic: it has, in point of fact, no aim and is incapable of obtaining complete satisfaction; and principally for that reason it is doomed to end in disappointment and to give place to a hostile attitude. Later on in life the lack of an ultimate satisfaction may favour a different result. This very factor may ensure the uninterrupted continuance of the libidinal cathexis, as happens with love-relations that are inhibited in their aim. But in the stress of the processes of development it regularly happens that the libido abandons its unsatisfying position in order to find a new one.

Another, much more specific motive for turning away from

the mother arises from the effect of the castration complex on the creature who is without a penis. At some time or other the little girl makes the discovery of her organic inferiority – earlier and more easily, of course, if there are brothers or other boys about. We have already taken note of the three paths which diverge from this point: (a) the one which leads to a cessation of her whole sexual life, (b) the one which leads to a defiant over-emphasis of her masculinity, and (c) the first steps towards definitive femininity. It is not easy to determine the exact timing here or the typical course of events. Even the point of time when the discovery of castration is made varies, and a number of other factors seem to be inconstant and to depend on chance. The state of the girl's own phallic activity plays a part; and so too does the question whether this activity was found out or not, and how much interference with it she experienced afterwards.

Little girls usually discover for themselves their characteristic phallic activity – masturbation of the clitoris;[1] and to begin with this is no doubt unaccompanied by phantasy. The part played in starting it by nursery hygiene is reflected in the very common phantasy which makes the mother or nurse into a seducer.[2] Whether little girls masturbate less frequently and from the first less energetically than little boys is not certain; quite possibly it is so. Actual seduction, too, is common enough; it is initiated either by other children or by someone in charge of the child who wants to soothe it, or send it to sleep or make it dependent on them. Where seduction intervenes it invariably disturbs the natural course of the developmental processes, and it often leaves behind extensive and lasting consequences.

A prohibition of masturbation, as we have seen, becomes an incentive for giving it up; but it also becomes a motive for rebelling against the person who prohibits it – that is to say, the mother, or the mother-substitute who later regularly

1. [Cf. *Three Essays* (1905d), p. 142 above.]
2. [Cf. a fuller discussion of this below, p. 386.]

merges with her. A defiant persistence in masturbation appears to open the way to masculinity. Even where the girl has not succeeded in suppressing her masturbation, the effect of the apparently vain prohibition is seen in her later efforts to free herself at all costs from a satisfaction which has been spoilt for her. When she reaches maturity her object-choice may still be influenced by this persisting purpose. Her resentment at being prevented from free sexual activity plays a big part in her detachment from her mother. The same motive comes into operation again after puberty, when her mother takes up her duty of guarding her daughter's chastity. We shall, of course, not forget that the mother is similarly opposed to a boy's masturbating and thus provides him, too, with a strong motive for rebellion.

When the little girl discovers her own deficiency, from seeing a male genital, it is only with hesitation and reluctance that she accepts the unwelcome knowledge. As we have seen, she clings obstinately to the expectation of one day having a genital of the same kind too, and her wish for it survives long after her hope has expired. The child invariably regards castration in the first instance as a misfortune peculiar to herself; only later does she realize that it extends to certain other children and lastly to certain grown-ups. When she comes to understand the general nature of this characteristic, it follows that femaleness – and with it, of course, her mother – suffers a great depreciation in her eyes.

This account of how girls respond to the impression of castration and the prohibition against masturbation will very probably strike the reader as confused and contradictory. This is not entirely the author's fault. In truth, it is hardly possible to give a description which has general validity. We find the most different reactions in different individuals, and in the same individual the contrary attitudes exist side by side. With the first intervention of the prohibition, the conflict is there, and from now on it will accompany the development of the sexual function. Insight into what takes place is made particularly difficult by the fact of its being so hard to distinguish the mental processes of this first phase from later ones by which they are overlaid and are distorted in memory. Thus, for instance, a girl may later construe the fact of castration as a punishment for her masturbatory activity, and she will attribute the carrying out of this punishment to her father, but neither of these ideas can have been a primary one. Similarly, boys regularly fear castration from their father, although in their case, too, the threat most usually comes from their mother.

However this may be, at the end of this first phase of attachment to the mother, there emerges, as the girl's strongest motive for turning away from her, the reproach that her mother did not give her a proper penis – that is to say, brought her into the world as a female.[1] A second reproach, which does not reach quite so far back, is rather a surprising one. It is that her mother did not give her enough milk, did not suckle her long enough. Under the conditions of modern civilization this may be true often enough, but certainly not so often as is asserted in analyses. It would seem rather that this accusation gives expression to the general dissatisfaction of children, who, in our monogamous civilization, are weaned from the breast after six or nine months, whereas the primitive mother devotes herself exclusively to her child for two or three years. It is as though our children had remained for ever unsated, as though they had never sucked long enough at their mother's breast. But I am not sure whether, if one analysed children who had been suckled as long as the children of primitive peoples, one would not come upon the same complaint. Such is the greed of a child's libido!

When we survey the whole range of motives for turning away from the mother which analysis brings to light – that she failed to provide the little girl with the only proper genital,

1. [Freud had pointed this out in the last paragraph of Section I of his paper on 'Some Character Types' (1916*d*).]

that she did not feed her sufficiently, that she compelled her to share her mother's love with others, that she never fulfilled all the girl's expectations of love, and, finally, that she first aroused her sexual activity and then forbade it – all these motives seem nevertheless insufficient to justify the girl's final hostility. Some of them follow inevitably from the nature of infantile sexuality; others appear like rationalizations devised later to account for the uncomprehended change in feeling. Perhaps the real fact is that the attachment to the mother is bound to perish, precisely because it was the first and was so intense; just as one can often see happen in the first marriages of young women which they have entered into when they were most passionately in love. In both situations the attitude of love probably comes to grief from the disappointments that are unavoidable and from the accumulation of occasions for aggression. As a rule, second marriages turn out much better.

We cannot go so far as to assert that the ambivalence of emotional cathexes is a universally valid law, and that it is absolutely impossible to feel great love for a person without its being accompanied by a hatred that is perhaps equally great, or vice versa. Normal adults do undoubtedly succeed in separating those two attitudes from each other, and do not find themselves obliged to hate their love-objects and to love their enemy as well as hate him. But this seems to be the result of later developments. In the first phases of erotic life, ambivalence is evidently the rule. Many people retain this archaic trait all through their lives. It is characteristic of obsessional neurotics that in their object-relationships love and hate counterbalance each other. In primitive races, too, we may say that ambivalence predominates.[1] We shall conclude, then, that the little girl's intense attachment to her mother is strongly ambivalent, and that it is in consequence precisely of this ambivalence that (with the assistance of the other factors we

1. [See *Totem and Taboo* (1912–13), passim, and especially the second essay.]

have adduced) her attachment is forced away from her mother – once again, that is to say, in consequence of a general characteristic of infantile sexuality.

The explanation I have attempted to give is at once met by a question: 'How is it, then, that boys are able to keep intact their attachment to their mother, which is certainly no less strong than that of girls?' The answer comes equally promptly: 'Because boys are able to deal with their ambivalent feelings towards their mother by directing all their hostility on to their father.' But, in the first place, we ought not to make this reply until we have made a close study of the pre-Oedipus phase in boys, and, in the second place, it is probably more prudent in general to admit that we have as yet no clear understanding of these processes, with which we have only just become acquainted.

3

A further question arises: 'What does the little girl require of her mother? What is the nature of her sexual aims during the time of exclusive attachment to her mother?' The answer we obtain from the analytic material is just what we should expect. The girl's sexual aims in regard to her mother are active as well as passive and are determined by the libidinal phases through which the child passes. Here the relation of activity to passivity is especially interesting. It can easily be observed that in every field of mental experience, not merely that of sexuality, when a child receives a passive impression it has a tendency to produce an active reaction. It tries to do itself what has just been done to it. This is part of the work imposed on it of mastering the external world and can even lead to its endeavouring to repeat an impression which it would have reason to avoid on account of its distressing content. Chilren's play, too, is made to serve this purpose of supplementing a passive experience with an active piece of behaviour and of thus, as it were, annulling it. When a doctor has opened a child's mouth, in spite of his resistance, to look down his throat, the same child, after the doctor has gone, will play at being the doctor himself, and will repeat the assault upon some small brother or sister who is as helpless in his hands as he was in the doctor's. Here we have an unmistakable revolt against passivity and a preference for the active role. This swing-over from passivity to activity does not take place with the same regularity or vigour in all chidren; in some it may not occur at all. A child's behaviour in this respect may enable us to draw conclusions as to the relative strength of the masculinity and femininity that it will exhibit in its sexuality.

The first sexual and sexually coloured experiences which a child has in relation to its mother are naturally of a passive character. It is suckled, fed, cleaned, and dressed by her, and taught to perform all its functions. A part of its libido goes on clinging to those experiences and enjoys the satisfactions bound up with them; but another part strives to turn them into activity. In the first place, being suckled at the breast gives place to active sucking. As regards the other experiences the child contents itself either with becoming self-sufficient – that is, with itself successfully carrying out what had hitherto been done for it – or with repeating its passive experiences in an active form in play; or else it actually makes its mother into the object and behaves as the active subject towards her. For a long time I was unable to credit this last behaviour, which takes place in the field of real action, until my observations removed all doubts on the matter.

We seldom hear of a little girl's wanting to wash or dress her mother, or tell her to perform her excretory functions. Sometimes, it is true, she says: 'Now let's play that I'm the mother and you're the child'; but generally she fulfils these active wishes in an indirect way, in her play with her doll, in which she represents the mother and the doll the child. The fondness girls have for playing with dolls, in contrast to boys, is commonly regarded as a sign of early awakened femininity.

Not unjustly so; but we must not overlook the fact that what finds expression here is the *active* side of femininity, and that the little girl's preference for dolls is probably evidence of the exclusiveness of her attachment to her mother, with complete neglect of her father-object.

The very surprising sexual activity of little girls in relation to their mother is manifested chronologically in oral, sadistic, and finally even in phallic trends directed towards her. It is difficult to give a detailed account of these because they are often obscure instinctual impulses which it was impossible for the child to grasp psychically at the time of their occurrence, which were therefore only interpreted by her later, and which then appear in the analysis in forms of expression that were certainly not the original ones. Sometimes we come across them as transferences on to the later, father-object, where they do not belong and where they seriously interfere with our understanding of the situation. We find the little girl's aggressive oral and sadistic wishes in a form forced on them by early repression, as a fear of being killed by her mother – a fear which, in turn, justifies her death-wish against her mother, if that becomes conscious. It is impossible to say how often this fear of the mother is supported by an unconscious hostility on the mother's part which is sensed by the girl. [Cf. p. 373 above.] (Hitherto, it is only in men that I have found the fear of being eaten up. This fear is referred to the father, but it is probably the product of a transformation of oral aggressivity directed to the mother. The child wants to eat up its mother from whom it has had its nourishment; in the case of the father there is no such obvious determinant for the wish.)

The women patients showing a strong attachment to their mother in whom I have been able to study the pre-Oedipus phase have all told me that when their mother gave them enemas or rectal douches they used to offer the greatest resistance and react with fear and screams of rage. This behaviour may be very frequent or even the habitual thing in children.

I only came to understand the reason for such a specially violent opposition from a remark made by Ruth Mack Brunswick, who was studying these problems at the same time as I was, to the effect that she was inclined to compare the outbreak of anger after an enema to the orgasm following genital excitation. The accompanying anxiety should, she thought, be construed as a transformation of the desire for aggression which had been stirred up. I believe that this is really so and that, at the sadistic-anal level, the intense passive stimulation of the intestinal zone is responded to by an outbreak of desire for aggression which is manifested either directly as rage, or, in consequence of its suppression, as anxiety. In later years this reaction seems to die away.

In regard to the passive impulses of the phallic phase, it is noteworthy that girls regularly accuse their mother of seducing them. This is because they necessarily received their first, or at any rate their strongest, genital sensations when they were being cleaned and having their toilet attended to by their mother (or by someone such as a nurse who took her place). Mothers have often told me, as a matter of observation, that their little daughters of two and three years old enjoy these sensations and try to get their mothers to make them more intense by repeated touching and rubbing. The fact that the mother thus unavoidably initiates the child into the phallic phase is, I think, the reason why, in phantasies of later years, the father so regularly appears as the sexual seducer. When the girl turns away from her mother, she also makes over to her father her introduction into sexual life.[1]

1. [This is the last phase of a long story. When, in his early analyses, Freud's hysterical patients told him that they had been seduced by their father in childhood, he accepted these tales as the truth and regarded the traumas as the cause of their illness. It was not long before he recognized his mistake, and grasped the important fact that these apparently false memories were wishful phantasies, which pointed the way to the existence of the Oedipus complex. It was only in the present passage, however, that Freud gave his full explanation of these ostensible

Lastly, intense *active* wishful impulses directed towards the mother also arise during the phallic phase. The sexual activity of this period culminates in clitoridal masturbation. This is probably accompanied by ideas of the mother, but whether the child attaches a sexual aim to the idea, and what that aim is, I have not been able to discover from my observations. It is only when all her interests have received a fresh impetus through the arrival of a baby brother or sister that we can clearly recognize such an aim. The little girl wants to believe that she has given her mother the new baby, just as the boy wants to; and her reaction to this event and her behaviour to the baby is exactly the same as his. No doubt this sounds quite absurd, but perhaps that is only because it sounds so unfamiliar.

The turning-way from her mother is an extremely important step in the course of a little girl's development. It is more than a mere change of object. We have already described what takes place in it and the many motives put forward for it; we may now add that hand in hand with it there is to be observed a marked lowering of the active sexual impulses and a rise of the passive ones. It is true that the active trends have been affected by frustration more strongly; they have proved totally unrealizable and are therefore abandoned by the libido more readily. But the passive trends have not escaped disappointment either. With the turning-away from the mother clitoridal masturbation frequently ceases as well; and often enough when the small girl represses her previous masculinity a considerable portion of her sexual trends in general is permanently injured too. The transition to the father-object is accomplished with the help of the passive trends in so far as they have escaped the catastrophe. The path to the development of femininity now lies open to the girl, to the extent to which it is not restricted by the remains of the

----

memories. He discusses this whole episode at greater length in Lecture 33 of his *New Introductory Lectures* (1933*a*), *P.F.L.*, **2**, 154.]

pre-Oedipus attachment to her mother which she has surmounted.

If we now survey the stage of sexual development in the
female which I have been describing, we cannot resist coming
to a definite conclusion about female sexuality as a whole. We
have found the same libidinal forces at work in it as in the
male child and we have been able to convince ourselves that
for a period of time these forces follow the same course and
have the same outcome in each.

Biological factors subsequently deflect those libidinal forces
[in the girl's case] from their original aims and conduct even
active and in every sense masculine trends into feminine
channels. Since we cannot dismiss the notion that sexual
excitation is derived from the operation of certain chemical
substances, it seems plausible at first to expect that biochemistry will one day disclose a substance to us whose presence
produces a male sexual excitation and another substance which
produces a female one. But this hope seems no less naïve than
the other one – happily obsolete today – that it may be
possible under the miscroscope to isolate the different exciting
factors of hysteria, obsessional neurosis, melancholia, and so
on.

Even in sexual chemistry things must be rather more complicated.[1] For psychology, however, it is a matter of indifference
whether there is a single sexually exciting substance in the
body or two or countless numbers of them. Psychoanalysis
teaches us to manage with a single libido, which, it is true,
has both active and passive aims (that is, modes of satisfaction).
This antithesis and, above all, the existence of libidinal trends
with passive aims, contains within itself the remainder of our
problem.

1. [Cf. the discussion of the chemistry of the sexual processes added
in 1920 to the Three Essays (1905d), pp. 136–7 above, where (in a footnote on pp. 137–8) the earlier version from the first edition of the book
will also be found.]

4

An examination of the analytic literature on the subject shows that everything that has been said by me here is already to be found in it.[1] It would have been superfluous to publish this paper if it were not that in a field of research which is so difficult of access every account of first-hand experiences or personal views may be of value. Moreover, there are a number of points which I have defined more sharply and isolated more carefully. In some of the other papers on the subject the description is obscured because they deal at the same time with the problems of the super-ego and the sense of guilt. This I have avoided doing. Also, in describing the various outcomes of this phase of development, I have refrained from discussing the complications which arise when a child, as a result of disappointment from her father, returns to the attachment to her mother which she had abandoned, or when, in the course of her life, she repeatedly changes over from one position to the other. But precisely because my paper is only one contribution among others, I may be spared an exhaustive survey of the literature, and I can confine myself to bringing out the more important points on which I agree or disagree with these other writings.

Abraham's (1921) description of the manifestations of the castration complex in the female is still unsurpassed; but one would be glad if it had included the factor of the girl's original exclusive attachment to her mother. I am in agreement with the principal points in Jeanne Lampl-de Groot's[2] important paper (1927). In this the complete identity of the pre-Oedipus phase in boys and girls is recognized, and the girl's sexual

1. [It should be pointed out that recent works by other writers discussed in what follows appeared *after* Freud's earlier paper on the anatomical distinction between the sexes (1925j). See the Editor's Note, p. 370 above.]

2. The author's name was given when it appeared in the *Zeitschrift* as 'A. Lampl-de-Groot', and I correct it here at her request.

(phallic) activity towards her mother is affirmed and substantiated by observations. The turning-away from the mother is traced to the influence of the girl's recognition of castration, which obliges her to give up her sexual object, and often masturbation along with it. The whole development is summed up in the formula that the girl goes through a phase of the 'negative' Oedipus complex before she can enter the positive one. A point on which I find the writer's account inadequate is that it represents the turning-away from the mother as being merely a change of object and does not discuss the fact that it is accompanied by the plainest manifestations of hostility. To this hostility full justice is done in Helene Deutsch's latest paper, on feminine masochism and its relation to frigidity (1930), in which she also recognizes the girl's phallic activity and the intensity of her attachment to her mother. Helene Deutsch states further that the girl's turning towards her father takes place *viâ* her passive trends (which have already been awakened in relation to her mother). In her earlier book (1925) the author had not yet set herself free from the endeavour to apply the Oedipus pattern to the pre-Oedipus phase, and she therefore interpreted the little girl's phallic activity as an identification with her father.

Fenichel (1930) rightly emphasizes the difficulty of recognizing in the material produced in analysis what parts of it represent the unchanged content of the pre-Oedipus phase and what parts have been distorted by regression (or in other ways). He does not accept Jeanne Lampl-de Groot's assertion of the little girl's active attitude in the phallic phase. He also rejects the 'displacement backwards' of the Oedipus complex proposed by Melanie Klein (1928), who places its beginnings as early as the commencement of the second year of life. This dating of it, which would also necessarily imply a modification of our view of all the rest of the child's development, does not in fact correspond to what we learn from the analyses of adults, and it is especially incompatible with my findings as to the long duration of the girl's pre-Oedipus

attachment to her mother. A means of softening this contradiction is afforded by the reflection that we are not as yet
able to distinguish in this field between what is rigidly fixed
by biological laws and what is open to movement and change
under the influence of accidental experience. The effect of
seduction has long been familiar to us and in just the same way
other factors – such as the date at which the child's brothers
and sisters are born or the time when it discovers the difference
between the sexes, or again its direct observations of sexual
intercourse or its parents' behaviour in encouraging or
repelling it – may hasten the child's sexual development and
bring it to maturity.

Some writers are inclined to reduce the importance of the
child's first and most original libidinal impulses in favour of
later developmental processes, so that – to put this view in its
most extreme form – the only role left to the former is
merely to indicate certain paths, while the [psychical] intensities[1] which flow along those paths are supplied by later
regressions and reaction-formations. Thus, for instance,
Karen Horney (1926) is of the opinion that we greatly overestimate the girl's primary penis-envy and that the strength
of the masculine trend which she develops later is to be
attributed to a *secondary* penis-envy which is used to fend off
her feminine impulses and, in particular, her feminine attachment to her father. This does not tally with my impressions.
Certain as is the occurrence of later reinforcements through
regression and reaction-formation, and difficult as it is to
estimate the relative strength of the confluent libidinal components, I nevertheless think that we should not overlook the
fact that the first libidinal impulses have an intensity of their

1. ['*Intensitäten*'. Freud does not often use the word, as here, without
any qualifying epithet. He is in fact using the word as an equivalent to
the term 'quantity' which he preferred in the earlier 'Project' of 1895
(Freud, 1950a). In the metapsychological paper on 'Repression' (1915d)
the term 'quantity' is equated with 'instinctual energy'; and in Chapter
V of his posthumous *Outline of Psychoanalysis* (1940a [1938]) he uses the
term 'psychical intensities' and adds in parentheses 'cathexes'.]

own which is superior to any that come later and which may indeed be termed incommensurable. It is undoubtedly true that there is an antithesis between the attachment to the father and the masculinity complex; it is the general antithesis that exists between activity and passivity, masculinity and femininity. But this gives us no right to assume that only one of them is primary and that the other owes its strength merely to the force of defence. And if the defence against femininity is so energetic, from what other source can it draw its strength than from the masculine trend which found its first expression in the child's penis-envy and therefore deserves to be named after it?

A similar objection applies to Ernest Jones's view (1927) that the phallic phase in girls is a secondary, protective reaction rather than a genuine developmental stage. This does not correspond either to the dynamic or the chronological position of things.

BIBLIOGRAPHY
AND AUTHOR INDEX

Titles of books and periodicals are in italics, titles of papers are in inverted commas. Abbreviations are in accordance with the *World List of Scientific Periodicals* (London, 1963–5). Further abbreviations used in this volume will be found in the List at the end of this bibliography. Numerals in bold type refer to volumes, ordinary numerals refer to pages. The figures in round brackets at the end of each entry indicate the page or pages of this volume on which the work in question is mentioned.

In the case of the Freud entries, only English translations are given. The initial dates are those of the German original publications. (The date of writing is added in square brackets where it differs from the latter.) The letters attached to the dates of publication are in accordance with the corresponding entries in the complete bibliography of Freud's writings included in Volume 24 of the *Standard Edition*. Details of the original publication, including the original German title, are given in the editorial introduction to each work in the *Penguin Freud Library*.

For non-technical authors, and for technical authors where no specific work is mentioned, see the General Index.

ABRAHAM, K. (1916) 'Untersuchungen über die früheste prägenitale Entwicklungsstufe der Libido', *Int. Z. ärztl. Psychoanal.*, **4**, 71. (117)
[*Trans.:* 'The First Pregenital Stage of the Libido', *Selected Papers*, London, 1927; New York, 1953, Chap. XII.]
(1921) 'Äusserungsformen des weiblichen Kastrationskomplexes', *Int. Z. Psychoanal.*, **7**, 422. (343, 389)
[*Trans.:* 'Manifestations of the Female Castration Complex', *Selected Papers*, London, 1927; New York, 1953, Chap. XXII.]
(1924) *Versuch einer Entwicklungsgeschichte der Libido*, Leipzig, Vienna, Zurich. (117, 118)
[*Trans.:* 'A Short Study of the Development of the Libido'.

Selected Papers, London, 1927; New York, 1953, Chap. XXVI.]

(1965) With FREUD, S. *See* FREUD, S. (1965a)

ADLER, A. (1907) *Studie über Minderwertigkeit von Organen*, Berlin and Vienna, (100)

[*Trans.: Study of Organ-Inferiority and its Psychical Compensation*, New York, 1917.]

(1910) 'Der psychische Hermaphroditismus im Leben und in der Neurose', *Fortschr. Med.*, **28**, 486. (278)

ANDREAS-SALOMÉ, L. (1916) '"Anal" und "Sexual"', *Imago*, **4**, 249. (104, 302) (1966) With FREUD, S. *See* FREUD, S. (1966a)

ARDUIN (1900) 'Die Frauenfrage und die sexuellen Zwischenstufen', *Jb. sex. Zwischenstufen*, **2**, 211. (54)

BALDWIN, J. M. (1895) *Mental Development in the Child and the Race*, New York, (89)

BARTELS, M., and PLOSS, H. H. *See* PLOSS, H. H. and BARTELS, M.

BAYER, H. (1902) 'Zur Entwicklungsgeschichte der Gebärmutter', *Dt. Arch. klin. Med.*, **73**, 422. (92)

BELL, J. SANFORD (1902) 'A Preliminary Study of the Emotion of Love between the Sexes'. *Am. J. Psychol.*, **13**, 325. (89, 112)

BINET, A. (1888) *Études de psychologie expérimentale: le fétichisme dans l'amour*, Paris. (67, 86–7)

BLEULER, E. (1908) 'Sexuelle Abnormitäten der Kinder', *Jb. schweiz. Ges. SchulgesundPfl.*, **9**, 623. (89)

(1913) 'Der Sexualwiderstand', *Jb. psychoanalyt. psychopath. Forsch.*, **5**, 442. (107)

BLOCH, I. (1902–3) *Beiträge zur Ätiologie der Psychopathia sexualis* (2 vols.), Dresden. (45, 50)

BREUER, J., and FREUD, S. (1893). *See* FREUD, S. (1893a)

(1895) *See* FREUD, S. (1895d)

BRUNSWICK, R. MACK (1928) 'Die Analyse eines Eifersuchts-wahnes', *Int. Z. Psychoanal.*, **14**, 458. (373)

[*English Text:* 'The Analysis of a Case of Paranoia', *J. nerv. ment. Dis.*, **70** (1929), 177.]

CHEVALIER, J. (1893) *L'inversion sexuelle*, Lyon. (52, 54)

CRAWLEY, E. (1902) *The Mystic Rose, A Study of Primitive Marriage*, London. (267)

DEKKER, E. D. *See* 'MULTATULI'

DESSOIR, M. (1894) 'Zur Psychologie der Vita sexualis', *Allg. Z. Psychiat.*, **50**, 941. (152–3)

DEUTSCH, H. (1925) *Psychoanalyse der weiblichen Sexualfunktionen*, Vienna. (343, 390)

(1930) 'Der feminine Masochismus und seine Beziehung zur Frigidität', *Int. Z. Psychoanal.*, **16**, 172. (390)
[*Trans.*: 'The Significance of Masochism in the Mental Life of Women', *Int. J. Psycho-Analysis*, **11** (1930), 48.]

DISKUSSIONEN DER WIENER PSYCHOANALYTISCHEN VEREINIGUNG, **2**, *Die Onanie*, Wiesbaden, 1912. (102, 105)

DULAURE, J. A. (1905) *Des divinités génératrices*, Paris. (1st ed., 1805.) (278)

ECKSTEIN, E. (1904) *Die Sexualfrage in der Erziehung des Kindes*, Leipzig. (179)

ELLIS, HAVELOCK (1897) *Studies in the Psychology of Sex*, Vol. II [first issued as Vol. I]: *Sexual Inversion*, London. (3rd ed., Philadelphia, 1915.) (51, 53)

(1898) 'Auto-Erotism; a Psychological Study', *Alien. & Neurol.*, **19**, 260. (97, 175).

(1903) *Studies in the Psychology of Sex, Vol. III: Analysis of the Sexual Impulse; Love and Pain; the Sexual Impulse in Women*, Philadelphia. (2nd ed., Philadelphia, 1913.) (73, 89, 108, 145–6, 189)

(1910) *Studies in the Psychology of Sex*, Vol. VI: *Sex in Relation to Society*, Philadelphia. (2nd ed., Philadelphia, 1913.) (267)

(1927) 'The Conception of Narcissism', *Psychoan. Rev.*, **14**, 129; *Studies in the Psychology of Sex*, Vol. VII: *Eonism and Other Supplementary Studies*, Philadelphia, 1928, Chap. VI. (140)

FEATHERMAN, A. (1885–91) *Social History of the Races of Mankind* (7 vols.), London. (268)

FENICHEL, O. (1930) 'Zur prägenitalen Vorgeschichte des Ödipuskomplexes', *Int. Z. Psychoanal.*, **16**, 139. (390)
[*Trans.*: 'The Pregenital Antecedents of the Oedipus Complex', *Int. J. Psycho-Analysis*, **12**, (1931), 141.]

FERENCZI, S. (1908) 'Analytische Deutung und Behandlung der psychosexuellen Impotenz beim Manne', *Psychiat.-neurol. Wschr.*, **10**, 298. (248)
[*Trans.*: 'The Analytic Interpretation and Treatment of Psychosexual Impotence', *First Contributions to Psycho-Analysis*, London, 1952, Chap. I.]

FERENCZI, S. (*contd*)

(1909) 'Introjektion und Übertragung', *Jb. psychoanalyt. psychopath. Forsch.*, **1**, 422. (63)

[*Trans.*: 'Introjection and Transference', *First Contributions to Psycho-Analysis*, London, 1952, Chap. II.]

(1914) 'Zur Nosologie der männlichen Homosexualität (Homoërotik)', *Int. Z. ärztl. Psychoanal.*, **2**, 131. (58)

[*Trans.*: 'The Nosology of Male Homosexuality (Homoerotism)', *First Contributions to Psycho-Analysis*, London, 1952, Chap. XII.]

(1920) Review of Lipschütz, *Die Pubertätsdrüse*, *Int. Z. Psychoanal.* **6**, 84. (93)

(1923) 'Zur Symbolik des Medusenhauptes', *Int. Z. Psychoanal.*, **9**, 69. (311)

[*Trans.*: 'On the Symbolism of the Head of Medusa', *Further Contributions to the Theory and Technique of Psycho-Analysis*, London, 1926. Chap. LXVI.]

(1924) *Versuch einer Genitaltheorie*, Leipzig and Vienna. (153, 279, 341)

[*Trans.*: *Thalassa, a Theory of Genitality*, New York, 1938.]

FLIESS, W. (1906) *Der Ablauf des Lebens*, Vienna. (54)

FLOERKE, G. (1902) *Zehn Jahre mit Böcklin* (2nd ed.), Munich. (258)

FRAZER, J. G. (1911) *Taboo and the Perils of the Soul* (*The Golden Bough*, 3rd ed., Part II), London. (267)

FREUD, M. (1957) *Glory Reflected*, London. (24)

FREUD, S. (1891*b*) *On Aphasia*, London and New York, 1953. (16, 28)

(1893*a*) With BREUER, J., 'On the Psychical Mechanism of Hysterical Phenomena: Preliminary Communication', in *Studies on Hysteria*, Standard Ed., **2**, 3; *P.F.L.*, **3.**, 53. (28, 77)

(1895*b* [1894]) 'On the Grounds for Detaching a Particular Syndrome from Neurasthenia under the Description "Anxiety Neurosis"', *Standard Ed.*, **3**, 87; *P.F.L.*, **10**, 31. (35, 134)

(1895*d*) With BREUER, J., *Studies on Hysteria*, London, 1956; *Standard Ed.*, **2**; *P.F.L.*, **3**. (28, 79)

(1896*c*) 'The Aetiology of Hysteria', *Standard Ed.*, **3**, 189. (91, 108)

(1898*a*) 'Sexuality in the Aetiology of the Neuroses', *Standard Ed.*, **3**, 261. (37)

(1899*a*) 'Screen Memories', *Standard Ed.*, **3**, 301. (90)

(1900*a*) *The Interpretation of Dreams*, London and New York, 1955;

Standard Ed., 4–5; *P.F.L.*, 4. (10, 23, 28, 34–7, 101, 110, 121, 149, 150, 191, 195, 225, 237, 241, 326, 332)

(1901a) *On Dreams*, London and New York, 1951; *Standard Ed.*, 5, 633. (37)

(1901b) *The Psychopathology of Everyday Life*, *Standard Ed.*, 6; *P.F.L.*, 5. (23, 28, 38, 90)

(1905c) *Jokes and their Relation to the Unconscious*, *Standard Ed.*, 8; *P.F.L.*, 6. (38, 131, 237)

(1905d) *Three Essays on the Theory of Sexuality*, London, 1962; *Standard Ed.*, 7, 130; *P.F.L.*, 7, 31. (28, 34, 36, 38, 39–40, 138, 173, 175, 177, 185, 195, 208, 210–11, 215, 245–6, 258, 294, 302, 305, 307–8, 312, 317, 326, 328, 335, 339, 348, 371, 379, 388)

(1905e [1901]) 'Fragment of an Analysis of a Case of Hysteria', *Standard Ed.*, 7, 3; *P.F.L.*, 8, 29. (37, 38, 69, 77, 80, 82, 327, 332)

(1906a [1905]) 'My Views on the Part played by Sexuality in the Aetiology of the Neuroses', *Standard Ed.*, 7, 271; *P.F.L.*, 10, 71. (108)

(1907a) *Delusions and Dreams in Jensen's 'Gradiva'*, *Standard Ed.*, 9, 3; *P.F.L.*, 14, 27. (347)

(1907c) 'The Sexual Enlightenment of Children', *Standard Ed.*, 9, 131; *P.F.L.*, 7, 171. (197, 336)

(1908a) 'Hysterical Phantasies and their Relation to Bisexuality', *Standard Ed.*, 9, 157; *P.F.L.*, 10, 83. (222)

(1908b) 'Character and Anal Erotism', *Standard Ed.*, 9, 169; *P.F.L.*, 7, 205. (102, 164, 241, 295, 296, 360)

(1908c) 'On the Sexual Theories of Children', *Standard Ed.*, 9, 207; *P.F.L.*, 7, 183. (108, 112, 172, 177, 178, 179, 237, 300, 306, 326, 328, 348)

(1908d) '"Civilized" Sexual Morality and Modern Nervous Illness', *Standard Ed.*, 9, 179; *P.F.L.*, 12, 27. (181, 246)

(1908e [1907]) 'Creative Writers and Day-Dreaming', *Standard Ed.*, 9, 143; *P.F.L.*, 14, 129. (132)

(1908f) Preface to Stekel's *Nervöse Angstzustände und ihre Behandlung*, *Standard Ed.*, 9, 250. (248)

(1909b) 'Analysis of a Phobia in a Five-Year-Old Boy', *Standard Ed.*, 14, 3; *P.F.L.*, 8, 165. (29, 112, 166, 172, 177, 185, 186, 192, 194, 196, 197–8, 299, 309, 310–11, 317)

(1909c) 'Family Romances', *Standard Ed.*, 9, 237; *P.F.L.*, 7, 217. (149, 238)

FREUD, S. (contd)

(1909d) 'Notes upon a Case of Obsessional Neurosis', Standard Ed., 10, 155; P.F.L., 9, 31. (68, 149, 192, 207, 275, 348)

(1910a [1909]) Five Lectures on Psycho-Analysis, Standard Ed., 11, 3; in Two Short Accounts of Psycho-Analysis, Penguin Books, Harmondsworth, 1962. (18, 29)

(1910c) Leonardo da Vinci and a Memory of his Childhood, Standard Ed., 11, 59; P.F.L., 14, 143. (196, 236, 348, 352, 357)

(1910h) 'A Special Type of Choice of Object made by Men', Standard Ed., 11, 165; P.F.L., 7, 227. (152, 192, 204, 223)

(1910i) 'The Psycho-Analytic View of Psychogenic Disturbance of Vision', Standard Ed., 11, 211; P.F.L., 10, 103. (126)

(1911c [1910]) 'Psycho-Analytic Notes on an Autobiographical Account of a Case of Paranoia (Dementia Paranoides)', Standard Ed., 12, 3; P.F.L., 9, 129. (29)

(1912c) 'Types of Onset of Neurosis', Standard Ed., 12, 229; P.F.L., 10, 115. (79)

(1912d) 'On the Universal Tendency to Debasement in the Sphere of Love', Standard Ed., 11, 179; P.F.L., 7, 243. (119, 276, 330).

(1912f) 'Contributions to a Discussion on Masturbation', Standard Ed., 12, 243. (102, 105, 339)

(1912–13) Totem and Taboo, London, 1950; New York, 1952; Standard Ed., 13, 1; P.F.L., 13, 43. (29, 148, 263, 269, 273, 382)

(1913i) 'The Disposition to Obsessional Neurosis', Standard Ed., 12, 313; P.F.L., 10, 129. (160, 207, 208, 295, 305)

(1914c) 'On Narcissism: an Introduction', Standard Ed., 14, 69; P.F.L., 11, 59. (94, 98, 138, 140, 145, 241, 298)

(1914d) 'On the History of the Psycho-Analytic Movement', Standard Ed., 14, 3; P.F.L., 15, 57. (29, 36, 337)

(1915c) 'Instincts and their Vicissitudes', Standard Ed., 14, 111; P.F.L., 11, 105. (82)

(1915d) 'Repression', Standard Ed., 14, 143; P.F.L., 11, 139. (91, 352, 391)

(1915f) 'A Case of Paranoia Running Counter to the Psycho-Analytic Theory of the Disease', Standard Ed., 14, 263; P.F.L., 10, 145. (327, 373)

(1916d) 'Some Character-Types Met with in Psycho-Analytic Work', Standard Ed., 14, 311; P.F.L., 14, 291. (208, 328, 381)

(1916–17 [1915–17]) Introductory Lectures on Psycho-Analysis, New

York, 1966; London, 1971; *Standard Ed.*, **15–16**; *P.F.L.*, **1.** (10, 29, 147, 149, 165, 168, 240, 326–7, 334, 348)

(1917c) 'On Transformations of Instinct as Exemplified in Anal Erotism', *Standard Ed.*, **17**, 127; *P.F.L.*, **7**, 293. (102, 103, 207, 208, 278, 321)

(1918a) 'The Taboo of Virginity', *Standard Ed.*, **11**, 193; *P.F.L.*, **7**, 261. (253, 255, 328, 377)

(1918b [1914]) 'From the History of an Infantile Neurosis', *Standard Ed.*, **17**, 3; *P.F.L.*, **9**, 225. (29, 198, 199, 207, 294, 334)

(1919e) 'A Child is Being Beaten', *Standard Ed.*, **17**, 177; *P.F.L.*, **10**, 159. (55, 327, 338)

(1920a) 'The Psychogenesis of a Case of Female Homosexuality', *Standard Ed.*, **18**, 147; *P.F.L.*, **9**, 367. (144, 242, 327)

(1920g) *Beyond the Pleasure Principle*, London, 1961; *Standard Ed.*, **18**, 7; *P.F.L.*, **11**, 269. (29, 46, 83)

(1921c) *Group Psychology and the Analysis of the Ego*, London and New York, 1959; *Standard Ed.*, **18**, 69; *P.F.L.*, **12.** (29, 63, 272)

(1923b) *The Ego and the Id*, London and New York, 1962; *Standard Ed.*, **19**, 3; *P.F.L.*, **11.** (29, 83, 94, 208, 314, 319, 327, 328, 372)

(1923d [1922]) 'A Seventeenth-Century Demonological Neurosis', *Standard Ed.*, **19**, 69; *P.F.L.*, **14**, 337. (214)

(1923e) 'The Infantile Genital Organization', *Standard Ed.*, **19**, 141; *P.F.L.*, **7**, 303. (34, 118, 194, 316, 317, 326, 336, 337, 349, 353)

(1924b [1923]) 'Neurosis and Psychosis', *Standard Ed.*, **19**, 149; *P.F.L.*, **10**, 209. (355)

(1924c) 'The Economic Problem of Masochism', *Standard Ed.*, **19**, 157; *P.F.L.*, **11**, 409. (72, 130, 310)

(1924d) 'The Dissolution of the Oedipus Complex', *Standard Ed.*, **19**, 173; *P.F.L.*, **7**, 313. (259, 311, 327, 333–4, 340, 341, 376)

(1924e) 'The Loss of Reality in Neurosis and Psychosis', *Standard Ed.*, **19**, 183; *P.F.L.*, **10**, 219. (355)

(1925d [1924]) *An Autobiographical Study*, *Standard Ed.*, **20**, 3; *P.F.L.*, **15**, 183. (14, 36)

(1925h) 'Negation', *Standard Ed.*, **19**, 235; *P.F.L.*, **11**, 435. (101, 310)

(1925j) 'Some Psychical Consequences of the Anatomical Distinction between the Sexes', *Standard Ed.*, **19**, 243; *P.F.L.*, **7**, 323. (113, 144, 177, 310, 314, 320, 321, 322, 357, 369, 389)

(1926d [1925]) *Inhibitions, Symptoms and Anxiety*, London, 1960; *Standard Ed.*, **20**, 77; *P.F.L.*, **10**, 227. (29, 147, 150, 241, 322)

FREUD, S. (*contd*)

(1926e) *The Question of Lay Analysis*, London, 1947; *Standard Ed.*, **20**, 179; P.F.L., **15**, 277. (326)

(1927a) 'Postscript to *The Question of Lay Analysis*', *Standard Ed.*, **20**, 251; P.F.L., **15**, 355. (14)

(1927c) *The Future of an Illusion*, London, 1962; *Standard Ed.*, **21**, 3; P.F.L., **12**, 179. (29–30)

(1927e) 'Fetishism', *Standard Ed.*, **21**, 149; P.F.L., **7**, 345. (68, 194, 310)

(1928b) Dostoevsky and Parricide', *Standard Ed.*, **21**, 175; P.F.L., **14**, 435. (377)

(1930a) *Civilization and its Discontents*, New York, 1961; London, 1963; *Standard Ed.*, **21**, 59; P.F.L., **12**, 243. (30, 68, 142, 168, 215, 246, 258, 272, 362)

(1931a) 'Libidinal Types', *Standard Ed.*, **21**, 215; P.F.L., **7**, 359. (208, 360)

(1931b) 'Female Sexuality', *Standard Ed.*, **21**, 223; P.F.L., **7**, 367. (138, 144, 320, 322, 326, 327, 360)

(1932a) 'The Acquisition and Control of Fire', *Standard Ed.*, **22**, 185; P.F.L., **13**, 225. (215)

(1933a) *New Introductory Lectures on Psycho-Analysis*, New York, 1966; London, 1971; *Standard Ed.*, **22**; P.F.L., **2**. (144, 147, 208, 327, 357, 370, 387)

(1935a) Postscript (1935) to *An Autobiographical Study*, new edition, London and New York; *Standard Ed.*, **20**, 71; P.F.L., **15**. (14)

(1939a [1934–8]) *Moses and Monotheism*, *Standard Ed.*, **23**, 3; P.F.L., **13**, 237. (30)

(1940a [1938]) *An Outline of Psycho-Analysis*, New York, 1968; London, 1969; *Standard Ed.*, **23**, 141; P.F.L., **15**, 369. (30, 68, 327, 349, 353, 391)

(1940c [1922]) 'Medusa's Head', *Standard Ed.*, **18**, 273. (311)

(1940e [1938]) 'Splitting of the Ego in the Process of Defence', *Standard Ed.*, **23**, 273; P.F.L., **11**, 457. (68, 349)

(1950a [1887–1902]) *The Origins of Psycho-Analysis*, London and New York, 1954. (Partly, including 'A Project for a Scientific Psychology', in *Standard Ed.*, **1**, 175.) (18, 26, 27, 28, 34–7, 138, 220, 328, 391)

(1960a) *Letters* 1873–1939 (ed. E. L. Freud) (trans. T. and J. Stern), New York, 1960; London, 1961. (25, 26)

(1963a [1909–39]) *Psycho-Analysis and Faith. The Letters of Sigmund Freud and Oskar Pfister* (ed. H. Meng and E. L. Freud) (trans. E. Mosbacher), London and New York, 1963. (26)

(1965a [1907–26]) *A Psycho-Analytic Dialogue. The Letters of Sigmund Freud and Karl Abraham* (ed. H. C. Abraham and E. L. Freud) (trans. B. Marsh and H. C. Abraham), London and New York, 1965. (26)

(1966a [1912–36]) *Sigmund Freud and Lou Andreas-Salomé: Letters* (ed. E. Pfeiffer) (trans. W. and E. Robson-Scott), London and New York, 1972. (26)

(1968a [1927–39]) *The Letters of Sigmund Freud and Arnold Zweig* (ed. E. L. Freud) (trans. W. and E. Robson-Scott), London and New York, 1970. (26)

(1970a [1919–35]) *Sigmund Freud as a Consultant. Recollections of a Pioneer in Psychoanalysis* (Letters from Freud to Edoardo Weiss, including a Memoir and Commentaries by Weiss, with Foreword and Introduction by M. Grotjahn), New York, 1970. (26)

(1974a [1906–23]) *The Freud/Jung Letters* (ed. W. McGuire) (trans. R. Manheim and R. F. C. Hull), London and Princeton, N.J., 1974. (26)

GALANT, S. (1919) 'Sexualleben im Säuglings- and Kindesalter', *Neurol. Zentbl.*, **38**, 652. Reprinted, *Int. Z. Psychoanal.*, **6** (1920), 164. (97)

GLEY, E. (1884) 'Les aberrations de l'instinct sexuel', *Rev. phil.*, **17**, 66. (54)

GROOS, C. (1899) *Die Spiele der Menschen*, Jena. (89)

(1904) *Das Seelenleben des Kindes*, Berlin. (89)

HALBAN, J. (1903) 'Die Entstehung der Geschlechtscharaktere', *Arch. Gynaek.*, **70**, 205. (53)

(1904) 'Schwangerschaftsreaktionen der fötalen Organe und ihre puerperale Involution', *Z. Geburtsh. Gynäk.*, **53**, 191. (92)

HALL, G. STANLEY (1904) *Adolescence: its Psychology and its relations to Physiology, Anthropology, Sociology, Sex, Crime, Religion and Education*, 2 vols., New York. (89)

HELLER, T. (1904) *Grundriss der Heilpädagogik*, Leipzig. (89)

HERMAN, G. (1903) *'Genesis', das Gesetz der Zeugung*, Bd. 5, *Libido und Mania*, Leipzig. (54)

HIRSCHFELD, M. (1899) 'Die objective Diagnose der Homosexualität', *Jb. sex. Zwischenstufen*, **1**, 4. (45, 54)

(1904) 'Statistische Untersuchungen über den Prozentsatz der Homosexuellen', *Jb. sex. Zwischenstufen*, 6. (45, 46)

HORNEY, K. (1923) 'Zur Genese des weiblichen Kastrationskomplexes', *Int. Z. Psychoanal.*, 9, 12. (343)

[*Trans.*: 'On the Genesis of the Castration Complex in Women', *Int. J. Psycho-Analysis*, 5, (1924), 50.]

(1926) 'Flucht aus der Weiblichkeit', *Int. Z. Psychoanal.*, 12, 360. (391)

[*Trans.*: 'The Flight from Womanhood', *Int. J. Psycho-Analysis*, 7 (1926), 324.]

HUG-HELLMUTH, H. VON (1913) *Aus dem Seelenleben des Kindes*, Leipzig and Vienna. (89)

JAHRBUCH FÜR SEXUELLE ZWISCHENSTUFEN (45, 52, 54)

JEREMIAS, A. (1904a) *Das alte Testament im Lichte des alten Orients*, Leipzig. (2nd, revised, ed., Leipzig, 1906.) (214)

(1904b) *Monotheistische Strömungen innerhalb der babylonischen Religion*, Leipzig. (214)

(1905) *Babylonisches im Neuen Testament*, Leipzig. (214)

JONES, E. (1927) 'The Early Development of Female Sexuality', *Int. J. Psycho-Analysis*, 8, 459; in *Papers on Psycho-Analysis*, 4th and 5th eds., London and New York, 1938; London and Baltimore, 1948. (392)

(1953) *Sigmund Freud: Life and Work*, Vol. 1, London and New York. (26)

(1955) *Sigmund Freud: Life and Work*, Vol. 2, London and New York. (Page references are to the English edition.) (26, 38, 230, 326, 348)

(1957) *Sigmund Freud: Life and Work*, Vol. 3, London and New York. (Page references are to the English edition.) (26, 305, 326, 347, 369)

JUNG, C. G. (1906, 1909) (ed.) *Diagnostische Assoziationsstudien* (2 vols.), Leipzig. (251)

[*Trans.*: *Studies in Word-Association*, London, 1918; New York, 1919.]

(1909) 'Die Bedeutung des Vaters für das Schicksal des Einzelnen', *Jb. psychoanalyt. psychopath. Forsch.*, 1, 155. (277)

[*Trans.*: 'The Significance of the Father in the Destiny of the Individual', *Collected Papers on Analytical Psychology*, London, 1916 (2nd ed., London, 1917; New York, 1920), Chap. III.]

(1911–12) 'Wandlungen und Symbole der Libido', *Jb. psychoanalyt. psychopath. Forsch.*, **3**, 120 and 4, 162; in book form, Leipzig and Vienna, 1912. (249)

[*Trans.: Psychology of the Unconscious*, New York, 1916; London, 1917.]

(1913) 'Versuch einer Darstellung der psychoanalytischen Theorie', *Jb. psychoanalyt. psychopath. Forsch.*, **5**, 307; in book form, Leipzig and Vienna, 1913. (375)

[*Trans.: The Theory of Psycho-Analysis*, New York, 1915.]

(1974) With FREUD, S. *See* FREUD, S. (1974*a*)

KIERNAN, J. G. (1888) 'Sexual Perversion and the Whitechapel Murders', *Med. Standard Chicago*, **4**, 170, (52)

KINDERFEHLER, DIE (89)

KLEIN, M. (1928) 'Frühstadien des Ödipuskonfliktes', *Int. Z. Psychoanal.*, **14**, 65. (390)

[*Trans.:* 'Early Stages of the Oedipus Conflict', *Int. J. Psycho-Analysis*, **9**, (1928), 167.]

KRAFFT-EBING, R. VON (1892) 'Bemerkungen über "geschlechtliche Hörigkeit" und Masochismus', *Jb. Psychiat. Neurol.*, **10**, 199. (45, 265–6)

(1895) 'Zur Erklärung der conträren Sexualempfindung', *Jb. Psychiat. Neurol.*, **13**, 1. (45, 54)

LAFORGUE, R. (1926) 'Verdrängung und Skotomisation', *Int. Z. Psychoanal.*, **12**, 54. (352)

LAMPL-DE GROOT, J. (1927) 'Zur Entwicklungsgeschichte des Ödipuskomplexes der Frau', *Int. Z. Psychoanal.*, **13**, 269. (389)

[*Trans.:* 'The Evolution of the Oedipus Complex in Women', *Int. J. Psycho-Analysis*, **9**, (1928), 332.]

LINDNER, S. (1879) 'Das Saugen an den Fingern, Lippen, etc., bei den Kindern (Ludeln)', *Jb. Kinderheilk.*, N.F., **14**, 68. (95–6, 335)

LIPSCHÜTZ, A. (1919) *Die Pubertätsdrüse und ihre Wirkungen*, Berne. (59, 92, 136)

LYDSTON, G. F. (1889) 'A Lecture on Sexual Perversion, Satyriasis and Nymphomania', *Med. Surg. Reporter*, Philadelphia, **61**, Sept. 7. (52)

MOEBIUS, P. J. (1900) 'Über Entartung', *Grenzfr. Nerv.- u. Seelenleb.* No. 3, 95, Weisbaden. (45, 49)

MOLL, A. (1898) *Untersuchungen über die Libido sexualis*, Vol. 1, Berlin. (45, 84, 96)

(1909) *Das Sexualleben des Kindes*, Berlin. (45, 89, 96)

'MULTATULI' [E. D. DEKKER] (1906) *Multatuli-Briefe* (2 vols.), Frankfurt. (175)

NACHMANSOHN, M. (1915) 'Freuds Libidotheorie verglichen mit der Eroslehre Platos', *Int. Z. ärztl. Psychoanal.*, 3, 65. (43)

OPHUIJSEN, J. H. W. VAN (1917) 'Beiträge zum Männlichkeitskomplex der Frau', *Int. Z. ärztl. Psychoanal.*, 4, 241. (336)
   [*Trans.:* 'Contributions to the Masculinity Complex in Women', *Int. J. Psycho-Analysis*, 5 (1924), 39.]

PÉREZ, B. (1886) *L'enfant de trois à sept ans*, Paris. (89)

PFISTER, O., and FREUD, S. (1963) *See* FREUD, S. (1963a)

PLOSS, H. H., and BARTELS, M. (1891) *Das Weib in der Natur-und Völkerkunde*, Leipzig. (267, 268, 278)

PREYER, W. (1882) *Die Seele des Kindes*, Leipzig. (89)

RANK, O. (1909) *Der Mythus von der Geburt des Helden*, Leipzig and Vienna. (149, 219, 238, 241)
   [*Trans.:* *The Myth of the Birth of the Hero*, New York, 1914.]
   (1924) *Das Trauma der Geburt*, Vienna. (150, 322, 355)
   [*Trans.:* *The Trauma of Birth*, London, 1929].

RIEGER, C. (1900) *Die Castration*, Jena. (135)

ROHLEDER, H. (1899) *Die Masturbation*, Berlin (102)

SACHS, H. (1945) *Freud, Master and Friend*, Cambridge (Mass.) and London. (Page reference is to the English edition.) (249)

SADGER, I. (1912) 'Von der Pathographie zur Psychographie', *Imago*, 1, 158. (281–2)

SCHRENCK-NOTZING, A. VON (1899) 'Literaturzusammenstellung über die Psychologie und Psychopathologie der Vita sexualis', *Z. Hypnot.*, 9, 98. (70)

SMITH, R. BROUGH (1878) *The Aborigines of Victora* (2 vols.), London. (267)

SPENCER, B., and GILLEN, F. J. (1899) *The Native Tribes of Central Australia*, London. (267)

STEINER, M. (1907) 'Die funktionelle Impotenz des Mannes und ihre Behandlung', *Wien. med. Pr.*, 48, 1535. (248)

STEKEL, W. (1908) *Nervöse Angstzustände und ihre Behandlung*, Berlin and Vienna. (248)

STORFER, A. J. (1911) *Zur Sonderstellung des Vatermords*, Leipzig and Vienna. (277)

STRÜMPELL, L. (1899) *Die padagogische Pathologie*. Leipzig. (89)

SULLY, J. (1895) *Studies of Childhood*, London. (89)

TARUFFI, C. (1903) *Hermaphroditismus und Zeugungsunfähigkeit* (German trans. by R. Teuscher), Berlin. (52)

THOMSON, J. (1887) *Through Masai Land*, London. (268)

WEININGER, O. (1903) *Geschlecht und Charakter*, Vienna. (55)
  [*Trans.: Sex and Character*, London, 1906.]

WEISS, E., and FREUD, S. (1970) *See* FREUD, S. (1970a)

ZWEIG, A., and FREUD, S. (1968) *See* FREUD, S. (1968a)

LIST OF ABBREVIATIONS

Gesammelte Schriften = Freud, *Gesammelte Schriften* (12 vols), Vienna, 1924–34.

Gesammelte Werke = Freud, *Gesammelte Werke* (18 vols), Vols 1–17 London, 1940–52, Vol. 18 Frankfurt am Main, 1968. From 1960 the whole edition published by S. Fischer Verlag, Frankfurt am Main.

S.K.S.N. = Freud, *Sammlung kleiner Schriften zur Neurosenlehre* (5 vols), Vienna, 1906–1922.

Almanach 1928 = *Almanach für das Jahr 1928*, Vienna, Internationaler Psychoanalytischer Verlag, 1927.

Neurosenlehre und Technik = Freud, *Schriften zur Neurosenlehre und zu psychoanalytischen Technik (1913–1926)*, Vienna, 1931.

Psychoanalyse der Neurosen = Freud, *Studien zur Psychoanalyse der Neurosen aus den Jahren 1913–1925*, Vienna, 1926.

Sexualtheorie und Traumlehre = Freud, *Kleine Schriften zur Sexualtheorie und zur Traumlehre*, Vienna, 1931.

Basic Writings = Freud, *The Basic Writings of Sigmund Freud*, New York, 1938.

Collected Papers = Freud, *Collected Papers* (5 vols), London, 1924–50.

Standard Edition = *The Standard Edition of the Complete Psychological Works of Sigmund Freud* (24 vols), Hogarth Press and The Institute of Psycho-Analysis, London, 1953–74.

P.F.L. = *Penguin Freud Library* (15 vols), Penguin Books, Harmondsworth, from 1973.

GENERAL INDEX

This index includes the names of non-technical authors. It also includes the names of technical authors where no reference is made in the text to specific works. For reference to specific technical works, the Bibliography should be consulted.

Jokes, 131 *n.*

Judas, 288

Judith and Holofernes (Hebbel), 281–2

Jung, C. J. (*see also* Bibliography), 18, 29, 140, 251 *n.*
 and theory of complexes, 188

Jungferngift, Das (Anzengruber), 280

Jus primae noctis, 277

Kinderfehler, Die, periodical, 89 *n.* 1

Kings and Emperors as father-symbols, 240

Kiss, the, 62, 63–4, 97 *n.* 1, 98, 145
 equated with sexual intercourse, 201

Knowledge, instinct for, 112–13

Koller, Carl, 15

Kraft-Ebbing, R. von (*see also* Bibliography), 45 *n.* 1, 70–71, 73 *n.* 2, 135

Lampl-de-Groot, J. (*see also* Bibliography), 373, 389 *n.* 3

Latency period, 92–5, 107–8, 128, 144–5, 149 *n.*, 156–7, 158–9, 163, 166, 315, 319–22

Legends, 177, 191, 195, 241
 and *n.* 3, 241

Leisenbogh, Freiherr von, 280 *n.* 2

Leonardo da Vinci, 348, 352 *n.* 1, 357 *n.* 1

Lettres de femmes (Prévost), 203

Libido (*see also* Sexual excitation; Sexual instinct)
 and anxiety, 147
 and character-types, 361–5
 and hunger, 45, 60
 and neuroses, 250–51, 277
 and object-choice, 235–6, 240
 backward flow of, 297–8
 collateral flow of, 63 *n.* 2, 85, 111, 156
 definition of, 45, 138
 development of, 248–50, 276–7, 295
 increase of, at puberty, 95, 143
 phases of, in female sexuality, 383, 388, 391–2
 pregenital organization, 306
 theory of, 35, 138–40

Liébeault, A.-A., 16

Lies told by children, 287–91

Lindner, S. (*see also* Bibliography), 95, 96

Lingam, defloration by, 277–8

'Little Hans', case of, 29, 111–112 *n.*, 166 *n.*, 172, 176–7, 185–6, 192, and *n.* 2, 194 and *n.* 2, 196 *n.* 1, 197 *n.* 1, 299, 309 *n.*, 310 *nn.* 2 and 3, 317 *n.* 2

'Little one' as symbol, 297, 301

Little Red Riding Hood, 197

Love, 75, 81, 90, 145–7, 152 *n.* 2
 children's capacity for, 176
 compulsive nature of, 234
 conflict between affectionate and sensual currents in, 248–56
 fear of loss of, 362
 for prostitutes, 233–42, 251–2

Neuroses (*contd*)
  and masturbation, 108 and *n*.
  and parents, 145–7, 151
  and repression, 42, 78, 85, 99,
    121, 144, 150, 156, 162–6
  and toxic states,138
  compared to psychoses,
    352 *n*. 2, 355
  negative of perversion, 79–
    80, 84–7, 155–6, 161
  nuclear complex of, 149 *n*.,
    192 and *n*. 1, 238 *n*. 1
  precipitating cause of, 297
  preconditions of, 363–5, 372
  psychoanalytic treatment of,
    77–9, 59–60 *n*.
  regressive character of, 296
  sexual aetiology of, 173, 176,
    178
  sexual instinct in, 77–87
Neurosis
  choice of, 160 *n*.
  obsessional, 58 *n*., 77, 118,
    139, 160 *n*s., 275
  sadistic-anal disposition
    associated with, 300
Neurotics
  perverse tendencies in, 79–82,
    84–6, 156–7, 161–3
  psychoanalysis of, 187–8,
    203–4, 213–15, 232, 235,
    278, 331
  withdrawal from reality, 250
Night fears (*Pavor nocturnis*),
  147 and *n*.
Nocturnal emissions, 108, 123,
  134
Normal and abnormal
  sexuality

  no hard and fast line between,
    50, 52, 54 *n*. 2, 54–5, 56 *n*.,
    60–63, 66–72, 73–6, 86–7,
    92 *n*. 1, 125 *n*.
Normal mental processes, 361,
  364
Normal sexuality, abortive
  beginnings of, in
  perversions, 47–8, 58 *n*.,
  66 *n*., 76 *n*. 2
Nutritional instinct, 45, 96,
  138–9, 145, 156
  and oral erotism, 95–9, 117,
    125–6, 144–5, 156
Nuclear complex of neurosis,
  149 *n*., 192 and *n*. 1, 238 *n*. 1

Object-choice (*see also* Infantile
  sexuality; Sexual object),
  112 *n*.
  accidental determinant, 58–
    59 *n*.
  anaclitic, 145 *n*., 249 *n*. 1
  debasement in, 232–42,
    251–2, 254
  diphasic, 119, 258
  early beginnings, 89 *n*., 109–
    110, 112 *n*., 118 and *n*.,
    127 *n*., 144–6, 158
  final, 258
  hetero-sexual, 45–6, 56 *n*.,
    151–4, 167
  in boys and girls compared,
    375–6, 378–80
  in fetishism, 351
  incestuous, 148–51, 159
  narcissistic, 56 *n*., 100 *n*.,
    139–40, 145 *n*.